The Story
of Classic Crime
in 100 Books

The Story
of Classic Crime
in 100 Books

Martin Edwards

Poisoned Pen Press

Poisoned Pen
PRESS

Copyright © 2017 by Martin Edwards

First U.S. Edition 2017

10 9 8 7 6 5 4 3 2 1

Library of Congress Catalog Card Number: 2017934126

ISBN: 9781464207211   Hardcover
     9781464207235   Trade Paperback

Poisoned Pen Press
6962 E. First Ave., Ste. 103
Scottsdale, AZ 85251
www.poisonedpenpress.com
info@poisonedpenpress.com

Printed in the United States of America

Contents

Introduction

This book tells the story of crime fiction published during the first half of the twentieth century. I see it as a tale of the unexpected. The diversity of this much-loved genre is breathtaking, and so much greater than many critics have suggested. To illustrate this, I have chosen one hundred examples of books which highlight the achievements, and sometimes the limitations, of popular fiction of that era. The main aim of detective stories is to entertain, but the best cast a light on human behaviour, and display both literary ambition and accomplishment. And there is another reason why millions of modern readers continue to appreciate classic crime fiction. Even unpretentious detective stories, written for unashamedly commercial reasons, can give us clues to the past, and give us insight into a long-vanished world that, for all its imperfections, continues to fascinate.

This book serves as a companion to the British Library's internationally acclaimed series of Crime Classics. Long-forgotten stories republished in the series have won a devoted new readership. Several titles have entered the bestseller charts, with sales outstripping those of highly acclaimed contemporary thrillers. Nostalgia for a bygone age is perhaps a factor, but it would be unwise to assume it is the main reason for the series' success in Britain, the United States and elsewhere. That success has been as surprising and gratifying as any of the plot twists that make the stories so delightful to read.

So how do we define 'crime classics'? The term has been adopted several times over the years by publishers who have sought to bring old mysteries back to life, but until recently, few of these ventures lasted long or gained much attention. Fashion counts in publishing, as in other walks of life, and a pleasing spin-off from the success of the British Library's Crime Classics has been that other publishers have followed the Library's lead, so that readers can now find scores of vintage detective stories that were previously difficult to find, and even harder to afford once traced.

In truth, 'crime classics' is—like 'vintage crime'—a broad term allowing a great deal of latitude. A convenient label is not a guarantee of literary quality, or even that the puzzle in the story is markedly original. But for a book to merit the description of a 'crime classic', it should surely offer the reader something of value over and above the fact that it was written in the distant past, and may have languished in obscurity for decades. That special something may concern plot, character, setting, humour, social or historic significance, or a mix of these. Crime fiction is a broad church; that breadth helps to explain its global appeal.

Here, I have defined a 'classic' crime book as a novel or story collection published between 1901 and 1950 which seems to me to remain of particular interest—for whatever reason—to present-day lovers of detective fiction. The British Library's series spans a slightly longer time frame, but for the present purposes, it makes sense to concentrate on the first half of the last century. The British Library also publishes a series of Classic Thrillers, but the focus here is on crime fiction (including many detective stories, but also some books where detection is not central to the story) rather than thrillers. One can debate endlessly the distinctions between 'detective stories' and 'crime stories', and between 'crime fiction' and 'thrillers', but for a book such as this, a pedantic insistence on strictness in definition seems futile. The term 'mystery', disliked by some purists, is used here interchangeably with 'crime story'. In the case of authors better known by their crime-writing pseudonyms, I have generally used those rather than the real names. Many classic crime novels have been published under more than one title; I have been selective in mentioning alternative titles, because although such minutiae are often valuable, one can have too much of a good thing.

My choice of books reflects a wish to present the genre's development in an accessible, informative, and engaging way. So far as possible, I have avoided including 'spoilers' revealing solutions to mysteries. Michael Innes, a learned academic as well as a renowned detective novelist, argued in a review for the *London Review of Books* in May 1983 that 'systematically to conceal the core of a story is surely to hamstring effective critical discussion'. I am not wholly convinced, but in any event, I suspect that most readers, like me, prefer not to have their surprises anticipated.

My emphasis is on topics that will, I hope, appeal to readers with no more than a casual interest in the older detective stories. Although I have not written this book primarily with the most widely read connoisseurs of the genre in mind, I hope that even they will find books (and trivia) with which they are unfamiliar. People who enjoy classic crime fiction love making new discoveries, and one of my priorities has been to help them to indulge in some happy hunting.

I have not attempted to list the 'best' books of the period, nor is this even a selection of all my own favourites, which would certainly include more titles by Agatha Christie, and novels such as Dorothy L. Sayers' *Murder Must Advertise*, Henry Wade's *Lonely Magdalen*, Robert Player's *The Ingenious Mr Stone*, and many others. The clue to this book is in its title—the aim is to tell a story. My account of the genre's development over the space of fifty years is highly selective; it could not be otherwise in a book of this length. This is not an encyclopedia. One would need much more space to explore every aspect of this fascinating branch of fiction throughout the course of one of the most turbulent half-centuries in the history of the world, but I hope that my references to scores of other books in the chapter introductions will encourage further investigations on the part of readers.

The 'Golden Age' of detective fiction is another familiar but vague concept that can be defined to suit one's purpose. Most people treat the Golden Age as roughly synonymous with the era between the two world wars, and I share that view. This book covers a much longer stretch of time than the Golden Age, though, and suggests ways in which keynote stories written before the First World War influenced those that followed, just as Golden Age mysteries inspired writers of later generations, including some of today's bestsellers.

This book overlaps with, but is very different from, *The Golden Age of Murder*, my study of the lives and work of members of the Detection Club in the Thirties, published in 2015. Many of the books discussed here were written by members of the Detection Club, the world's first association of crime writers, an elite social network with a limited membership elected by secret ballot. But the Detection Club only came into existence in 1930, and some of the genre's foundation stones were laid before then. The hundred chosen titles are set in a wider context, but the book is designed so that those who prefer to do so may dip in randomly to read about specific topics, titles or authors.

This is not the first book to examine fifty or one hundred note-worthy crime novels, but it offers more contextual background to the chosen titles than its predecessors. Jacques Barzun and Wendell Hertig Taylor gathered together their introductions to the books described in *A Book of Prefaces to Fifty Classics of Crime Fiction: 1900–50* (1976). Julian Symons had previously produced *The Hundred Best Crime Stories* for the *Sunday Times* in 1957–8, an undertaking that, in his characteristically modest manner, he later described as 'dubiously useful'. Undeterred by Symons' reservations, almost forty years later, his friend and successor as President of the Detection Club, H.R.F. Keating, published *Crime and Mystery: The 100 Best Books*. In addition, there are 'Cornerstones' listed by two distinguished American authorities, Howard Haycraft and Ellery Queen, and a more recent 'hundred best' selection edited on behalf of the Crime Writers' Association by Susan Moody. In the internet age, the list of lists is endless.

Plenty of titles featured here appear in one or more of the earlier lists, but I was not content simply to round up the usual suspects. Several of my more obscure choices are unashamedly idiosyncratic. This is partly because unpredictability appeals to crime fans, including me, and partly because of my wish to demonstrate the sheer variety of the genre. Some forgotten books, of course, are forgotten for reasons that become obvious as soon as one reads them, but even some of the flimsier stories offer pictures of character or society, even if that was not the authors' intention. I have discussed the work of journeymen and journeywomen alongside that of writers whose fiction displays literary aspiration and, sometimes, conspicuous achievement.

The book's structure is, in very broad terms, chronological; it starts with an undoubted classic, *The Hound of the Baskervilles*, and ends with a novel by Julian Symons that set the tone for British crime fiction in the second half of the twentieth century. To highlight some of the patterns in the genre, I have divided the book into thematic chapters, although many of the novels discussed illustrate several of the highlighted themes. Because this story about classic crime does not always follow a well-trodden path, I hope it offers something fresh even to those who have, like me, misspent their youth and much of the rest of their lives delving into the dusty corners of this hugely enjoyable branch of literary entertainment.

A surprising number of my chosen books were collaborative efforts, rather than the work of a single author. Similarly, it is striking that, although only two of the books selected from the years before 1920 were written by women, female authors wrote, or co-wrote, a much higher proportion of novels during the next three decades. While the never-ending success story of Agatha Christie is unique, she was not the only 'Crime Queen' of the Golden Age; her achievements, and those of Dorothy L. Sayers, Ngaio Marsh, Margery Allingham and company have overshadowed those of their male contemporaries, many of whom deserve to be better known.

Classic crime novels have long been popular with book collectors. A dust-jacketed first edition in good condition of most of the titles discussed here will often fetch an eye-watering sum, and all the more so if it benefits from a signature or inscription from the author. Such hard-to-find copies may be out of the reach of most readers, but it is a source of delight to the British Library, and to me, that titles in the Crime Classics series, so attractively packaged, are themselves now being widely collected.

Novels published in that series come, unsurprisingly, from authors born or writing in Britain, and this presented me with a dilemma. The story told here concerns, first and foremost, British detective fiction. Yet in the first half of the century, many crime novels and short stories of distinction were produced in other parts of the world. This has often been overlooked, perhaps because of insularity, but also for the very good reason that, even today, some excellent work has yet to be translated into English. Space simply does not permit an extended discussion of books from overseas, but I was reluctant to ignore them altogether. In sharing my love of the genre, I seek to emphasise its extraordinary range, and so I have included a small sampling of key titles from the United States and elsewhere.

This book does not pretend to be the last word on its subject—far from it. Its overriding aim is to provide a launch point that enables readers to embark on their own voyages of discovery. My hope is to encourage an increasing number of readers to share my delight in the diverse riches that classic crime fiction has to offer.

Chapter One

A New Era Dawns

As the Victorian era gave way to a short-lived phase of Edwardian elegance, detective fiction was, like Britain itself, in a state of transition. Readers continued to mourn the loss of Sherlock Holmes, killed (or so it seemed) at the Reichenbach Falls because his creator Arthur Conan Doyle felt the need to save his mind 'for better things'. Doyle's fellow writers struggled to fill the vacuum. As his brother-in-law, E.W. Hornung put it, 'there is no police like Holmes'. The sheer ordinariness of stout and cordial private detective Martin Hewitt, created by Arthur Morrison, made a striking contrast to Holmes' brilliant eccentricity, but also meant Hewitt was easily forgotten.

More exotic and interesting was Hornung's gentleman-burglar A.J. Raffles. The moral unorthodoxy of the stories was intriguing, but when Raffles joined the forces of law and order, before dying a hero in the Boer War, he sacrificed his dangerous charm. His fellow anti-heroes, notably Morrison's amiable sociopath Horace Dorrington, and the crafty Romney Pringle, created by Clifford Ashdown (a pen-name for R. Austin Freeman and John J. Pitcairn) were in some respects years ahead of their time, but they soon disappeared from sight.

Writers strove for originality, none more energetically than Baroness Orczy. In addition to the Old Man in the Corner, she created a second-string detective, Patrick Mulligan, an Irish solicitor with dingy offices in Finsbury Square and a confidential clerk who narrates his cases and rejoices in the name Alexander Stanislaus Mullins. Mulligan is known as Skin O' My Tooth in tribute to his flair for securing the acquittal of clients whose conviction seemed certain. Ostracised by dignified fellow lawyers for being so unprofessional as to act as an amateur detective when the case demands it, Mulligan is unprepossessing, but he gets results. His cases, belatedly gathered together in *Skin O' My Tooth* (1928), illustrated the fictional potential of the single-minded and sometimes unscrupulous solicitor-detective, which was further developed by H.C. Bailey in his books about Joshua Clunk, and by Anthony Gilbert (a pen-name of Lucy Malleson) in her long series featuring Arthur Crook.

Nor did the Baroness stop there. She also created Lady Molly Robertson-Kirk, an unlikely Head of Scotland Yard, who achieves eminence as a woman detective for the sole purpose of helping to free her husband from Dartmoor, where he has been incarcerated since his wrongful conviction for murder. Richard Marsh created Judith Lee, a teacher of the deaf and dumb, who found that her ability to lip-read was an invaluable aid to solving crime. There was a vogue for female sleuths around the turn of the century, and Matthias McDonnell Bodkin was quick to jump on the bandwagon, introducing Dora Myrl, 'the famous lady detective, whose subtle wit had foiled the most cunning criminals, whose cool courage had faced the most appalling dangers'. But if Bodkin ever intended to strike a blow for feminism, he changed his mind; Dora's ultimate fate was to marry his male protagonist Paul Beck, 'the rule of thumb detective', and resign herself to domesticity. Their union produced Paul Beck Jr., whose genetic inheritance made it inevitable that he too became a capable sleuth; his achievements were recorded in *Young Beck, a Chip off the Old Block* (1911).

Holmes and his rivals were seen at their best in short stories. After Wilkie Collins' masterpiece *The Moonstone* appeared in 1868, only a handful of first-rate British detective novels were published in the next thirty years. Crime writers had not learned how to combine a memorable detective, capable of solving a series of baffling crimes, with the form of a novel. A short story can succeed through a single trick; the length of a detective novel demands a complicated plot, or development of character, or both.

In his essay 'A Defence of Detective Stories', published in 1901, G.K. Chesterton argued that 'the first essential value of the detective story lies in this, that it is the earliest and only form of popular literature in which is expressed some sense of the poetry of modern life'. Chesterton, a poet, journalist and much else besides, created in Father Brown the outstanding new detective of Edwardian England, and became a powerful and passionate advocate for the genre: 'Not only is a detective story a perfectly legitimate form of art, but it has…real advantages as an agent of the public weal…When the detective in a police romance stands alone…it does certainly serve to make us remember that it is the agent of social justice who is the original and poetic figure.'

Crime writers began to explore the possibilities that Chesterton had identified. They tackled a dazzling variety of subjects: political unrest (Edgar Wallace), philosophy about human nature (Godfrey Benson), scientific enquiry (R. Austin Freeman), and social class (Roy Horniman). Meanwhile, Sherlock Holmes came back from the dead by public request, although it was widely accepted that despite escaping the icy torrents, he was never quite the same man again.

Times were changing. In 1912, the sinking of the 'unsinkable' RMS *Titanic* resulted in the death of one of the most talented American writers of detective fiction, Jacques Futrelle. The tragedy also seemed to herald a transition from confidence to unease and uncertainty. At much the same time, novels such as *At the Villa Rose* signalled the changing nature of crime fiction.

A.E.W. Mason's book was inspired by a real-life murder case, and so was Marie Belloc Lowndes' *The Lodger*.

• • ● • •

The detective short story was giving way to the detective novel. As crime writers struggled with the challenge of maintaining suspense and an air of mystery for the whole length of a novel, they experimented with techniques that their successors would refine. The significance of these developments went far beyond much-increased word counts. The genre was undergoing a metamorphosis that opened up opportunities for a brand new type of crime writing.

The Hound of the Baskervilles
by Arthur Conan Doyle (1902)

Sherlock Holmes is so closely associated with Victorian London's foggy, gas-lit streets in the popular imagination that it is surprising to realise that Arthur Conan Doyle wrote more stories about him in the twentieth century than in the nineteenth. Similarly, more of his cases were recorded after his apparent demise at the Reichenbach Falls in 'The Final Problem', in 1893, than before.

The idea for *The Hound of the Baskervilles* came from a young journalist (and occasional crime writer) called Bertram Fletcher Robinson, who told Doyle about a legend concerning a gigantic hound which terrorised the people of Dartmoor. The two contemplated co-authorship, but the story needed to be built around a compelling central character. Once Doyle decided that the material suited Sherlock Holmes, it became inevitable that he would write the book alone, although Robinson shared in the proceeds. Holmes experts disagree about the precise date when the story was set, but Doyle was untroubled by the fact that he had killed off the great detective: 'there was no limit to the number of papers he left behind or the reminiscences in the brain of his biographer'.

The story opens with a superb *tour de force* of deduction from the evidence of a walking stick (a 'Penang lawyer') left by a caller at 221b Baker Street, Dr James Mortimer. When Mortimer returns, he reads out to Holmes and Watson a story in an old manuscript about the ancient curse of the Baskervilles, and a recent newspaper account of the mysterious death of Mortimer's friend and patient, Sir Charles Baskerville. No signs of violence were found on Sir Charles' corpse, but there was 'an almost incredible facial distortion'. Mortimer reveals that he found footprints close to the body: 'Mr Holmes, they were the footprints of a gigantic hound!'

Sir Henry Baskerville, last of the line, is determined to live in the family home on Dartmoor, but Mortimer fears that 'every Baskerville who goes there meets with an evil fate'. Are they victims of a diabolical curse, or is there a more rational explanation? Holmes agrees to investigate.

Atmospheric and gripping, *The Hound of the Baskervilles* is the best of the four long stories about Holmes, although the structure is unsatisfactory, with Holmes off-stage for too long. Melodramatic elements such as the hereditary curse hark back to the Victorian 'novel of sensation', and it is easy to identify the villain. But Conan Doyle was not writing a tightly plotted whodunit of the kind that was to become so popular during the Golden Age of detective fiction. His fascination with the macabre, and his brisk, memorable descriptions of people and places, suited him ideally to writing short stories.

Sir Arthur Conan Doyle wrote tales of historical romance, horror and the supernatural, as well as non-fiction, but his fame rests primarily on his creation of the most famous of all detectives. Shortly after *The Hound of the Baskervilles* was published (it was serialised in the *Strand* magazine in 1901 before appearing in volume form the following year), the offer of a huge fee persuaded him to bring Holmes back from the dead in 'The Empty House' in 1903, and Holmes stories continued to appear until 1927. To this day, the great consulting detective enjoys worldwide popularity, fuelled in part by successful film and television adaptations, and a never-ending flow of pastiche stories by authors who find the appeal of the character, and the chance to write in Watson's distinctive narrative voice, impossible to resist.

The Four Just Men
by Edgar Wallace (1905)

The Four Just Men launched Edgar Wallace's career as a popular novelist in a blaze of publicity—and scandal. While working as a journalist for the *Daily Mail*, Wallace came up with the idea of writing a crime novel with a difference: the public was to be invited to solve the mystery. A man whose reckless self-confidence was matched only by his energy and vivid imagination, he dashed off the novel in a burst of feverish activity, but found it harder to interest a publisher than he had expected.

Undaunted, he set up his own business, the Tallis Press, and published the story himself, with a massive advertising campaign, including the offer of prizes totalling £500 to readers who deduced the correct solution to the mystery. The book was bound with a detachable competition form at the back, but the interactive publicity stunt proved so successful that it almost ruined Wallace financially. A large number of correct solutions were sent in, and he could not afford the prize money. His delay in announcing the winners led to suggestions that he was a swindler. To avoid bankruptcy, he had to borrow the money from Alfred Harmsworth, owner of the *Daily Mail*. He sold the copyright in the book cheaply, and failed to profit from later sales.

The Four Just Men amounted to an innovative example of the 'challenge to the reader' which—stripped of cash prizes—became a popular feature of later detective stories. Wallace's thriller was not only highly topical at the time it first appeared, but also, more than a century later, seems strikingly modern in its concerns—immigration and international terrorism.

A shadowy group, the 'Four Just Men' threaten to kill the British Foreign Secretary, Sir Philip Ramon, if he does not abandon the Aliens Extradition (Political Offences) Bill. The new law will, they claim, 'hand over to a corrupt and vengeful government men who now in England find an asylum from the persecution of despots and tyrants'. Ramon, cold-blooded but courageous, refuses to bow to intimidation, and the authorities take every precaution to protect him. The tension mounts as Wallace evokes the febrile atmosphere of a London gripped by fear of anarchy and assassinations. When death occurs, it takes place in a locked room, and appears inexplicable.

The attitudes of the Four Just Men seem, to say the least, morally ambiguous, and when Wallace resurrected them in later books, he aligned them more closely with the forces of law and order. A later move towards respectability has often been made by the genre's anti-heroes, but it is striking that the leading exception to the rule, Patricia Highsmith's Tom Ripley, remains the most memorable and consistently interesting homicidal protagonist.

The Four Just Men's ambivalent nature reflected the personality of their creator. Even when Richard Horatio Edgar Wallace became not merely a bestselling author but a high-profile celebrity, he remained a maverick and an outsider, rather than a pillar of the establishment. His gift for capturing a scene or character in a few vivid strokes compensated for the often slapdash nature of much of his work. For all his success, his extravagance meant that he died in debt, while working in Hollywood on the film *King Kong*. Like the fictional ape, Wallace was larger than life, and doomed to die too soon.

The Case of Miss Elliott
by Baroness Orczy (1905)

In 1901, Baroness Orczy published 'The Fenchurch Street Mystery', which introduced an unusual and distinctive detective, the Old Man in the Corner. This was the first of a series of half a dozen magazine stories, 'Mysteries of London', which were swiftly followed by seven more stories, each concerning mysteries in major cities such as Liverpool, Glasgow and Dublin. The stories about the Old Man in the Corner were eventually revised and collected in three volumes, of which *The Case of Miss Elliott* was the second in chronological terms, but the first to be published.

The Old Man sits at the same table in an ABC tea shop (one of a large chain of popular self-service tea shops operated by the Aerated Bread Company) on the corner of Norfolk Street and the Strand. There he drinks milk, eats cheesecake and fidgets incessantly with a piece of string. He acts as an armchair detective, with a 'Watson' who is a female journalist, originally unnamed but later called Polly Burton. The focus of the stories is on solving the puzzles rather than on ensuring that the guilty are punished for their crimes. The Old Man is not one of those detectives with a passion for justice, and he is dismissive of the forces of law and order, maintaining that the police 'always prefer a mystery to any logical conclusion, if it is arrived at by an outsider'.

The title story is typical of the series as a whole, as Polly and the Old Man discuss the discovery in Maida Vale of the body of a young woman, Miss Elliott, whose throat had been cut. The dead woman was clutching a surgical knife in her clenched hand, and at first it was unclear whether she had committed suicide or had been murdered. Miss Elliott was matron of a convalescent home, and then, as now, the finances of care homes were often in a perilous state. The Old Man has stirred himself to attend the inquest, where he learns enough to deduce the truth about a seemingly perfect alibi.

The Old Man is conceited and misanthropic, and even, it appears, capable of committing murder and getting away with it. The story-telling formula, although inherently limited, was neat and original, and the book enjoyed considerable popularity; it was included in the tiny library taken by Sir Ernest Shackleton on his ill-fated expedition to the South Pole in 1915. In later years Orczy wrote a further set of stories about the Old Man which were collected in a third volume, *Unravelled Knots* (1925), but by then his moment had passed.

Baroness Orczy liked to be called 'Emmuska'; her full name was Emma Magdolna Rozalia Maria Jozefa B0rbala Orczy di Orci. She was born in Hungary of noble descent, and moved to Britain with her family in 1880. She was a talented artist, but found fame and fortune as a writer, eventually earning enough money to buy an estate in Monte Carlo. Her increasing focus on historical fiction meant that she contributed little of note to the crime genre after the First World War. She became a founder member of the Detection Club, established in 1930, although by that time her main claim to literary fame lay in her stories about Sir Percy Blakeney, alias the Scarlet Pimpernel.

Tracks in the Snow
by Godfrey R. Benson (1906)

Godfrey Benson enjoyed a career of distinction before and after making a solitary venture into crime fiction. *Tracks in the Snow: Being the History of a Crime* is narrated by Robert Driver, rector of a country parish, and opens crisply: 'On the morning of the 29th of January, 1896, Eustace Peters was found murdered in his bed…Much mystery attached to the circumstances of his death. It was into my hands that chance threw the clue to this mystery.'

Peters is a former official with the Consular Service who retired early after years spent in the East, inherited a country house, Grenville Combe, and indulged himself in the leisure pursuits of an Edwardian gentleman. On the last night of his life, his guests were Driver, an Irishman called Callaghan, a German businessman called Thalberg, and the wealthy, enigmatic William Vane-Cartwright. By the time Driver awakes the next morning, snow lies on the ground outside Grenville Combe, and the master of the house has been stabbed to death. Footprints found in the snow appear to implicate the dead man's gardener, Reuben Trethewy, who had recently expressed a wish to kill his employer. Trethewy is arrested, but it soon becomes clear that the explanation for the crime lies elsewhere.

The quest for the truth about Peters' death proceeds at a leisurely pace characteristic of its period. Driver, appointed the dead man's executor, stumbles across correspondence which points the finger of guilt at one of his fellow supper guests, and despite a number of twists in a tale of jealousy and revenge, the identity of the culprit is easy to spot. Benson was not trying to write a complex whodunit, but simply to tell, as his subtitle indicates, a story about a crime with its roots in the past, and in lands far distant from England.

More than a year passes before the criminal is brought to justice, but occasional moments of tension occur, as when Driver is accompanied on an evening stroll by someone he believes to be a double murderer: 'It is not safe to be dealing with a desperate man, but, if you happen not to pity him, it is not a disagreeable sensation.'

Godfrey Rathbone Benson was educated at Winchester and Balliol College, Oxford, and became a lecturer in philosophy at Balliol. A man of many parts, he served as Liberal MP for Woodstock and later as Mayor of Lichfield, and held various public offices. His biography of Abraham Lincoln is to this day admired for its focus on character analysis and political philosophy. After Benson was elevated to the peerage in 1911, editions of *Tracks in the Snow* appeared under the name of Lord Charnwood. Later it sank into oblivion, but Benson's thoughtful, well-crafted prose, his insights into human behaviour, and the way in which the story touches on issues such as free will and the ramifications of Britain's imperial past combine to make his brief venture into the crime genre notable.

Israel Rank
by Roy Horniman (1907)

A polished and distinctive novel, *Israel Rank* is a black comedy whose cynical and ruthless narrator resorts to multiple murder with a view to inheriting a fortune. The story formed the basis of one of the most admired British films of the twentieth century, so it is surprising that the book has often been overlooked by historians of crime fiction. Subtitled *The Autobiography of a Criminal*, the book's ironic and amoral flavour is neatly captured in a preliminary note by the eponymous narrator: 'I am convinced that many a delightful member of society has found it necessary at some time or other to remove a human obstacle, and has done so undetected and undisturbed by those pangs of conscience which Society, afraid of itself, would have us believe wait upon the sinner.'

Israel Gascoyne Rank is the son of a woman who has 'married beneath her'; she is a member of the aristocratic Gascoyne family, and her husband is a Jewish commercial traveller. Israel is a dark and handsome young man who, despite being baptised a Christian, suffers because of anti-Semitism. He becomes obsessed with his remote connection to the Gascoyne peerage, and ascertains that eight lives separate him from the earldom. Of his decision to remove everyone who stands in his way, he explains coolly: 'I am not conscious of a natural wickedness staining and perverting all my actions. My career has been simply the result of an immense desire to be somebody of importance.'

Israel's relentless progress towards his goal makes for a compelling narrative, but in the years after Horniman's death, *Israel Rank* faded from the public mind. Graham Greene, working as an editor, included it in the Century Library, a series of reprints of unjustly forgotten books, and in 1949, a year after its reappearance in print, it formed the basis for the Ealing Studios black comedy *Kind Hearts and Coronets*. Robert Hamer's screenplay differed greatly from the novel, with Israel Rank transformed into Louis Mazzini, whose father was an Italian opera singer, and a brand new (and superior) conclusion. The changes may have been influenced by a desire, in the aftermath of the Second World War, to avoid any debate as to whether the portrayal of such a ruthless and egotistic (if charming) murderer was anti-Semitic.

The novel is edgy and provocative, perhaps reflecting the author's complex personality. Horniman devoted much of his life to vigorous campaigns for unpopular causes, and overall, it seems fair to regard his book as a condemnation of anti-Semitism, rather than some form of endorsement of it, while there is something quite modern about the book's flourishes of irony.

Roy Horniman, the son of a naval paymaster, became an actor and playwright, and was at one time tenant and manager of the Criterion Theatre. A wealthy bachelor and admirer of Oscar Wilde, he was prompted by a distaste for profiteering by private rail firms to write *How to Make the Railway Companies Pay for the War*, which ran to three editions. A vegetarian, antivivisectionist and crusader against censorship, he was closely associated with several charities, especially in the field of animal welfare. His other books included *The Viper* (1928), in which a sociopathic confidence trickster resorts to murder in the hope of profiting from an inheritance, but among his varied achievements, *Israel Rank* remains supreme.

The Blotting Book
by E.F. Benson (1908)

Morris Assheton, who has returned to live with his mother at the comfortable family home in Brighton after four years at Cambridge, is heir to a fortune. He will come in to the money if he marries with his mother's consent, and in any event when he reaches twenty-five. The two trustees in charge of the funds are solicitors in partnership, the seemingly benevolent and plausible Edward Taynton, and the younger, sharper Godfrey Mills.

Morris declines Taynton's suggestion that he should check through the accounts of the trust, which is precisely as Taynton had hoped, since otherwise, as he says to his partner, 'you and I would find it impossible to live elsewhere than in the Argentine Republic, were we so fortunate as to get there'. The two lawyers have unwisely gambled Morris' money on a hopeless investment in South African mines, and their attempts to recover their losses have ended in financial disaster.

The story unfolds slowly, reflecting the unhurried nature of life among the well-to-do in Edwardian Britain. Eventually, murder occurs, and the final scenes are devoted to courtroom drama. The solution, in a book with a small cast list, is far from surprising, but the quality of the writing keeps the reader wanting to turn the pages.

Edward Frederic Benson, no relation to the author of *Tracks in the Snow* (page 17), belonged to a brilliant if eccentric family. His father was Archbishop of Canterbury, his mother was described by Gladstone as 'the cleverest woman in England', and 'Fred' and three siblings who survived infancy all achieved distinction in their chosen fields. Fred published his first book while still a student at Cambridge, and his debut novel appeared in 1893 while he was working as an archaeologist in Athens. Later in life, he became Mayor of Rye in Sussex, and by the time of his death he had produced almost one hundred books, one of them devoted to figure skating, in which he was a skilled exponent who represented England. His most popular fiction was the Mapp and Lucia stories, which present an entertaining view of English social life and have twice been successfully televised.

Even Benson's lighter work occasionally displays his keen interest in the macabre. He wrote highly regarded ghost stories, sometimes humorous in tone, including 'The Bus-Conductor', which in 1945 supplied one element of the classic horror portmanteau film *Dead of Night*. In 1901, he tried his hand at crime fiction with *The Luck of the Vails*, his only other full-length work in the genre.

Introducing a reprint of *The Blotting Book* in 1987, Stephen Knight argued that the book may have influenced Agatha Christie, and that it amounts to 'a psychodrama among well-known people, looking forward to the methods of A.B. Cox, especially when he wrote as Francis Iles. Here there is no real detective; Superintendent Figgis thinks with his mouth open most of the time...the elements of a classic clue-puzzle are also present, time and place are as important as they would be to the Detection Club.' The plot is much less elaborate than those of the Golden Age of murder between the world wars, but the agreeable writing and delineation of character supply ample compensation.

The Innocence of Father Brown
by G.K. Chesterton (1911)

The Innocence of Father Brown was the first and best collection of stories about the little priest whose insight into human nature makes him a formidable amateur detective. Chesterton took a real-life friend, a Bradford priest, as his model, 'knocking him about; beating his hat and umbrella shapeless, untidying his clothes, punching his intelligent countenance into a condition of pudding-faced fatuity, and generally disguising Father O'Connor as Father Brown'. Father Brown became a convenient mouthpiece for Chesterton's opinions, and shared his creator's humanity and fascination with paradox.

The first Father Brown story, 'The Blue Cross', introduces the arch-criminal Flambeau and the policeman who pursues him, Valentin. Father Brown outwits Flambeau 'by being a celibate simpleton, I suppose…Has it never struck you that a man who does next to nothing but hear men's real sins is not likely to be wholly unaware of human evil?' He sees through Flambeau's attempt to disguise himself as a priest, because the villain attacks reason, which amounts to 'bad theology'.

Other stories make equally telling points. In 'The Invisible Man', Father Brown solves a perplexing case of murder by pointing out that an ordinary working person can seem 'mentally invisible' to others. Consequently, his presence at the scene of a crime may not be remembered by a witness. As he says, 'Nobody ever notices postmen somehow, yet they have passions like other men.'

Father Brown was suited to the short story form, and Chesterton wisely avoided attempting to include him in a novel. One unusual experiment, a forerunner of the game-playing that became common during the Golden Age of detective fiction, came in 1914 with 'The Donnington Affair'. Sir Max Pemberton, a journalist, dandy and author of crime and mystery fiction, wrote the first part of the story for a magazine, and invited Chesterton to try his hand at unravelling the mystery. Chesterton rose to the challenge, and Father Brown solved the case.

Gilbert Keith Chesterton loved detective stories, although one biographer, Michael Ffinch, has said: 'It is ironic that Chesterton is best known today for what he himself considered his least important work.' In later years, Chesterton wrote the Father Brown stories primarily to fund other activities. Like Arthur Conan Doyle before him, and novelists such as G.D.H. Cole in the Golden Age, he never expected his mysteries to survive long after his other writing faded from the public memory. At the time of writing, a daytime television series which shifts Father Brown to the Fifties, and offers storylines with scant resemblance to the originals, was enjoying perhaps unexpected popularity.

Chesterton's other detectives included Horne Fisher, who appeared in *The Man Who Knew Too Much* (1922; the title was later given by Alfred Hitchcock to two films unconnected with Chesterton), and Gabriel Gale, who features in *The Poet and the Lunatics* (1929). *The Man Who Was Thursday* (1908), which is prefaced by a poem addressed to his lifelong friend E.C. Bentley, is a metaphysical thriller reflecting his enthusiasm for the fantastic. Chesterton believed that: 'The whole point of a sensational story is that the secret should be simple. The whole story exists for the moment of surprise...It should not be something that it takes twenty minutes to explain.' The convoluted plotting of the full-length Golden Age whodunits was not for him, but in

1930 he accepted Anthony Berkeley's invitation to become first President of the Detection Club, and participated in the Club's activities with characteristic gusto.

At the Villa Rose
by A.E.W. Mason (1910)

Crime writers have always drawn on real-life cases when seeking inspiration for their fiction. Edgar Allan Poe, Wilkie Collins and Arthur Conan Doyle all wrote detective stories based on 'true crimes' that caught their interest, and so do many authors of today. In the hands of a talented novelist, the facts of a seemingly mundane or commonplace crime may be fashioned into an intriguing mystery, focusing on plot, character, setting or all three.

On a visit to the then-renowned Star and Garter hotel at Richmond, A.E.W. Mason saw two names scratched on a window-pane by a diamond ring: 'One was of Madame Fougere, a wealthy elderly woman who a year before had been murdered in her villa at Aix-les-Bains, the second was that of her maid and companion, who had been discovered…bound and chloroformed in her bed.' The incident stuck in his mind, and visits to a provincial conjuring show, a murder trial at the Old Bailey, and a restaurant in Geneva supplied him with further material for the plot of a detective novel. He conceived a French police professional, Inspector Hanaud, who was 'as physically unlike Mr Sherlock Holmes as he could possibly be'. Mason gave Hanaud a 'Dr Watson' in Mr Julius Ricardo, a fastidious dilettante who had made a fortune in the City of London.

At the Villa Rose opens with Ricardo spending the summer in Aix-les-Bains. On a visit to the baccarat table, he encounters a young Englishman, Harry Wethermill, together with Celia Harland, the pretty but impecunious girl to whom Harry has become attached. Less than forty-eight hours later, Harry calls on Ricardo for help. Celia's employer, Madame Dauvray, has been strangled, and her maid bound and chloroformed. Celia is missing, and is the obvious suspect. Presuming on a slight acquaintance, Ricardo persuades Hanaud to become involved in the case, and the legendary detective proceeds to unmask an unexpected culprit.

Already a well-regarded novelist and playwright, Mason wanted 'to make the story of what actually happened more intriguing and dramatic than the unravelling of the mystery and the detection of the criminal…to combine the crime story which produces a shiver with the detective story which aims at a surprise'. This worthy aim caused him to reveal whodunit long before the end of the book, with later chapters amounting to an extended explanatory flashback.

Albert Edward Woodley Mason was an accomplished all-rounder: an actor, politician, writer and spy. His novel of courage and adventure, *The Four Feathers* (1902), has been filmed no fewer than seven times. Hanaud is a memorable creation, and his friendship with Ricardo one of the most attractive early variations on the theme of detective and admiring stooge. The cosmopolitan backdrop of the story adds further appeal, while the plot blends the real-life source material with phoney spiritualism, baffling but logical detective work, and a 'least likely suspect' as villain. Its main flaw is the lop-sided story structure.

Mason waited for more than a decade before bringing Hanaud back in *The House of the Arrow* (1924). This time, he resolved 'to leave as little as possible, once the mystery was solved, to be cleared up and explained'. The result was an even better book, but *At the Villa Rose* remains a landmark in the genre. Three more Hanaud novels appeared at intervals; he made his final appearance as late as 1946 in *The House in Lordship Lane*, his only recorded case to take place in England.

The Eye of Osiris
by R. Austin Freeman (1911)

The Eye of Osiris blends elements of an actual murder in Boston, Massachusetts with forensic science, Egyptology and romance. The result is a memorable challenge for Dr John Thorndyke, an expert in medical jurisprudence, and the first major scientific detective to appear in twentieth-century crime fiction.

The Thorndyke stories occasionally drew on real-life mysteries, and in this novel the detective talks about how the murder in 1849 of a Boston businessman, George Parkman, by an impecunious lecturer, John Webster, resulted in an early triumph for forensic detection, and Webster's conviction and public hanging. The dead man's remains had been partially cremated, and as Thorndyke explains to his friend, Christopher Jervis, 'identification was actually effected by means of remains collected from the ashes of a furnace'. The human body is, Thorndyke says, 'a very remarkable object...it is extremely difficult to preserve unchanged, and it is still more difficult completely to destroy.'

Jervis narrates many of Thorndyke's cases, but here the story is told by a young physician called Paul Berkeley. A wealthy Egyptologist called John Bellingham has been missing for two years, leaving behind a strange and convoluted will. Berkeley becomes personally involved when he falls in love with the missing man's niece Ruth, who is living in poverty with her father Godfrey. When human remains come to light, it falls to

Thorndyke to identify them, and discover what happened to John Bellingham, and why.

The puzzle is cleverly constructed, and Freeman's meticulous handling of technical detail makes Thorndyke's investigation highly credible, even though the prose lacks sparkle, and the story proceeds at a stately pace. The 'love interest' did not appeal to every reader; even Dorothy L. Sayers—a fervent admirer of Freeman—deplored it. Thorndyke is, however, bluntly unapologetic. Perhaps speaking for Freeman, he insists: 'We should be bad biologists and worse physicians if we should underestimate the…paramount importance of sex; and we are deaf and blind if we do not hear and see it in everything that lives when we look around the world.'

Richard Austin Freeman qualified as a doctor before joining the Colonial Service and serving in Africa. Ill-health disrupted his medical career, and he turned to writing to supplement his income. He co-wrote two collections of short detective stories under a pseudonym prior to creating Thorndyke. *The Singing Bone* (1912) was an innovative collection of 'inverted' detective stories, in which the culprit is seen carrying out his criminal scheme before Thorndyke sets about unravelling it, although the book's originality and significance was not appreciated for many years.

Forensic detective work had already featured in Sherlock Holmes' cases (written by a doctor) and also in the stories co-authored by L.T. Meade and Robert Eustace. Freeman's discussions of science carried even greater authority, and Raymond Chandler, author of detective novels of a very different type, described him in a letter as 'a wonderful performer…he is also a much better writer than you might think, if you were superficially inclined, because in spite of the immense leisure of his writing, he accomplishes an even suspense which is quite unexpected.'

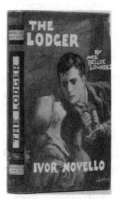

The Lodger
by Marie Belloc Lowndes (1913)

The Lodger began life as a short story inspired by a conversation which its author had overheard at a dinner party. A fellow guest's mother employed a butler and cook who married, and took in lodgers. The couple were convinced that Jack the Ripper had spent one night in their house, and Marie Belloc Lowndes became intrigued by the idea of living under the same roof as someone who proves to be a multiple murderer. After the story 'The Lodger' was published in the final issue of the American magazine *McClure's* in 1911, she was commissioned by the *Daily Telegraph* to write a novel for serialisation in the newspaper. The editor agreed to her proposed expansion of the short story, and the result was a notable early example of the novel of psychological suspense.

The strength of *The Lodger* derives from its focus on the tensions of domestic life rather than lurid melodrama. Robert and Ellen Bunting, who live in a 'grimy if not exactly sordid' street in west London (rather than Whitechapel, the actual scene of the Ripper's crimes), appear to present a cosy picture of comfortable married life. But appearances are deceptive; the couple are desperately short of money: 'Already they had learnt to go hungry and now they were beginning to learn to go cold.'

Financial salvation arrives in the form of a long, lanky man 'clad in an Inverness cape and an old-fashioned top hat', who knocks on the Buntings' door. He is looking for quiet rooms, and is willing to pay a good price. He says his name is Mr Sleuth, and his habit of quoting the Bible seems to Mrs Bunting to set the seal on his respectability. But four brutal murders have been committed in London over the past fortnight by someone calling himself 'the Avenger'. Before long, it begins to dawn on Mrs Bunting that her lodger may be nursing a very dark secret. But she is reluctant to betray him.

• • ● • •

The Lodger became a bestseller, and its popularity endured; later admirers included Ernest Hemingway and Gertrude Stein. The story was adapted for the stage, filmed four times (once by Alfred Hitchcock) and even, in 1960, turned into an opera by Phyllis Tate, with a libretto by the broadcaster David Franklin.

Marie Adelaide Belloc Lowndes had an English mother and a French father. Her younger brother, the poet and satirist Hilaire Belloc, was a close friend of G.K. Chesterton, and himself dabbled briefly in light-hearted fiction on the fringe of the crime genre. A feminist like her mother, Belloc Lowndes was an early member of the Women Writers' Suffrage League, and in *The Lodger* she observes: 'perhaps because she is subject rather than citizen, her duty as a component part of civilised society weighs but lightly on woman's shoulders'.

Her fascination with real-life crime led her to attend the trial of the Seddons, a husband and wife accused of poisoning an eccentric spinster. In her diary, she recorded that 'watching the prisoners was to me intensely interesting. They were the most respectable, commonplace-looking people imaginable.' *The Chink in the Armour* (1912) was inspired by the murder of Marie Lavin at Monte Carlo; *What Really Happened* (1926) drew on the unsolved Victorian murder of Charles Bravo; and *Letty Lynton* (1931) fictionalised the Madeleine Smith case, and was filmed with Joan Crawford in the lead. Belloc Lowndes also created a series detective, Hercule Popeau, whose name may have been lurking in Agatha Christie's subconscious when she came to christen the Belgian detective who appeared in her first novel.

Max Carrados
by Ernest Bramah (1914)

'The Coin of Dionysios' opens this first book of short stories about Max Carrados. It begins with a private enquiry agent, Louis Carlyle, visiting the home of an expert on numismatics. Ushered into the library, he is shocked when the expert, Max Carrados, asks if his name is Louis Calling. The men, it emerges, are old friends who have for contrasting reasons changed their names. Carlyle was a solicitor who was struck off after being wrongly accused of falsifying a trust account. He changed his appearance and became a private detective. Max Wynn inherited a fortune from an American cousin on condition that he changed his surname to Carrados. But he cannot see: as a result of being struck in the eye by a branch while out riding, he suffers from a form of blindness called amaurosis. Carlyle had changed his appearance, yet Carrados still recognised his voice: 'I had no blundering, self-confident eyes to be hoodwinked.'

Carrados' remaining senses are acute, and he admits to a secret hankering to become a detective. Carlyle's initial scepticism turns to astonishment when, after handing Carrados an ancient Greek coin which is a clue to the fraud he is investigating, the blind man solves the case with a flourish worthy of Sherlock Holmes: 'I should advise you to arrest [the culprit]…communicate with the police authorities of Padua for particulars of the career of Helene Brunesi, and suggest to Lord Seastoke that he should return to London to see what further depredations have been made in his cabinet.'

Although Carlyle is the professional, he acts as Carrados' Watson, while his friend's valet, Parkinson, usefully possesses a photographic memory. Carrados sees detection as a game comparable to cricket, and in 'The Game Played in the Dark', Carrados puts himself on a more than equal footing with the villains by extinguishing the lights. This plot device has been borrowed many times, for instance by Nigel Balchin in his screenplay for *23 Paces to Baker Street*, a film based on Philip MacDonald's *The Nursemaid Who Disappeared* (1938); Balchin dispensed with MacDonald's sleuth Anthony Gethryn and substituted a blind protagonist.

Introducing a subsequent collection of stories, *The Eyes of Max Carrados* (1923), Ernest Bramah described the extraordinary achievements of blind people over the years, adding that 'many of the realities of fact have been deemed too improbable to be transferred to fiction'. Carrados was far from being the only blind detective in fiction, and the early stories about him appeared at much the same time that the American Clinton H. Stagg created Thornley Colton, a sightless investigator known as 'the Problemist'. Colton appeared in eight short stories and a novel before Stagg was killed in a car crash at the age of twenty-six, but Carrados' career continued until 1934, when he appeared for the one and only time in a novel, *The Bravo of London*.

Ernest Brammah Smith started to write while unsuccessfully following in his father's footsteps as a farmer, and his first published book was *English Farming, and Why I Turned it Up* (1894). His stories about the itinerant Chinese story-teller Kai Lung achieved a vogue, but it is his detective stories which have stood the test of time. George Orwell, a critic with stern opinions about the genre, said that Carrados' cases were, together with those of Arthur Conan Doyle and R. Austin Freeman, 'the only detective stories since Poe that are worth rereading'.

Chapter Two

The Birth of the Golden Age

When E.C. Bentley decided to poke fun at the notion of the omniscient fictional detective, by creating a sleuth who proved all too fallible, he could not have imagined the consequences. Not only was the resulting novel, *Trent's Last Case* (page 36), a runaway bestseller, it also had lasting consequences for the genre. Other writers, as well as readers, were fascinated by the cleverness of the plot, and the story's lightness of touch. The carnage of the so-called 'war to end all wars' between 1914 and 1918 made people increasingly desperate for escapism and entertainment, and they fell on ingenious murder mysteries with delight.

Bentley's Philip Trent talks about 'detective sportsmanship', and the concept of the 'fair play' mystery was beginning to catch on. 'The game is afoot!' Sherlock Holmes had cried in 'The Abbey Grange', borrowing Shakespeare's phrase, but his was a game where readers were spectators, not fellow players. Holmes' admirers had no more chance of beating him to the truth of a case than did Dr Watson. Conan Doyle's stories were supremely atmospheric, frequently macabre and invariably gripping, but they were not elaborate fair-play whodunits. While some cases investigated by Holmes concerned murder, many did not. In a short story, an author did not necessarily need to introduce the ultimate crime in order to keep the reader engaged from start to finish.

Other than Wilkie Collins, relatively few Victorian authors had mastered the challenge of writing an intricate detective novel. Their successors in the first quarter of the twentieth century realised that, as murder was the ultimate crime, it was easier to sustain interest in a murder mystery, than, say, into a detailed investigation of a jewel robbery. In a full-length book, it was possible to introduce more suspects, and more clues and red herrings. High-quality fair-play detective short stories remained relatively uncommon, but novelists with a taste for the complex whodunit began to emerge, many of them influenced by the success of *Trent's Last Case*.

A handful of writers made effective use of the potential offered by exploration of criminal psychology (and a larger number soon started paying lip-service to it), while others focused on the detail of police investigation. As a war-weary public demanded escapism, and interesting games to play, a growing number of detective novelists began to invite readers to pit their wits against those of fictional sleuths. This was the genesis of new age of light literary entertainment—still remembered today as a Golden Age.

'The Golden Age of detective fiction' is a phrase which seems to have been coined by John Strachey, in an article which appeared in *The Saturday Review* in 1939. Strachey, a Marxist who later became a minister in Clement Attlee's post-war Labour government, was a detective-fiction addict, and the term was quickly adopted by fellow enthusiasts on both sides of the Atlantic. The 'Golden Age' is commonly regarded as the period between the two world wars; books by authors who came to prominence during that time continued to be published long after the Second World War ended, and so did books of a similar type, but the inter-war years saw the most innovative and ingenious work in the field of the classic, cerebral detective story.

Trent's Last Case
by E.C. Bentley (1913)

In writing *Trent's Last Case*, Bentley set out 'to write a detective story of a new sort'. A journalist who had in his youth invented the clerihew verse form, Bentley succeeded in that aim beyond his wildest dreams. Yet he embarked on his project in conventional fashion, drawing up a list of standard ingredients: 'a millionaire—murdered, of course; a police detective who fails where the gifted amateur succeeds; an apparently perfect alibi...a crew of regulation suspects, to include the victim's widow, his secretary, his wife's maid, his butler, and a person who had quarrelled openly with him ...'

Bentley's stroke of genius was to come up with an ironic twist: 'making the hero's hard-won and obviously correct solution of the mystery turn out to be completely wrong'. He was poking fun at the infallibility of 'great detectives' such as Sherlock Holmes, but what impressed readers was Bentley's combination of stylish writing and clever surprise solution. The book opens with a scathing denunciation of the ruthless American magnate Sigsbee Manderson. More than a century after the book was published, this passage retains its power, and reminds us that there is nothing new about the unpopularity of financiers:

> 'Many a time when he "took hold" to smash a strike,
> or to federate the ownership of some great field of

labour, [Manderson] sent ruin upon a multitude of tiny homes; and if miners or steelworkers or cattlemen defied him and invoked disorder, he could be more lawless and ruthless than they...Tens of thousands of the poor might curse his name, but the financier and the speculator execrated him no more. He stretched a hand to protect or to manipulate the power of wealth in every corner of the country. Forcible, cold, and unerring, in all he did he ministered to the national lust for magnitude; and a grateful country surnamed him the Colossus.'

Manderson is a striking example of the unpleasant victim, so invaluable to writers of Golden Age fiction. Odious characters like Manderson supplied suspects with plausible motives for murder, and their passing was not so tragic as to distract readers from matching their wits with the detective's.

Philip Trent is an artist who dabbles in journalism and amateur sleuthing, and even falls in love with Manderson's widow. When he learns, at the end of the story, that he had misunderstood the dead man's fate, he is abashed: "'I am cured. I will never touch a crime-mystery again. The Manderson affair shall be Philip Trent's last case. His high-blown pride at length breaks under him." Trent's smile suddenly returned. "I could have borne everything but that last revelation of the impotence of human reason.'"

Just as Trent was wrong about the killing of Sigsbee Manderson, he was mistaken in saying that he would never again touch a mysterious crime. He reappeared in short stories eventually collected in *Trent Intervenes* (1938) and in a second novel, *Trent's Own Case* (1936). Despite Bentley's exposure of 'the impotence of human reason', *Trent's Last Case* paved the way for the ingenious detective puzzles created by Agatha Christie, Dorothy L. Sayers and a host of other writers whose detectives excelled at solving those puzzles through reason.

Edmund Clerihew Bentley succeeded his lifelong friend G.K. Chesterton as President of the Detection Club. His later work even included a story parodying Lord Peter Wimsey, 'Greedy Night', but his enduring contribution to the genre remains his debut novel. It has been filmed three times, most notably in 1952, with Orson Welles cast as Manderson. *Trent's Own Case* (1936) was co-authored by Bentley and Herbert Warner Allen, a wine buff who had already created a sleuthing wine merchant called, in Bentley's honour, Mr Clerihew. Mr Clerihew makes a guest appearance in the jointly written novel. Warner Allen's own detective novels include *The Uncounted Hour* (1936).

In the Night
by Lord Gorell (1917)

In the Night, oddly neglected by many historians of the genre, is an early example of fair-play detective fiction. Lord Gorell sets out his manifesto in the foreword: 'Every essential fact is related as it is discovered and readers are, as far as possible, given the eyes of the investigators and equal opportunities with them of arriving at the truth.'

Writing about the history of crime fiction in the preface to *Great Short Stories of Detection, Mystery and Horror* (1928), Dorothy L. Sayers bracketed Gorell's novel with *Trent's Last Case*, and with George Pleydell's *The Ware Case* (a novel and play published in 1913, and filmed three times) when offering examples of one of the key strategies that detective story writers used to mislead readers. The method is 'to tell the reader what the detective has observed and deduced—but to make the observations and deductions turn out to be incorrect, thus leading up to a carefully manufactured surprise packet in the last chapter.'

Gorell offers a country-house murder mystery of the kind that became highly popular during the Golden Age. Sir Roger Penterton, owner of Salting Towers, and a wealthy businessman with few friends and many enemies, is found with a head wound, lying dead in the hall. Inspector Emmanuel Humblethorne of Scotland Yard happens to be holidaying in the neighbourhood, and takes a hand in the investigation.

A prodigal son is among the suspects, and it is even possible that the butler did it. Soon Evelyn Temple, a young woman with 'transparent vivacity and charm' finds herself indulging in amateur detective work. But she, like Philip Trent, is confounded in the end. As Humblethorne points out, 'the same facts can often be explained in several different ways.'

To help the reader grasp the detail of the layout of the scene of the crime, Gorell supplied a ground floor plan of Salting Towers. Soon, floor plans and maps became almost as common in whodunits as solutions in which 'the least likely person' proved to be the culprit.

The carnage of the First World War does not intrude on the storyline, although it had life-changing consequences for the author in the year the book was published. Ronald Gorell Barnes, the second son of the first baron Gorell, served in the Rifle Brigade, earning the Military Cross. In January 1917, his elder brother was killed in the conflict, and Ronald became the third baron Gorell. He was a man of many accomplishments: a journalist, poet and cricketer, who found time to serve as Under-Secretary of State for Air in the coalition government led by David Lloyd George. Four years later, he defected to the Labour Party, from which he was later expelled, along with Ramsay MacDonald.

He continued to write crime fiction intermittently, boasting that Arthur Conan Doyle said that *The Devouring Fire* (1928) 'had him guessing completely'. Evelyn Temple eventually returned in *Red Lilac* (1935), in which her cousin's unpleasant husband is murdered. Sayers praised the book, saying: 'Lord Gorell has a nice ear for dialogue, and a light and pleasant touch with description.' It has even been suggested that Gorell was a prototype for Lord Peter Wimsey. *In the Night* remains, however, his most significant contribution to the genre.

The Middle Temple Murder
by J.S. Fletcher (1919)

The Middle Temple Murder would nowadays be described as J.S. Fletcher's 'breakthrough' crime novel. When President Woodrow Wilson read the story while recovering from illness and heaped praise upon it, Fletcher's American publishers made the most of the encomium. Sales of his fiction surged, and he was for a time regarded in the US as the finest crime writer to have emerged since Arthur Conan Doyle.

Frank Spargo, who works for the *Watchman* newspaper, is walking home from Fleet Street early on a June morning in 1912 when he learns that a body has been discovered in the entrance to chambers in Middle Temple Lane. The victim, an elderly man, has been battered to death, but is still clutching a piece of paper bearing the name and address of Ronald Breton, a young barrister. Inspector Rathbury proves remarkably accommodating in providing Spargo with inside information about the case, and the journalist pursues his own enquiries with youthful vigour. Spargo discovers that the dead man had recently returned to England from Australia, and was seen in the company of a Member of Parliament called Stephen Aylmore. It emerges that Aylmore was an old acquaintance of the deceased, and his evasiveness arouses suspicion. The police arrest him, but Spargo persists with an investigation which ultimately takes him to the fell country of the north. There he finally discovers the identity of the killer.

Joseph Smith Fletcher was born in Halifax in 1863, and worked as a journalist and sub-editor (like Frank Spargo), sometimes writing under the by-line 'A Son of the Soil'. He produced novels in the dialect of his native Yorkshire, guidebooks, poetry, biography and historical romances; his regional writing led to him being called 'the Yorkshire Hardy'. As the twentieth century dawned, he began to concentrate on crime fiction, and *The Adventures of Archer Dawe, Sleuth Hound* (1909) gathered short stories about a Yorkshire detective; elements from one, 'The Contents of the Coffin', were refashioned for *The Middle Temple Murder*.

Spargo did not appear in any more novels, and although Paul Campenhaye, a 'specialist in criminology', appeared in a book of short stories, it was not until late in his career that Fletcher bowed to fashion and created a series detective, the London-based Ronald Camberwell. He died before completing his final novel, *Todmanhawe Grange* (1937), and the book was finished by Edward Powys Mathers, better known as 'Torquemada', a crossword compiler and crime fiction reviewer for the *Observer*.

Mathers explained in an introductory note that Fletcher 'left clear notes outlining the third murder, indicating the party guilty of the first and second murders, and even providing the last sentence of the book.'

Fletcher produced considerably in excess of two hundred books in his lifetime; inevitably, the quality of his work fluctuated. He belonged to an older generation of writers than Agatha Christie and other dominant figures of the Golden Age, and his work began to seem dated even during his lifetime. After his death in 1935, his reputation went into steep decline, and has never fully recovered. *The Middle Temple Murder* remains, however, one of the most enjoyable crime novels of its period. The plot ingredients—false identities and long-ago swindles—often crop up in Fletcher's work, but the book is skilfully structured. The pace and the plot twists (with the revelation in the closing paragraphs of an unexpected culprit) make for entertainment lively enough to take even a President's mind off ill-health and the cares of office.

The Skeleton Key
by Bernard Capes (1919)

It is symptomatic of Bernard Capes' successful yet unlucky life
that his solitary, yet substantial, contribution to the crime genre
was only published after his death in 1918; he died from heart
failure after being struck down by the epidemic of influenza.
Introducing *The Skeleton Key*, G.K. Chesterton highlighted the
quality of Capes' writing: 'From the first his prose had a strong
element of poetry.' Julian Symons, in his seminal study of the
genre, *Bloody Murder*, described the book as 'a neglected *tour
de force*'.

The story opens with an extract from a manuscript written
by Vivian Bickerdike; further segments are interspersed with a
third-person narrative throughout the book. Capes plays with
viewpoint in order to heighten suspense and facilitate plot twists,
just as Wilkie Collins had done long before in *The Moonstone*
(1868), and as Agatha Christie, Dorothy L. Sayers and countless others (not least Gillian Flynn in the twenty-first-century
bestseller *Gone Girl*) would do in the future.

Capes injected glamour into his story with a scene set in
Paris, where Bickerdike meets the Baron Le Sage, an affable
adventurer who plays chess for money. A road accident occurs,
but its significance only becomes clear at the end of the book. A
year later, the pair join a country-house party at Wildshott, the
Hampshire seat of Sir Calvin Kennett. Le Sage's Gascon valet,

Louis Cabanis, quickly falls for an attractive under-housemaid, but she rejects his advances. Tension builds during a dinner conversation when Le Sage argues that 'a successful crime is not a crime which baffles its investigators, but a crime which does not appear as a crime at all'.

Next day, a shooting party takes place. Shooting parties proved an invaluable pastime over many years for writers of country-house mysteries, ranging from the unlikely (Anton Chekhov's entertaining novel of 1884, *The Shooting Party*) to the rather more conventional, such as two novels of 1934, John Ferguson's *The Grouse Moor Mystery*, and J.J. Connington's *The Ha-Ha Case*. The outcome is that a member of Le Sage's household is shot dead.

Sergeant Ridgway of Scotland Yard is summoned to investigate; as Bickerdike says, 'A notable writer has somewhat humoured a belief in the fatuity of the professional detective; but that was with a view, I think, to exalt his own incomparable amateur.' A lengthy chapter is devoted to an account of the inquest, a pattern that became commonplace in detective novels of the Golden Age, but the jury's conclusion that Cabanis is guilty is soon disproved.

Subtle touches of plotting as well as characterisation lift *The Skeleton Key* out of the ordinary. The story illustrates Chesterton's claim that: 'A detective story might well be in a special sense a spiritual tragedy; since it is a story in which even the moral sympathies may be in doubt. A police romance is almost the only romance in which the hero may turn out to be the villain, or the villain to be the hero.'

Bernard Capes worked as a tea broker before studying at the Slade School of Art. He edited a periodical called *The Theatre*, and later had a brief and unsuccessful stint as a rabbit farmer. He turned to fiction in his forties, novels and short stories pouring from his pen. His 'strange stories' were highly accomplished, and Chesterton, a lover of contradictions, pointed out the paradox that Capes 'was insufficiently appreciated because he did popular things well.'

The Cask
by Freeman Wills Crofts (1920)

Set in 1912, *The Cask* opens with a minor accident at St Katherine Docks. Dock workers unloading casks that have arrived in London from continental Europe drop one, causing it to split slightly. They discover that it contains gold sovereigns, but more than that, a woman's hand is visible inside. The police are called, but by the time they arrive, the cask has vanished. A mysterious Frenchman has claimed the cask as his own.

Aided by good work from a police constable who 'had read Conan Doyle, Austin Freeman and other masters of detective fiction', Inspector Burnley of Scotland Yard traces the Frenchman, Felix Leon, together with the cask. Inside the cask is the body of a beautiful woman, who has been strangled. This remains a vivid and memorable image, even when described in Crofts' sober, functional prose.

Who is the woman, and how did she meet her fate? To find the answers, Burnley and his colleagues embark on a lengthy investigation. One suspect possesses an apparently impregnable alibi, and the action switches back and forth between England and France as the police struggle to break it. They call on Georges La Touche, 'the smartest private detective in London', for help; La Touche is half-English, half-French, and he plays a crucial part in unravelling a mystery with a cosmopolitan flavour.

The meticulous account of detective work, coupled with the ingenuity of the construction (and deconstruction) of the alibi were to become Freeman Wills Crofts' hallmarks, and they set his debut novel apart from the competition. Over the next twenty years, the book sold more than 100,000 copies.

Dublin-born Crofts became a crime novelist by accident. A railway engineer, he started writing the book 'as an escape from boredom during recovery from a long illness'. After much revision, it was accepted for publication, and its immediate success prompted him to keep writing. He continued to make use of interesting foreign locations; Inspector Tanner journeys to Portugal in *The Ponson Case* (1921), a disappointingly anti-climactic follow-up to *The Cask*, while the first part of *The Groote Park Murder* (1923) is set in South Africa. Travel, whether by road, train, boat, or plane, plays an important part in many of his books, and trickery with journey times is often crucial to his culprits' cleverly constructed alibis.

In his fifth book, he introduced the good-natured but relentless Inspector Joseph French, who became his most famous detective. By the end of the decade, Crofts had earned the admiration of no less an authority than T.S. Eliot, retired from the Belfast and Northern Counties Railway, and settled in England to write full-time. Even Raymond Chandler, no fan of this type of story, acknowledged him as the 'best plodding detail man'. Introducing a reprint of *The Cask*, Crofts modestly admitted the book's shortcomings—thin characterisation and an excess of padding—but it represents a milestone in the evolution of the detective story.

The Red House Mystery
by A.A. Milne (1922)

A.A. Milne is now so closely associated with Winnie-the-Pooh and children's fiction that it comes as a surprise to many readers to learn that, prior to creating Pooh, Eeyore, Piglet and their friends, he wrote an immensely popular detective novel. *The Red House Mystery* is a country-house mystery, so deftly written that it achieved widespread acclaim.

Mark Ablett, wealthy owner of the eponymous Red House, has been hosting a party of guests when Antony Gillingham, an affable and well-travelled young man, calls, hoping to catch up with his old friend Bill Beverley. He stumbles upon a locked-room mystery: Mark's 'black sheep' brother Robert has apparently been shot between the eyes, and Mark, a selfish drunkard, is nowhere to be found. Antony takes it upon himself to investigate, with Bill acting as his Watson.

Milne was well known for his humorous writing in *Punch* at the time the book was published, and despite the change of direction, his tone is characteristically light-hearted. In the aftermath of a bloody war, whodunit puzzles offered an ideal form of escapism, and Bill finds it hard to think of Mark Ablett 'as an escaped murderer, a fugitive from justice, when everything was going on just as it did yesterday, and the sun was shining…How could you help feeling that this was not a real tragedy, but merely a jolly kind of detective game that he and Antony were playing?'

Despite moving on to books for children, Milne retained his 'passion for detective stories' and wrote a witty and incisive introduction to a new edition of this novel, four years after its first publication. He insisted that detective fiction should be written in 'good English' and abhorred the complications that ensue from 'love interest'. He favoured amateur detectives and fair play, arguing that 'the detective must have no more special knowledge than the reader'. Readers should know what was in the detective's mind, and for that reason a 'Watson' figure was invaluable: the sleuth must 'watsonise or soliloquise; the one is merely a dialogue form of the other, and for that, more readable'.

Such was the popularity of Winnie-the-Pooh that it is often forgotten that, apart from this novel, Alan Alexander Milne also enjoyed success as a screenwriter and a playwright. His play *The Fourth Wall* (1929) is on the fringe of the crime genre, and he also wrote crime short stories, but although the closing lines of *The Red House Mystery* suggest that Antony will tackle further cases, Milne never wrote a second detective novel. The chances are that, like E.C. Bentley, he would have struggled to improve upon his enjoyable debut.

Chapter Three

The Great Detectives

The decade following the end of the First World War saw the emergence of a new generation of detective novelists. Many were young—sometimes *very* young; Margery Allingham's first novel appeared when she was only nineteen—but also ambitious and dynamic. They had survived the carnage, but none of them had been left unscathed. Many had lost friends and family members; some had themselves been wounded. With the coming of peace, they were, like the public at large, in the mood for fun and games.

Agatha Christie, Dorothy L. Sayers, Philip MacDonald and their colleagues wanted to write lively mysteries that tested readers' wits. Their task was to create a post-war incarnation of the 'Great Detective', someone who could solve a fiendishly complex puzzle before anyone else. But these detectives, and their creators, had to jump a hurdle that Sherlock Holmes and Arthur Conan Doyle never faced. Fair play demanded that all the clues should be laid out in the story, so that readers had an opportunity to test their own skills in deductive reasoning before the truth was finally revealed.

The broader canvas afforded by a novel made this possible. Red herrings abounded, as well as clues. The pool of suspects—typically in a 'closed community', such as the guests at a traditional country-house party—became larger, presenting more options for mystification. Authors developed increasingly sophisticated techniques of misdirection, none more so than Agatha Christie. Her special gift was the ability to deceive readers time and again without having her detectives rely upon sophisticated scientific or technical expertise or other esoteric knowledge. This set her apart from writers such as R. Austin Freeman, of whom Sayers said: 'Thorndyke can cheerfully show you all his finds. You will be none the wiser, unless you happen to have an intimate acquaintance with the fauna of local ponds; the effect of belladonna on rabbits; the physical and chemical properties of blood; optics; tropical diseases; metallurgy; hieroglyphics, and a few other trifles.'

Sayers thought that 'the modern revolution' in the direction of playing fair was 'a recoil from the Holmes influence and a turning back to *The Moonstone* (1868) and its contemporaries', but Sergeant Cuff, although a memorable and significant character, did not dominate *The Moonstone* in the way that Great Detectives towered over the mysteries in which they appeared. Cuff was much more fallible than the relentlessly brilliant Hercule Poirot. Even Philip Trent, whose flawed deductions lay at the heart of the narrative in *Trent's Last Case*, soon returned to prove his worth as a sleuth. The question for readers of Golden Age detective stories was whether, if they too were presented with all the clues to a baffling puzzle or whodunit or howdunit, they might be sharp-witted enough to work out the solution before the Great Detective revealed all in the closing pages.

Sergeant Cuff was, above all, a professional police officer, with a real-life model in Inspector Whicher. The Great Detectives of the Golden Age were almost invariably amateurs who were fascinated by criminology, such as Lord Peter Wimsey, or professionals who worked alongside the police but were not part of the force. A diverse bunch, they included H.C. Bailey's Reggie Fortune, Christopher Bush's Ludovic Travers, and Maud Silver, created by Patricia Wentworth, a pen-name for Dora Amy Elles. Miss Silver was a former governess who became a private detective in order to supplement her retirement income, and flourished in her unlikely second career, solving mysteries flavoured with romance.

J.J. Connington's Sir Clinton Driffield was exceptional, a unique example of a Great Detective who is also a Chief Constable, his flair underlined by his elevation to that high office at the tender age of thirty-five. Even he retired to enjoy an interlude as an amateur sleuth, as Connington experimented with a new police detective, Superintendent Ross, before changing his mind, and restoring Sir Clinton to his original post in charge of the county force. Writing about professional police officers, as Freeman Wills Crofts demonstrated, required paying at least some attention to procedure and plausibility, even if authors such as Ngaio Marsh allowed their policemen the luxury of an occasional flash of deductive brilliance.

Writing about the genre in 1928, Sayers argued that 'love interest' was a potential impediment to the success of a detective novel, but she recognised that times were changing: 'As the detective ceases to be impenetrable and infallible and becomes a man touched with the feelings of our infirmities, so the rigid technique of the art necessarily expands a little.' Her own development as a crime writer reflected this, and she transformed Lord Peter Wimsey from a sleuthing equivalent of Bertie Wooster into a mature and rounded character. She even gave him a 'love interest', in the form of an extensive courtship of Harriet Vane, which reached a successful conclusion in *Gaudy Night* (1935). Two years later, Sayers denied that marriage would be the end of him as a detective: 'I can see no end to Peter this side of the grave.... His affairs are more real to me than my own.' But her crystal ball proved cloudy. Although she kept writing until her death in 1957, to all intents and purposes, Wimsey's career was already over.

Lesser writers struggled to create memorable Great Detectives. Brian Flynn's long-forgotten Anthony Bathurst made his debut in *The Billiard-Room Mystery* (1927), set in a country house during Cricket Week, in which he was critical of some fictional sleuths. This was rather rash – especially given that the American critics Jacques Barzun and Wendell Hertig Taylor dismissed one of his own later cases, *Conspiracy at Angel* (1947) as "straight tripe" – but Bathurst enjoyed a long career as a private investigator, and some of the mysteries he solved were ingeniously contrived. The concept of the Great Detective was, however, starting to seem shop-worn even during the Golden Age.

Just as E.C. Bentley had meant to do with *Trent's Last Case*, and as Anthony Berkeley did in creating the error-prone Roger Sheringham, novelists with a more original turn of mind began to enjoy subverting the notion of the Great Detective. Their chosen method was often parody, but the most original novel of this kind appeared as late as 1945. This was *The Ingenious Mr Stone* by Robert Player.

Player gave a neat twist to Golden Age conventions. A pleasingly differentiated trio of narrators tell, in leisurely fashion, a story set in part at a girls' school in Torquay whose head teacher is murdered. The eponymous Lysander Stone, an idiosyncratic private investigator said to be the most suitable man in Europe to investigate the case, does not even make a formal appearance until the second half of the story. A bewildering sequence of strange and suggestive incidents make it impossible for the reader to be quite sure what is going on until the final narrator, the elderly Mrs Bradford, 'describes the methods used by Lysander Stone in solving the Langdon-Miles problem'. The diversity of voices adds to the delights of a story packed with plot twists and wit. But despite the fact that Poirot and some of his peers continued to ply their trade long after the Second World War, their greatest days belonged to the past. *The Ingenious Mr Stone* signalled the end of the era.

The Mysterious Affair at Styles
by Agatha Christie (1920)

The First World War cast a long shadow over the Twenties. Its impact on people's lives is evident from the outset of Agatha Christie's first novel, which she began writing in 1916. Captain Arthur Hastings, recently invalided home from the Western Front, is invited to spend his sick leave with friends at Styles Court. In the green and peaceful Essex countryside, Hastings finds it almost impossible to believe that war is raging not so very far away: 'I felt I had suddenly strayed into another world.' He confesses to his hosts that, when the war is over, he has 'a secret hankering to be a detective'; before long, he bumps into the little man who had fired his imagination years earlier in Belgium, and whose name is Hercule Poirot.

Poirot, once a famous detective but now a refugee from the conflict, is living nearby. He and some fellow countrymen have benefited from the charitable work of Mrs Emily Inglethorp, wealthy chatelaine of Styles, whose recent marriage to a much younger man has proved unpopular with other members of her family. When Mrs Inglethorp dies of strychnine poisoning, Hastings seeks Poirot's aid, and they form an updated version of the Holmes–Watson partnership.

Hastings describes Poirot as an 'extraordinary-looking man'; he is short, with an egg-shaped head and stiff moustache. 'The neatness of his attire was almost incredible', Hastings says, choosing a topical comparison to emphasise his point: 'I believe a speck of dust would have caused him more pain than a bullet wound.' Poirot is vain, obsessed with order and method, and a master of the enigmatic remark that misleads Hastings, as well as the reader, as to where his suspicions really lie.

Christie blends a rich variety of ingredients, including floor plans, facsimile documents, an inheritance tangle, impersonation, forgery and courtroom drama. The originality of her approach lay in the way she prioritised the springing of a surprise solution ahead of everything else—including characterisation and description of setting.

Her prose is economical, rather than evocative, but *The Mysterious Affair at Styles* set the pattern for dozens of Christie's later novels. Poirot made a successful return in *The Murder on the Links* (1923), much of which is set in France, although the short stories gathered in *Poirot Investigates* (1924) show that Christie's method of hiding clues among red herrings was better suited to a longer story. The third Poirot novel, *The Murder of Roger Ackroyd* (1926), notable for a solution so daring that it briefly created controversy, remains one of the most famous of all detective novels, and secured the reputation of both character and author. The little Belgian ranks second only to Holmes in the pantheon of Great Detectives.

Agatha Mary Clarissa Christie (née Miller) worked in a pharmacy during the First World War, and put her knowledge of poisons to good use in *The Mysterious Affair at Styles* and many other stories. Speculation about the reasons for her brief, highly publicised disappearance in 1926, at a time when her marriage was in crisis, continues, but her fame rests on the enduring worldwide popularity of her books. Nobody has ever written ingenious whodunits with such consistency, and nobody has ever matched her worldwide sales. More than half a century after her death, she remains a household name.

Clouds of Witness
by Dorothy L. Sayers (1926)

Lord Peter Wimsey was created as a conscious act of escapism by a young writer who was short of money, and experiencing one unsatisfactory love affair after another. Peter Death Bredon Wimsey, second son of the Duke of Denver, began his fictional life as a fantasy figure. He was rich, handsome, charming and above all, highly intelligent. At Eton, he earned a reputation as an outstanding cricketer, cemented during his years at Balliol College, Oxford, where, naturally, he took First Class honours in History. During the Great War, he earned the Distinguished Service Order for 'recklessly good intelligence work behind the German front', before being blown up and buried in a shell-hole, and suffering post-traumatic stress disorder (as it would now be called) as a result. His convalescence was aided by a love of music and books shared with his creator, and he set himself up in a flat in Piccadilly with a devoted manservant, Mervyn Bunter, who had served as his sergeant during the war.

Wimsey's life took a new turn when he indulged in detective work to help solve 'the business of the Attenbury Emeralds' (eventually written up as a 'continuation novel', *The Attenbury Emeralds*, by Jill Paton Walsh in 2010). He befriended Charles Parker of Scotland Yard, and as his uncle said: 'The only trouble about Peter's new hobby was that it had to be more than a hobby...You cannot get murderers hanged for your own private entertainment. Peter's intellect pulled him one way, and his nerves another...At the end of every case we had the old nightmares and shell-shock all over again. And then Denver [Peter's elder brother, Gerald, Duke of Denver]...must needs get himself indicted on a murder charge and stand his trial in the House of Lords.'

Clouds of Witness tells the story of the Denver case, Wimsey's second recorded investigation. He is enjoying an extended holiday in Corsica when he learns that the man engaged to his sister Mary, Captain Denis Cathcart, has been found shot dead shortly after quarrelling with Denver. At the inquest, a coroner's jury returned a verdict finding Denver guilty of the murder. Wimsey and Parker investigate, and soon become convinced that both Denver and Mary have something to hide.

While Wimsey makes a transatlantic dash to attend the trial after pursuing his enquiries in the USA, the lawyer Sir Impey Biggs describes him as 'cleaving the air high above the wide Atlantic. In this wintry weather he is braving a peril which would appal any heart but his own and that of the world-famous aviator whose help he has enlisted so that no moment may be lost in freeing his noble brother from this terrible charge.' His Lordship is not only a Great Detective but also (unlike Poirot) a dashing man of action. At this stage of his career, Sayers' portrayal of him verged on caricature, but as her confidence grew, she sought to characterise him in greater depth; the turning point came in *Strong Poison* (1930), when he fell in love with Harriet Vane, who had been charged with murdering her lover.

Clouds of Witness is the work of a novelist learning her craft, but manifests the story-telling qualities that soon earned fame for Dorothy Leigh Sayers. An Oxford-educated intellectual, she was also a notable historian and critic of the genre whose reviews for the *Sunday Times* display erudition, energy and enthusiasm in equal measure. Together with Anthony Berkeley, she became a driving force in the Detection Club, using experience gained in the advertising world to help build its reputation; she succeeded E.C. Bentley as President in 1949. Her detective fiction became increasingly ambitious, and although opinion remains divided as to the extent of its success, her contribution to the development of the genre was highly significant before she abandoned crime writing at the end of the Thirties to concentrate on religious writing and translating Dante.

The Rasp
by Philip MacDonald (1924)

Among the Great Detectives suited to crime-solving in the Twenties were several men who had experienced 'a good war'. Colonel Anthony Ruthven Gethryn, who first appeared in *The Rasp*, was a prime example. He is introduced as 'something of an oddity. A man of action who dreamed while he acted; a dreamer who acted while he dreamed.' His parents were 'a hunting country gentleman' who was also a brilliant mathematician, and a Spanish woman who had been a dancer, mannequin, actress and portrait painter. The vivid if exaggerated characterisation is symptomatic of a young, energetic author serving his literary apprenticeship; MacDonald was still in his early twenties.

As if being courageous, handsome, modest and likeable were not enough, Gethryn was in addition an excellent sportsman, and an Oxford graduate skilled in mathematics; he 'also became known as a historian and man of classics'. He was called to the Bar, wrote novels and poetry, worked in politics, and then served with distinction in the infantry before being wounded in action. Recruited by the Secret Service, he went undercover in Germany: 'It was queer work, funny work, work in the dark, work in strange places.' Showered with decorations by 'a grateful Government' and 'a baker's dozen of other orders (foreign)', he inherited a fortune, and invested in a periodical called *The Owl*.

When the editor of *The Owl* urges him to look into the sensational murder of John Hoode, Gethryn leaps at the chance. Hoode is Minister of Imperial Finance, and one of many politicians who are murder victims in Golden Age mysteries, perhaps because countless people had motives to kill them. He has been bludgeoned to death, with a wood-rasp, in the study of his country house, Abbotshall. Gethryn falls in love with a young widow, Lucia Lemesurier, who lives across the river from the scene of the crime, but his pursuit of her is complicated by the fact that the man her sister loves is a prime suspect.

Gethryn often mentions detective stories, and intertextuality of this kind became commonplace in Golden Age fiction. Scientific know-how culled from Dr Thorndyke's debut, *The Red Thumb-Mark* (1907) helps him to solve a puzzle about fingerprints. He makes use of his acting ability in unmasking the culprit, and wins over Lucia. The zest of MacDonald's prose contributed to the book's success, and compensated for flaws such as Gethryn's very lengthy explanation of the mystery at the end. During the Twenties, 'love interest' in detective stories was frowned on by purists such as A.A. Milne and Dorothy L. Sayers, but MacDonald's romantic sub-plot proved to be ahead of its time. Gethryn's lead was followed by several Golden Age detectives—even Sayers' Lord Peter Wimsey—who married a woman they met through solving a murder.

Gethryn returned in books which demonstrate MacDonald's gift for building suspense, such as *The Noose* (1930), where he races against time to save an innocent man from the gallows; the surprise solution is a variant of that in *The Skeleton Key* (page 43). Gethryn's appearances became infrequent after the mid-Thirties, but he did not take his final bow until 1959, in *The List of Adrian Messenger*, an extraordinary story of multiple murder that was later filmed by John Huston.

Philip MacDonald came from a distinguished literary family; his grandfather, George Fraser MacDonald, was an inspiration to Chesterton and C.S. Lewis, and he co-wrote his first two novels with his father Ronald MacDonald. MacDonald and J.

Jefferson Farjeon co-wrote a screenplay based on *The Rasp* which was filmed by the legendary Michael Powell in 1932. MacDonald became a versatile scriptwriter, working on projects as varied as *Raise the Roof*, said to be the first British film musical, and—after relocating to the United States—the classic movies *Rebecca* and *Forbidden Planet*. Hollywood's gain was crime fiction's loss.

Mr Fortune, Please
by H.C. Bailey (1927)

In 'The Missing Husband', first of the half-dozen stories in this volume, Reggie Fortune is encountered lazing in a hammock in 'an orchard where the apple-blossom rose out of a flood of bluebells', but H.C. Bailey soon reminds his reader of the darker side of life. Reggie is recovering from 'the blood-poisoning which he acquired in his work as medical expert for the Crown upon the historic crime of the abominable Armenian, Commensus'. He is consulted by his friend the Hon. Sidney Lomas, Chief of the CID, and a missing person inquiry develops into a murder investigation. When Lomas says that the culprit would have escaped justice if the local police had handled the case, Reggie muses, in his customary languid way, 'I wonder how many clever fellows do get away with it?'

Reggie Fortune was unique among Great Detectives to emerge after the First World War in that he was seen to best advantage in short stories rather than in novels. The stories were longer than the typical detective short story, and often explore intense human passions which seldom darken detective stories of the Twenties written by Bailey's peers.

In 'The Quiet Lady', Reggie discusses criminal motivation with an elderly doctor: 'Fellow thinks he's a very important fellow. Ought to have more than he's got. Ought to have his own way. So he takes it...Conceit...Desire to show what a wonderful fellow he is. To prove his power over people's lives. Some fellows will do anything for that.' The telegraphic style of dialogue is characteristic, and so is the horrific behaviour of the culprit; Reggie summarises the case as: 'Not a nice business.' When the old doctor accuses him of being 'rather terrible…if you're not sure, let's have mercy', Reggie's bleak response is: 'Mercy—that's not my department. I work for justice.'

'The Little House' sees Reggie dealing with 'one of the few cases that have frightened him'. A seemingly innocuous, if puzzling, incident concerning a lost kitten introduces a grim tale about cruelty. The mistreatment of children is a subject that recurs in Bailey's work, as does the stinging cynicism in Reggie's remark: 'I use only evidence. That's why I don't get on with lawyers and policemen.'

Henry Christopher Bailey began his literary career as an author of historical and romantic fiction, publishing his first novel shortly after leaving Oxford. He became a journalist, spending many years with the *Daily Telegraph*, where he was a colleague of E.C. Bentley. He turned to detective fiction after the First World War, perhaps partly influenced by Bentley's success, at much the same time as younger writers such as Christie and Sayers, but he lacked their interest in playing elaborate games with readers.

Reggie Fortune, adviser to the Home Office, appeared in no fewer than eight collections of stories before his first appearance in a novel, *Shadow on the Wall* (1934). Agatha Christie was among his admirers: 'The stories stand or fall by Mr Fortune. It is not the cases themselves but Mr Fortune's handling of them wherein lies the fascination. For Mr Fortune is, undeniably, a great man…His method is the method of the knife, ruthless and incisive…Some of the best Fortune stories show the deduction of a whole malignant growth from one small isolated incident.' Bailey also created another long-running series character in the solicitor Joshua Clunk, whose path occasionally crosses that of Reggie Fortune. During the Golden Age itself, Bailey was one of the most highly regarded detective writers, but his reputation went into sharp decline after the Second World War. His mannered style of writing became deeply unfashionable, and is likely to remain so, but today his concerns as a crime writer seem rather more modern than those of many of his contemporaries.

The Poisoned Chocolates Case
by Anthony Berkeley (1929)

Roger Sheringham was the most fallible of Great Detectives. Anthony Berkeley's desire to debunk the notion of the omniscient crime-solver is made plain by the number of occasions when Roger—like Philip Trent in *Trent's Last Case* (page 36)—came up with an ingenious solution to a baffling mystery, only to discover that his theory was hopelessly mistaken. As Roger reflects in *Jumping Jenny* (1933), also known as *Dead Mrs Stratton*: 'That was the trouble with the old-fashioned detective-story. One deduction only was drawn from each fact, and it was invariably the right deduction. The Great Detectives of the past certainly had luck. In real life one can draw a hundred plausible deductions from one fact, and they're all equally wrong.'

No detective novel offers a more entertaining illustration of this principle than *The Poisoned Chocolates Case*. The genesis of the plot can be found in a clever short story, 'The Avenging Chance', in which Roger solves the murder of Joan Beresford. Berkeley expanded the story, making changes in the process, above all by having Roger's solution shown to be mistaken. In an odd twist somehow typical of Berkeley's contrariness, the novel appears to have been published before the short story; perhaps he realised that he had come up with a superb concept, and felt it made commercial sense for the novel to appear first.

Roger has founded the Crimes Circle, a select dining club for people with a passion for criminology. There are just five other members: a famous lawyer, a leading woman dramatist, a prominent detective novelist, and the meek and modest Ambrose Chitterwick. Their guest, Roger's old sparring partner Chief Inspector Moresby, is prevailed upon to recount the story of an apparently insoluble murder committed by means of poisoned chocolates. Each of the six members in turn comes up with a proposed solution to the mystery, and all of them except Chitterwick cite actual cases in support of their theories—a reminder of Berkeley's acute interest in real-life crime. One after another, the superficially plausible explanations of the mystery are dismantled.

To reinforce the point about the almost infinite possible interpretations of evidence, in 1979, Christianna Brand, a member of the Detection Club elected after the Second World War, and a friend of Berkeley's, came up with a seventh solution to the puzzle of the poisoned chocolates, and in 2016, the present writer published an eighth. The American critic James Sandoe noted that in *The Dain Curse*, also published in 1929, Dashiell Hammett 'solved' that case no fewer than four times. This is almost certainly a coincidence, but Hammett reviewed at least one of Berkeley's novels, and did find Roger Sheringham amusing.

Unwise characters in detective novels continued to consume chocolates from questionable sources with predictably calamitous results; the device was used by such diverse and gifted writers as Agatha Christie, in *Three-Act Tragedy*, (1934), the American Helen McCloy in *Who's Calling?* (1942), and by Edmund Crispin in *Buried for Pleasure*, as late as 1948.

Sheringham's life bore a striking resemblance to his creator's. Sheringham too was an Oxford graduate who fought and was wounded during the war, and then tried his hand at various jobs before making an unexpected success of writing a novel. He also shared Berkeley's fascination with criminology, 'which appealed not only to his sense of the dramatic but to his feeling for character'. Berkeley modelled the get-togethers of the Crimes

Circle on the dinners he hosted at his home in Watford that led
to his founding the Detection Club, a prestigious organisation
for detective writers which elected its members by secret ballot,
and subjected them to an initiation ritual which entailed swear-
ing an oath on a skull.

Anthony Berkeley was a pseudonym of Anthony Berkeley
Cox. After war service, Cox worked as a freelance journalist;
like his fellow Detection Club members A.A. Milne and Ronald
Knox, he contributed humorous columns to *Punch* before turning to detective fiction. His ingenious and innovative plotting
won immediate admiration, but he became increasingly interested in criminal psychology, which lay at the heart of the novels
he wrote as Francis Iles (page 259).

The Mystery of a Butcher's Shop
by Gladys Mitchell (1929)

Great Detectives are distinctive characters, none more so than Mrs Beatrice Adela Lestrange Bradley, described in this, her second appearance, as 'a small, shrivelled, bird-like woman, who might have been thirty-five and who might have been ninety, clad in a blue and sulphur jumper like the plumage of a macaw'. She greets the vicar of Wandles Parva with 'that air of easy condescension which is usually achieved by royalty only.'

Mrs Bradley is the author of a *Small Handbook of Psycho-Analysis*, and has moved to the Stone House in Wandles Parva fresh from her exploits in *Speedy Death* (1929), in which she not only solved the killing of a transvestite explorer, but took quite extraordinary measures in order to prevent another murder. Wandles Parva boasts a manor house owned by a blackmailer, a wood which is the scene of all manner of nefarious activities, and a pagan stone circle complete with blood-splashed 'Stone of Sacrifice'. After the blackmailer goes missing, human remains are found in the village butcher's shop, but neither decapitation nor dismemberment disturb the relentlessly playful tone of the narrative.

Mrs Bradley's idiosyncratic worldview is reflected in her comparison of a murderer with a doctor who is responsible for the birth of an illegitimate child: 'The population of this country is so excessive that, looked at from the purely common-sense point of view, a person who decreases it is considerably more public-spirited than one who adds to it, and he should be dealt with accordingly.'

Mitchell's ironic tone and ability to conjure up multiple solutions to a murder mystery are reminiscent of the work of Anthony Berkeley. In a satirical twist, the obvious suspect is neatly transformed into the least likely culprit before the final revelation. The ingenuity is worthy of Agatha Christie, but the flavour of Mitchell's writing is distinctive. To help draw together the threads of a complicated and coincidence-laden sequence of events, she supplies, in classic Golden Age fashion, not only entries from Mrs Bradley's notebook but also a timetable and two plans of the rural neighbourhood.

As in her debut novel, Mitchell was confident enough to confront convention head-on. Through Mrs Bradley, she makes it plain that it is 'retrogressive' to teach children that it is proper for factory owners to 'pay women about half what they would pay men are doing exactly the same work'. For her, 'it's a frightfully progressive sign that so few intelligent people go to church', given that plutocrats invoke 'the will of Heaven' to make their workers put up with unacceptable conditions.

Gladys Mitchell was a schoolteacher whose varied interests, including Freud and witchcraft, often found their way into her fiction. She also wrote mysteries as Malcolm Torrie, and historical novels as Stephen Hockaby. Mrs Bradley eventually appeared in no fewer than sixty-six novels as well as numerous short stories, and although their quality varied wildly, the best of them were amusingly original. Just as improbable as many of the plots was the casting of Diana Rigg as the star of *The Mrs Bradley Mysteries*, a short-lived BBC TV series first screened in 1998.

The Murder at the Vicarage
by Agatha Christie (1930)

Jane Marple, the second Great Detective created by Agatha Christie, less than a decade after Hercule Poirot's first appearance, was very different from the little Belgian. Far from having professional experience as a detective, she was an elderly spinster who had spent her life in the tranquil Home Counties village of St Mary Mead. But as she says to her condescending nephew, the avant-garde novelist Raymond West, 'You don't know as much of life as I do.' Her genius lies in her understanding of human nature. Drawing parallels between people and incidents in her own, ostensibly limited, experience, and the circumstances surrounding baffling cases of crime, she solves puzzles that have defeated others who seem, superficially, to be more worldly wise.

The Murder at the Vicarage is narrated by Leonard Clement, vicar of St Mary Mead. He appreciates Miss Marple's sense of humour, and realises that although she is 'a white-haired old lady with a gentle, appealing manner', she 'always sees everything. Gardening is as good as a smoke screen, and the habit of observing birds through powerful glasses can always be turned to account.' She makes no secret of her cynicism, and not long after Colonel Protheroe is found murdered in the vicar's study, she tells the Chief Constable: 'I'm afraid there's a lot of wickedness in the world. A nice upright honourable soldier like you doesn't know about these things.'

With quiet humour, Christie skewers the pretensions of Raymond West, and the narrow-mindedness of the zealous Inspector

Slack. They and the murderer underestimate her acumen, and she has the last laugh. In due course, she wrongfoots the police by revealing whodunit and suggests, for good measure, setting a trap to supply proof of the culprit's guilt.

Christie's sly wit is also evident in the presentation of village life. When Raymond West compares St Mary Mead to a stagnant pool, Miss Marple reminds him that life teems beneath the surface of stagnant pools. Her almost equally inquisitive elderly neighbours indulge in gossip and petty intrigue, and the neighbourhood is also home to adulterers and a well-known cracksman, who is masquerading as an archaeologist.

Christie herself acknowledged that Jane Marple resembled the sister of the doctor who narrates the classic Poirot novel, *The Murder of Roger Ackroyd* (1926), a gossip-loving spinster who is one of her most rounded and pleasing characters. Caroline Sheppard is not, however, a detective, and fails to deduce who did kill Roger Ackroyd. When Miss Marple first appeared, few imagined that a crime-solving spinster in a small village would become one of fiction's most iconic sleuths. Her career as an amateur detective was late-flowering, but long-lasting, and the stories about her have been successfully adapted for radio, television and film. As time passed, Christie's portrayal softened, and the old lady became unexpectedly adventurous; in her post-war incarnation, she unravelled mysteries in a London hotel, while travelling on a coach tour, and even during a Caribbean holiday. She remained, in true Christie fashion, the last person one would suspect of being a Great Detective.

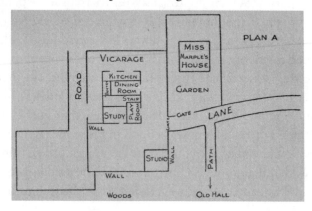

The Case of the Late Pig
by Margery Allingham (1937)

Great Detectives rarely tell their own stories. Sherlock Holmes' two accounts of his own investigations, for instance, rank among the less notable entries in his casebook, and serve as reminders of the benefits of having a 'Watson' as admiring narrator of the exploits of a much more gifted friend. But *The Case of the Late Pig* is a successful exception to the general rule, in part because Albert Campion's distinctive voice is captured from the outset:

'The main thing in autobiography, I have always thought, is not to let any damned modesty creep in to spoil the story. This adventure is mine…and I am fairly certain that I was pretty nearly brilliant in it in spite of the fact that I so nearly got myself and old Lugg killed that I hear a harp quintet whenever I consider it.'

Significantly, the book—the only one narrated by Campion—is short. Just as Great Detectives do not take their colleagues into their confidence, they like to keep their readers at arm's length; their conjuring tricks work best when watched from a distance. If events are seen from the sleuth's viewpoint, how can the element of surprise be maintained, and how can the author justify keeping us in the dark? The brevity and pace of the story help Allingham's narrative experiment to succeed, although Campion teases an amiable but naive chief constable when declining to explain what is in his mind:

"'Look here, Leo," I said. "I know how the first murder was done, and I think I know who did it, but at this stage proof is absolutely impossible…Give me a day or two longer.'"

A perplexing puzzle is the story's starting point. An intriguing but unsigned letter persuades Campion to attend the funeral of 'Pig' Peters, whom he remembers without affection from his school days at Botolph's Abbey. Five months later, he is summoned to the parish of Kepesake—only to be confronted by the corpse of 'Pig' Peters. The mystery of the man who died twice is enhanced by Allingham's evocation of rural England: 'Kepesake, which is a frankly picturesque village by day, was mysterious in the false light. The high trees were deep and shadowy…while the square tower of the church looked squat and menacing against the transparent sky. It was a secret village through which we sped on…our rather ghastly errand.'

As the plot thickens, a familiar rural scene takes on a macabre character: 'About half a mile away, in the middle of a field waist high in green corn, there was a dilapidated scarecrow, a grotesque, unnatural creature…But about this particular effigy there was a difference. Far from being frightened, the rooks were swarming upon it.' On looking through a telescope, Campion feels sick and giddy: a missing man has been found.

The Case of the Late Pig began life as a paperback original, and the first British hardback edition did not appear for more than half a century, but the story is an example of Margery Allingham at her best. Its high spirits are not a means of disguising a thin plot, but complementary to an intriguing mystery. She was an unorthodox novelist, whose work was correspondingly uneven, but her admirers remain legion, and to this day the Margery Allingham Society flourishes. A.S. Byatt described *Traitor's Purse* (1941), in which Campion loses his memory, as 'startlingly good', and added that it boasted 'the most amazing plot of any thriller I know'. Allingham's gift for evoking atmosphere won praise from Christie in an essay written for Russian mystery fans: 'You can *feel* the sinister influences behind the scenes; and her characters live on in your memory long after you have put the book away.'

'SEND FOR PAUL TEMPLE!'. . . A New Serial Thriller
Episode 1 today at 12.20

Send for Paul Temple
by Francis Durbridge and John Thewes (1938)

Paul Temple is unique among Great Detectives of the Golden Age in that he made his first appearance in a radio serial rather than in print. The storyline was turned into a novel shortly after the serial was first broadcast by the BBC (in the Midlands only). Its radio origins are betrayed in the cliff-hanger chapter endings, the heavy reliance on dialogue, and the absence of superfluous characterisation or other matters of detail.

Sir Graham Forbes, the monocled former military man who is Commissioner of the Metropolitan Police, confers with Superintendent Harvey and Chief Inspector Dale about a wave of diamond robberies. During the latest raid, a night watchman has died from chloroform poisoning. The man had been working under a false name, and it looks like an inside job. His dying exclamation was 'The Green Finger!', and in an earlier robbery, another man apparently hand in glove with the criminals had with his last breath uttered the same mysterious words. The police conclude that they are up against 'one of the greatest criminal organisations in Europe.' But, despite having the benefit of an enigmatic 'dying message' clue, they have not the faintest idea how to smash the gang.

Their helplessness has provoked the press into demanding that they 'Send for Paul Temple!' Suave and handsome, Temple is a former journalist who turned to writing thrillers for the stage with such phenomenal success that he has become a household name, and rich enough to own a country house near Evesham in addition to his London flat. He has also developed a sideline in criminology, investigating sensational crimes for the newspapers, and being responsible for the arrest of a string of notorious criminals.

Temple is duly consulted by Superintendent Harvey, who books a room at the Little General, an inn close to Temple's rural retreat. Shortly afterwards, Harvey is found there, shot dead in an apparent suicide. Temple is wisely dissatisfied with the easy explanation, and he is aided and abetted in his efforts to solve the mystery by an intrepid young newspaper reporter, Louise Harvey, who is the dead policeman's sister, and uses the name Steve Trent.

Once the master-criminal is unmasked, Temple marries Steve. Their creation may have been influenced by the popularity of Nick and Nora Charles, who do the detecting in Dashiell Hammett's final novel, *The Thin Man* (1934), and its film spin-offs. Temple, whose favourite catchphrase is 'By Timothy!', and Steve remain an idealised version of a quintessentially British couple. They are as brave and adventurous as Agatha Christie's Tommy and Tuppence Beresford.

Francis Henry Durbridge wrote diverse plays and sketches for the BBC before creating Paul Temple at the age of twenty-five. Durbridge shared the writing of *Send for Paul Temple* with John Thewes, which may have been an alias for Charles Hatton, who co-wrote the next four Temple books. Durbridge often reused material, and after adapting it for stage and film, he rewrote the first Temple novel in 1951 as *Beware of Johnny Washington*. He became a prolific writer for radio, and later television, finally concentrating on the stage. As a writer of breathless mysteries with multiple twists he had few peers.

Chapter Four

'Play Up! Play Up! and Play the Game!'

Arthur Conan Doyle, a sturdy patriot, surely endorsed the sentiments of Sir Henry Newbolt's once-famous poem 'Vitai Lampada'. Despite this, and his love of cricket and other sports, he did not really play the game with the Sherlock Holmes stories, in terms of presenting them as a contest between author and reader. In making his deductions, the great consulting detective usually benefited from information withheld from the reader. The game-playing aspects of detective fiction came into prominence only after the First World War, as a symptom of people's reaction to carnage and bereavement; there was a hunger for escapism, and readers relished having the chance to solve a puzzle set in a detective story.

Where there is a game, there must be rules, and such luminaries as the American aesthete Willard Huntington Wright (author of elaborate and wildly popular detective novels under the name S.S. Van Dine), A.A. Milne and T.S. Eliot published their opinions about the requirements of fair play in detective fiction. Towards the end of the Twenties, Monsignor Ronald Knox came up with 'the Detective Decalogue', a list of rules which commentators have sometimes taken much more seriously than he did. 'The criminal must be someone mentioned in the early part of the story, but must not be anyone whose thoughts the reader has been allowed to follow' was an example of a rule that did make artistic sense, while 'No Chinaman must figure in the story' was merely a light-hearted rebuke to thriller writers whose yarns made fanciful and sometimes xenophobic use of sinister Oriental bogeymen. Highly questionable principles included Knox's insistence that 'The detective must not himself commit the crime', a commandment flouted to brilliant effect before, during and after the Golden Age. The importance of playing fair was echoed in the rules and constitution of the Detection Club, of which Knox was a founder member, and in the Club's jokey initiation ritual for new members.

Philip MacDonald emphasised his commitment to fair play in a preface to one of the best Gethryn novels, *Persons Unknown* (1931, revised as *The Maze* a year later): 'In this book I have striven to be absolutely fair to the reader. There is *nothing* –nothing at all—for the detective that the reader has not had. More, the reader has had his information in exactly the same form as the detective—that is, the verbatim report of evidence.' Occasionally, writers such as J.J. Connington would be so lavish with the clues that the person guilty of an ingenious crime became evident a little too soon, but that was a better fault than the tendency of some writers to conceal vital information from the reader. Vernon Loder, at his best an entertaining puzzle-maker, sometimes sinned in this way. This may explain why John George Hazlette Vahey, who wrote as Loder, Henrietta Clandon and under other pseudonyms, was never elected to the Detection Club.

In its simplest form, the detective puzzle was a parlour game which had little or nothing to do with literature. F. Tennyson Jesse, a criminologist, novelist of distinction and author of interesting detective stories in the traditional mould, also edited the British edition of *The Baffle Book* (1930), the first of three collections of mystery puzzles put together by the Americans Lassiter Wren and Randle McKay. Diagrams, maps, plans of scenes of crime, and tantalising fragments of torn letters garnished dozens of detective stories; more unusual gimmicks included photographs and artists' sketches. Codes and ciphers were popular, although sometimes the explanation about how to interpret them proved lengthy and tedious.

The Documents in the Case by Dorothy L. Sayers and Robert Eustace (page 186) experimented with narrative structure, and so did the much more obscure *Documentary Evidence* (1936), a thriller by Robertson Halket (a pseudonym for E.R. Punshon). In both books, the story is told through letters, newspaper clippings and other documentation. *Murder off Miami* (1936), compiled by Dennis Wheatley and J.G. Links, took the concept to extremes. This was the first of four 'murder dossiers' containing physical evidence—clues in the form of hair samples, matches and illustrations—as well as telegrams, facsimile police reports and so on. The dossiers were gimmicky and expensive to produce, but at first they sold well, and inspired imitations in the United States; two of the American 'Crimefiles' were the work of Richard Wilson Webb and Hugh Wheeler, writing as Q. Patrick. The dossiers' popularity proved short-lived, however, and failed to survive the outbreak of war.

Equally artificial was *Cain's Jawbone*, a novella included in *The Torquemada Puzzle Book* (1934) compiled by the detective fiction critic of the *Observer*. In real life 'Torquemada' was Edward Powys Mathers, an expert compiler of cryptic crossword puzzles. The unique feature of *Cain's Jawbone* was that the pages were printed in the wrong order. Even when one knew the correct order (and very few people have ever risen to the challenge unaided), the story was not especially readable.

Ingredients of classic crime fiction such as impossible crimes and enigmatic dying message clues undeniably called for readers to make a herculean effort to suspend disbelief; whether they were willing to do so depended on the skill of the author, and Christie, Berkeley and John Dickson Carr often skated on thin ice. They took fair play seriously, and although Christie's *The Murder of Roger Ackroyd* (1926), a masterly example of the 'least likely person' solution to a murder puzzle, provoked controversy, the consensus was that she had not betrayed her readers. Their task, as Dorothy L. Sayers pointed out, was to suspect *everyone*.

Berkeley, Milward Kennedy and Rupert Penny were among those who adopted a favourite device of the American author Ellery Queen, the 'challenge to the reader' to solve the mystery, laid down at a point in the story when all the clues had been supplied.

Occasionally, ingenious authors liked to rub salt in the wounds of their hapless readers by making their obtuseness crystal clear. This was achieved by including at the end of the novel a 'cluefinder' providing, via footnotes or a table, a guide to those earlier pages where vital pieces of information were mentioned. The cluefinder, apparently invented by J.J. Connington in *The Eye in the Museum* (1929), was soon borrowed by others. They included Freeman Wills Crofts, who used a cluefinder in one of his most satisfying novels, *The Hog's Back Mystery* (1933), John Dickson Carr, Rupert Penny and Elspeth Huxley. Huxley was a cousin of Aldous, and an expert on colonial Kenya, whose occasional mysteries included *Murder on Safari* (1938) and *Death of an Aryan* (1939), also known as *The African Poison Murders.*

The most elaborate of all cluefinders appeared in C. Daly King's *Obelists Fly High* (1935), a labyrinthine mystery about a shooting on board an aeroplane, which begins with an epilogue and ends with a prologue. Even Julian Symons, a stern critic of the more artificial products of the Golden Age, could not help but admire the outrageous originality of King's novel, which he ranked alongside 'the detective story to end detective stories', Cameron McCabe's *The Face on the Cutting-Room Floor* (1937). McCabe's protagonist Muller says, in the course of a lengthy epilogue debating the nature of detective fiction, 'the possibilities for alternative endings to any detective story are infinite'. This echoing of Berkeley, one of several novelists and critics whose views are discussed, was entirely deliberate.

A very different kind of gimmick made Stella Tower's *Dumb Vengeance* (1933) memorable. The country-house setting is conventional enough, but the narrator, Miss Jenkins, is soon revealed to be a dog. The concept would have been better suited to a short story than a novel, but the quality of the writing compensates for the slenderness of the plot, and the book is the literary ancestor of those perhaps surprisingly popular crime novels featuring sleuthing animals, and in particular cats.

The best writers, having mastered the rules, became adept at breaking them, and Agatha Christie and Anthony Berkeley led the way in doing just that. As the Thirties drew to an end, it seemed that the detective novel in the form of a game was becoming played out. The Second World War and its aftermath wrought lasting changes to the genre, as had the previous global conflict. Detective novels continued to be written and enjoyed, however, and new exponents of the puzzle mystery kept coming on to the scene.

Crime writing evolves over time, but game-playing remains a feature of the genre. This is so, despite the fact that the era of challenges to the reader and cluefinders is long gone. It is worth noting the words of two major crime writers who emerged shortly after the Second World War, and whose work is widely regarded, quite reasonably, as having made a break with the past. Patricia Highsmith, a distinguished novelist with little interest in, or aptitude for, writing whodunits, declared in *Plotting and Writing Suspense Fiction* (1966): 'Writing fiction is a game, and one must be amused all the time to do it.'

As for Julian Symons, sometimes seen as a scourge of Golden Age detection, he acknowledged in *The Modern Crime Story* (1980) that he had come 'to realise how completely my stories were based on the conception that we are all playing games in our lives'. It is no coincidence that one of his finest novels resembles the best Golden Age fiction in various respects. The events in the story are influenced by a notorious real-life murder case—the Moors Murders—the reader is supplied with the private journal of an unnamed culprit, and there is a clever 'least likely person' solution. The book's title is *The Players and the Game* (1972).

The Floating Admiral
by certain members of the Detection Club
(1931)

Founded in 1930, the Detection Club attracted the great and the good of British detective writers. Chesterton was the Club's first President, and E.C. Bentley, A.A. Milne, A.E.W. Mason and Baroness Orczy were among the founder members. But the Club's driving force was a core of younger and highly energetic and enthusiastic writers with strong commercial instincts, and a fondness for game-playing. In the vanguard were Anthony Berkeley, the Club's founder, and Dorothy L. Sayers. From the start, they immersed themselves in collaborative projects, writing two 'round-robin' mysteries together. *Behind the Screen* (1930) and *The Scoop* (1931) were each the length of a novella, produced by half a dozen writers, broadcast by the BBC and serialised in *The Listener*; they were published together in book form in 1983.

The popular success of these ventures encouraged Club members to become even more ambitious, and they decided to co-author a full-length novel. Sayers began work on an expanded version of *The Scoop*, but soon it was decided to come up with a brand new storyline. The result was *The Floating Admiral*. In her introduction, Sayers explained the authors' approach:

'Here, the problem was made to approach as closely as possible to a problem of real detection. Except in the case of Mr Chesterton's picturesque Prologue, which was written last, each contributor tackled the mystery presented to him in the preceding chapters without having slightest idea what solution or solutions the previous authors had in mind. Two rules only were imposed. Each writer must construct his instalment with a definite solution in view: that is, he must not introduce new complications merely 'to make it more difficult'...Secondly, each writer was bound to deal faithfully with *all* the difficulties left for his consideration by his predecessors.

'Where one writer may have laid down a clue, thinking that it could point only in one obvious direction, succeeding writers have managed to make it point in a direction exactly opposite. And it is here, perhaps, that the game approximates most closely to real life. We judge one another by our outward actions, but in the motive underlying those actions our judgment may be widely at fault. Preoccupied by our own private interpretations of the matter, we can see only the one possible motive behind the action, so that our solution may be quite coherent, quite plausible and quite wrong.'

Chesterton's prologue is set in Hong Kong, before in the first chapter ('Corpse Ahoy!', written by Canon Victor L. Whitechurch) the action switches to a country river, and the discovery in a small boat of the corpse of Admiral Penistone. The story is progressed in lively fashion by a formidable team of literary conspirators: G.D.H. and M. Cole, Henry Wade, Agatha Christie, John Rhode, Milward Kennedy, Dorothy L. Sayers, Ronald Knox, Freeman Wills Crofts, Edgar Jepson, Clemence Dane and Anthony Berkeley. Berkeley's lengthy concluding chapter was called, with evident feeling, 'Clearing Up The Mess'.

An appendix contained the solutions put forward by the earlier contributors (apart from the authors of the first two chapters). Christie's idea involves transvestism, while Knox, famous for insisting that there should be 'no Chinamen' in a detective story, complains that having five characters associated with China is overdoing it. Another appendix presents notes on the mooring of the boat by John Rhode. 'Counsel's Opinion on Fitzgerald's Will' was included. There is also a map of Whynmouth and its environs. Any book written in such a fashion is bound to be idiosyncratic, but *The Floating Admiral* remains an exuberant and enjoyable example of a round-robin detective novel; eighty-five years later, the current generation of Detection Club members paid tribute to it with a new collaborative mystery, *The Sinking Admiral* (2016).

The Body in the Silo
by Ronald Knox (1933)

No detective novelist was better equipped for game-playing than Ronald Knox. Brother of a famous cryptographer, author of a book of acrostics and Sherlockian scholar, he also devised the genre's ten commandments, a 'Decalogue' for detective writers. Of his six crime novels, *The Body in the Silo* is a country-house mystery, complete with a map showing the grounds of Astbury Hall, a timeline of key events, a cipher based on an early form of shorthand, cluefinder footnotes—and even a chapter entitled 'The Rules of the Game'.

Knox's regular sleuth was Miles Bredon, an astute, crossword-loving investigator with the Indescribable Insurance Company. Most Golden Age detectives, other than stolid policemen like Crofts' Inspector French, seemed to find family ties an encumbrance. Miles' wife Angela, however, frequently played an active part in his cases. The Bredons—happily married in a way that would become deeply unfashionable for fictional detectives of later generations—are invited by their acquaintances the Hallifords to join a house party in Herefordshire.

They become involved in an 'elopement hunt', a variation on the idea of a scavenger hunt or treasure hunt, but the following morning one of their fellow guests is found dead in the hosts' grain silo. The hunt provides the perfect cover for a killer; as Bredon says, 'When everybody is plotting in fun, you get a good opportunity of plotting in earnest.' But even Knox factors into his highly elaborate story the psychological make-up of the culprit, who is fundamentally cruel yet at the same time squeamish, someone who 'recoils from the circumstances of violent death, the messiness, the twitching of the corpse.'

The mystery is so convoluted that Bredon's explanation of what actually happened takes up many pages; it is typical of Knox that the two deaths in the story occur as a result of a dark comedy of errors. In the end, a likeable character unintentionally acts as executioner, but Bredon reassures him: 'Nothing could possibly be more just than what has happened this time; the miscarriage of the plan brings death, not to a harmless stranger, but to the criminal.' This is a story brimming with Chestertonian paradoxes, written by a friend and admirer of Chesterton, who gave the address at the great man's funeral.

Ronald Arbuthnot Knox, a member of an intellectually gifted family, was educated at Eton and Balliol, where he excelled as a classicist. He became an Anglican priest before converting to Catholicism in 1918. He translated the Latin Vulgate Bible into English, and wrote on a wide range of subjects. His tongue-in-cheek paper 'Studies in the Literature of Sherlock Holmes', presented in 1911, earned the admiration of Arthur Conan Doyle, who said: 'You know a great deal more about it than I.' He was a founder member of the Detection Club, but eventually tired of writing detective stories. Knox was also a popular broadcaster, and his hoax 'Broadcasting from the Barricades', a radio programme about a revolution supposedly taking place in Britain, caused a sensation in the early days of the BBC. The trouble arose because so many listeners took his joke seriously.

She Had to Have Gas
by Rupert Penny (1939)

Agatha Topley, a widow who owns a modest boarding-house at Craybourne, a watering-place in East Anglia, worries about her sole lodger's creditworthiness. Alice Carter, a young woman whom Mrs Topley instinctively distrusts, is behind with her rent. Not long after Alice received a mysterious male visitor called Ellis, Mrs Topley discovers that Alice has gassed herself. But then the body of the apparent victim disappears—what can possibly be going on? Meanwhile, the spoiled niece of a famous crime writer has vanished, and the reader is tempted to believe that she was living a double life in the guest-house. With Rupert Penny, however, nothing is ever straightforward.

Penny's regular sleuth, the affable Inspector Beale, leads the investigation, and as usual his friend, stockbroker and journalist Tony Purdon is on hand to act as a rather superfluous version of Dr Watson. Penny was dedicated to playing fair with his reader, and the novel includes both a challenge to the reader and a scattering of cluefinder footnotes as the truth is revealed in the closing pages.

Rupert Penny was a pen-name of Ernest Basil Charles Thornett, who also wrote one thriller as Martin Tanner. Thornett was a crossword-puzzle fan who during the Second World War worked at Bletchley Park as a cryptographer. After the war, he continued to work for GCHQ (Government Communications

Headquarters), and for some years his superior was C.H.O'D. Alexander, head of cryptanalysis and a well-known chess champion.

Unsurprisingly, he found it easy to come up with clever puzzles for Chief Inspector Beale to solve. His novels are plotted with an elaboration that is extraordinary even by Golden Age standards, and feature a plethora of tropes of the genre such as maps, charts and timetables. He relished teasing his readers, and a typical example is the challenge laid down in an 'Interlude' in *Policeman in Armour* (1937): 'Who stabbed Sir Raymond Everett? How was the murder carried out? These are not unfair questions, the answers being discoverable from the foregoing evidence. It is hoped that at least one reader in ten will give five minutes' attention to the matter, and more than one in a hundred do so with satisfactory results. There is not much point in setting a problem that nobody can solve except the setter and his puppets.' *Sealed Room Murder* (1941) offers an impossible crime for solution, as does *Policeman's Evidence* (1938), which includes a cipher so fiendishly convoluted that it is hard to imagine anyone solving it.

Penny sometimes allowed himself to become carried away with complicated plotting, but his stories are sprinkled with welcome touches of humour. Had he begun to publish a decade earlier, he might have built a considerable reputation. By the time of the appearance of his first mystery, *The Talkative Policeman* (1936), however, Sayers, Berkeley and their followers had begun to shift the focus of the genre away from intellectual game-playing.

Penny recognised that the puzzle-based type of fiction at which he excelled was falling out of fashion. Even his first novel included a prefatory note discussing the likely fate of the detective story: 'By its nature it is for today and possibly for tomorrow and perhaps its highest hope is to pass from dustbin to dustman, and back again to bin, until...[it] is allowed to go the inevitable way of all rubbish. The detective shall find his grave at last as surely as the lifeless flesh he theorised upon.'

Penny felt that Holmes was the sole exception, although Wimsey (whose last case had actually been written by then) might become another, but his crystal ball failed him as regards Poirot and Miss Marple, and as to the future popularity of classic detective stories. He would be amazed, and perhaps appalled, to find that, eighty years after they were published, jacketed first edition copies of his novels can change hands for thousands of pounds. After a burst of activity yielding nine books in six years, he stopped writing fiction in the early Forties; in later life, his principal literary activity involved editing the annual journal of the British Iris Society, of which he was a doyen.

Chapter Five

Miraculous Murders

A dead body is found in a locked room. Murder has been done—and yet there is no sign of the murderer, perhaps not even of a weapon. It is an impossible crime—for how can it have been committed? The appeal of this puzzling paradox is intense and enduring. Locked-room mysteries have fascinated and entertained readers for as long as detective fiction has been written, while apparently impossible crimes have in recent years featured in popular television series as well as in novels written not only by English-speaking writers, but also by French and Japanese authors such as Paul Halter and Soji Shimada.

Locked-room and impossible crime stories flourished during the Golden Age, when ingenuity of plotting was so highly prized. John Dickson Carr, the anglophile American who is universally acknowledged as the supreme master of the locked-room mystery, summed up the appeal of these stories with typical gusto: 'When…we find ourselves flumdiddled by some master stroke of ingenuity which has turned our suspicion legitimately in the wrong direction, we can only salute the author and close the book with a kind of admiring curse.'

Edgar Allan Poe's 'The Murders in the Rue Morgue', published in 1841 and generally regarded as the first detective story, posed a fascinating problem for Poe's great detective, the

Chevalier C. Auguste Dupin, to solve. A woman was found dead in Paris, her body locked inside a room from which there appeared to be no means of escape for her killer. Yet this was not the first locked-room story. Two years earlier, Sheridan Le Fanu had published 'A Passage in the Secret History of an Irish Countess' anonymously, although this spooky story can scarcely be described as detective fiction. Antecedents of the locked-room mystery may also be discerned in Ann Radcliffe's *The Mysteries of Udolpho* (1794) and E.T.A. Hoffman's novella *Mademoiselle de Scuderi* (1819).

Wilkie Collins' short story 'A Terribly Strange Bed' poses a situation faintly reminiscent of that in an episode in Chretien de Troyes' *Lancelot of the Knight of the Cart*, written in the twelfth century. In the final decade of the nineteenth century, Israel Zangwill's *The Big Bow Mystery* (1892) earned widespread acclaim, while Arthur Conan Doyle's superb Sherlock Holmes story 'The Speckled Band' also exploited the potential of the locked-room mystery to excellent effect. Even Joseph Conrad dabbled with an impossible crime scenario similar to Collins', in his story 'The Inn of the Two Witches'.

The twentieth century saw a host of writers conjuring up ingenious variations of the impossible crime. Among the more talented were the American Jacques Futrelle, creator of Professor S.F.X. Van Dusen, alias 'the Thinking Machine', who was the epitome of a cerebral Great Detective, and France's Gaston Leroux, author of *The Mystery of the Yellow Room* (1907), whose detective was a journalist called Joseph Rouletabille. In Britain, G.K. Chesterton regularly confronted Father Brown with seemingly impossible crimes, a device which enabled him to indulge in his love of paradox.

Many Golden Age novelists—including Agatha Christie, Dorothy L. Sayers, Margery Allingham and Ngaio Marsh—found themselves unable to resist the challenge of concocting stories about apparently impossible crimes, while Anthony Wynne made a speciality of them. The prolific Frank King—the pseudonym of Clive Conrad—published four locked-room mysteries, notably *Terror at Staups House* (1927), in which the loathsome and miserly old Amos Brankard, a receiver of stolen property, gets his come-uppance in a sealed room one stormy winter's night.

The best work of Virgil Markham, son of the poet Edwin Markham, brims with youthful daring. *Death in the Dusk* (1928), set in Radnorshire on the border between England and Wales, combines an extraordinary plot with lashings of Gothic atmosphere. In the prefatory notes, one character whets the reader's appetite for the puzzle by describing it as 'a compendium of the bedevilment of Parson Lolly, the mad behaviour of the milkman, the invisible omnipresence of Sir Brooke Mortimer, the enigma of the mystic bone, the legend of Sir Pharamond's imperishable arm, and the machinations of the ultimate contriver'. Even this list omits 'the fiendish cat of the Sisters Delambre'. The key twist, although not wholly original, is cleverly disguised. *Shock!* (1930), known as *The Black Door* in the US, was subtitled *The Mystery of the Fate of Sir Anthony Veryan's Heirs in Kestrel's Eyrie Castle near the Coast of Wales*, and features a seemingly impossible disappearance. The Collins Crime Club first edition described the book as "a super-thriller" and included not only a map of St David's and Ramsey Island, but also a highly elaborate pull-out family tree detailing the 'descendants of Horace Veryan, of Coniston Park, Westmorland'. *The Devil Drives* (1932), concerning death by drowning in a locked cabin, is highly regarded, but Markham's output as a detective novelist extended to a mere eight books, the last appearing in 1936.

• • ● • •

John Dickson Carr enjoyed a much longer career. In three successful series, he rang variation upon variation upon his favourite theme. Dickson Carr was an anglophile who set most of his mysteries in Britain, although like Markham, and many other leading exponents of the impossible crime story, he was American. Carr's closest rival as a specialist in miracle problems was a professional magician called Clayton Rawson. Rawson's Great Detective was also a magician, the Great Merlini; writing as Stuart Towne, Rawson created another sleuthing conjurer, Don Diavolo. Henning Nelms, also American, wrote one of the finest impossible crime stories, *Rim of the Pit* (1944) under the name Hake Talbot. The rapid decline in popularity of this type of story after the Second World War is illustrated by the fact that the next Hake Talbot novel never found a publisher.

The inherent artificiality of the 'impossible crime' device might be thought to make it ill-suited to any fiction with pretensions to a degree of realism, but as ever with detective fiction, all is not as it seems. Impossible crimes feature in books focusing on psychological suspense, such as Helen McCloy's *Mr Splitfoot* (1968) and police procedurals, including Ed McBain's 87th Precinct novel *Killer's Wedge* (1959). Per Wahloo and Maj Sjowall produced a series of ten police novels that amounted to a Marxist critique of Swedish society which proved hugely influential, and Sjowall, sometimes described as 'the godmother of Nordic Noir', has picked as her favourite the ninth of the books, *The Locked Room* (1973), in which an investigation of a robbery is combined with Inspector Martin Beck's attempt to discover the truth about the death of a man found in a locked room.

Any idea that locked-room mysteries ended with the demise of the Golden Age of detective fiction was put to rest in the latter part of the twentieth century and the early years of the twenty-first, by successful television series on both sides of the Atlantic, such as *Banacek*, *Monk*, *Jonathan Creek* and *Death in Paradise*. And the international appeal of an apparently impossible crime has been confirmed by the popularity of Soji Shimada's *The Tokyo Zodiac Murders*, published in Japan in 1981, but not translated into English until more than twenty years later. It is a striking example of a story that combines Golden Age trappings such as a locked-room mystery and a 'challenge to the reader' with startling descriptions of violence that to Anthony Wynne or John Dickson Carr would have been unthinkable.

The Medbury Fort Murder
by George Limnelius (1929)

A memorable setting, strong characterisation and sound plotting distinguish George Limnelius' crime-writing debut. This locked-room mystery begins quietly, with background and character sketched at some length. When Major Hugh Preece of the Royal Army Medical Corps is consulted by a subaltern called Lepean, his realisation that he has encountered the man before triggers memories of past indiscretions.

As a young man, Preece had become infatuated with a ruthlessly ambitious showgirl called Prunella Lake. The outbreak of war brought their relationship to an end, and they both married other people, although a subsequent reunion had far-reaching consequences. In the meantime, while serving in West Africa, Preece had seen his friend and colleague Victor Wape kill a man, but escape punishment.

Old sins cast long shadows, as Preece discovers when he begins a stint as Medical Officer at Medbury Fort. The fort lies on the Thames estuary, one of the chain of forts forming the Thames and Medway defences before improvements to coastal defence artillery rendered it obsolete. Preece and Victor Wape are thrown together with Lepean, and the subaltern soon reveals himself to be an unscrupulous blackmailer who has learned Preece's darkest secret.

Preece finds himself driven to contemplate Lepean's murder, and he devises a plan inspired by Israel Zangwill's famous locked room story *The Big Bow Mystery* (1892). When Lepean is duly found dead in almost precisely the circumstances envisaged by Preece, Scotland Yard is called in. It soon emerges that Preece has something to hide, but a sequence of plot twists complicate his investigation. Preece proves not to be the only man present at Medbury Fort with a reason to kill Lepean, and the police are confronted with an unexpectedly testing puzzle of character, means and motive.

The cast of suspects is small, but Limnelius handles his narrative with aplomb, engaging the reader's sympathy with both the hunters and the hunted. His no-nonsense treatment of sex and violence is hardly in keeping with the lazily conventional view of Golden Age fiction as 'cosy', and the attention he pays to characterisation is equally striking. Why the novel has often been overlooked by historians of the genre is itself a mystery, but its merits were long championed by the late Robert Adey, the leading expert on locked-room mysteries and impossible crime stories.

The authentic flavour of military life conveyed throughout the novel provides a clue to the author's real identity; it is evident from the wealth of detail that Limnelius is painting an insider's picture of the army. His real name was Lewis George Robinson, and during the course of a long and distinguished service career, he rose to the rank of Colonel before retiring due to ill-health. He published a handful of novels, including *The Manuscript Murder* (1934); as the title of *The General Goes Too Far* (1935) indicates, he continued to mine his experience of soldiers and their way of life for his fiction, but *The Medbury Fort Murder* remains his outstanding contribution to the genre.

Murder of a Lady
by Anthony Wynne (1931)

Set in the author's native Scotland, this intricate story opens in fine dramatic fashion with the Procurator Fiscal calling late one evening on Colonel John MacCullen. He brings news that Mary Gregor has been stabbed to death in nearby Duchlan Castle: 'I have never seen so terrible a wound.' The dead woman was found crouching by her bed, but there is no trace of a murder weapon. The door of her room was locked, and so were all the windows.

A second murder follows, and suspicion shifts around a small cast of suspects. The book's alternative title, *The Silver Scale Mystery*, refers to the puzzling presence of herring scales at the crime scenes. Luckily, MacCullen is playing host to Dr Eustace Hailey, who has a knack of solving apparently impossible crimes. The puzzle is cleverly contrived, and the explanation is not—as is often the risk with a locked-room mystery—a let-down.

Hailey maintains that: 'Detective work is like looking at a puzzle. The solution is there before one's eyes, only one can't see it…because some detail, more aggressive than the others, leads one's eyes away from the essential detail.' His focus was on criminal psychology, and in particular 'the special stresses' to which the murderer was subject prior to committing the crime.' Hailey enjoyed a long career as a sleuth, first appearing in short stories in the mid-Twenties, and making his final bow in *Death of a Shadow* (1950). In an essay published in 1934,

Wynne explains Hailey's preference for working independently of the police: 'My studies of crime are undertaken only because they interest me…I follow a line of investigation often without knowing exactly why I'm following it—it would be intolerable to have to justify and explain every step.' Unexpectedly, he adds that: 'The detection of crime, I think, is an art more than a science, like the practice of medicine.'

His creator, like Hailey, knew a good deal about the practice of medicine. Wynne's real name was Robert McNair Wilson, and he was a Glasgow-born physician specialising in cardiology who served as medical correspondent of *The Times* for almost thirty years. His publications ranged over a variety of scientific, medical and historical subjects. Politics fascinated him, and he twice stood unsuccessfully for Parliament as a Liberal Party candidate. Another abiding interest was economics, discussion of which intrudes into a novel with a teasing impossible crime scenario, *Death of a Banker* (1934); the first-edition dust-jacket blurb mused that: 'It is possible that most of us, at one time or another, has contemplated the murder of a Banker…in this novel Mr Wynne shows us how it should be done—provided, of course, that there exists no Dr Eustace Hailey to undertake the solution of the crime!' In the same year, Wilson published his less racily titled work of non-fiction, *Promise to Pay: An Inquiry into the Principles and Practice of the Latter-Day Magic Sometimes Called High Finance.*

The definitive study of this sub-genre, *Locked Room Murders* by Robert Adey, lists no fewer than twenty-three books and stories written by Wynne which feature impossible-crime elements, typically involving 'death by invisible agent'. The Hailey mysteries often display considerable ingenuity, but never matched the popularity of John Dickson Carr's novels featuring Dr Gideon Fell and Sir Henry Merrivale. Carr's stories derive much of their appeal from lashings of macabre—and splendidly evoked—atmosphere, and a good deal of humour. By contrast, Wynne's stories often lacked verve. *Murder of a Lady* is enjoyable enough to suggest that this was due not to a lack of ability, but to his writing too much—a recurrent failing of Golden Age writers.

The Hollow Man
by John Dickson Carr (1935)

John Dickson Carr wastes no time in telling readers of *The Hollow Man* (published as *The Three Coffins* in the US) what lies in store for them. In a dazzling first paragraph, he proclaims that the murder of Professor Grimaud and the equally impossible crime in Caglisotro Street were as baffling and terrifying as any in the casebook of his sleuth Dr Gideon Fell: 'two murders were committed, in such fashion that the murderer must have been not only invisible, but lighter than air. According to the evidence, this person killed his first victim and literally disappeared. Again according to the evidence, he killed his second victim in the middle of an empty street, with watchers at either end; yet not a soul saw him, and no footprint appeared in the snow.'

The puzzles are skilfully constructed, but what lifts the novel into the highest rank of classic mystery is Carr's flair for creepy atmospherics. Vivid descriptive writing, coupled with a host of small, deft touches (even names like Grimaud and Cagliostro have a memorable quality), contribute to the overall impression of baffling unreality. The crimes appear miraculous (might a vampire be involved? The book was originally to be called *Vampire Tower*); yet it is the promise of a rational solution which makes the story so gripping.

In an extraordinarily bold move, Carr allows Fell in chapter seventeen to address the reader directly, giving a disquisition on the locked-room mystery that has often been reprinted as an essay on the subject: 'We're in a detective story, and we don't fool the reader by pretending we're not...Let's candidly glory in the noblest pursuit possible to characters in a book...When I say that a story about a hermetically sealed chamber is more interesting than anything else in detective fiction, that's merely prejudice. I like my murders to be frequent, gory, and grotesque. I like some vividness of colour and imagination flashing out of my plot, since I cannot find a story enthralling solely on the grounds that it sounds as though it might really have happened.' Fell proceeds to offer an analysis of different types of locked-room scenarios so impressively detailed that it has never been surpassed.

Gideon Fell's vast physique, rumpled appearance and larger-than-life personality were conscious tributes to G.K. Chesterton, whom Carr much admired. Dorothy L. Sayers, one of the most perceptive reviewers of detective fiction, spotted the parallels: 'Chestertonian also are the touches of extravagance in character and plot, and the sensitiveness to symbolism, to historical association...to the crazy terror of the incongruous.'

This is a remarkably assured novel, displaying in addition to its flair and originality the craftsmanship of an author who had already published more than a dozen books to widespread acclaim. Astonishingly, however, John Dickson Carr wrote it before reaching the age of thirty. And this reflects a truth about Golden Age detective fiction that has often been overlooked. Much of the best work of the period was produced by relatively young writers whose boundless energy and zest contributed significantly to the quality of the books—and their daring.

Carr's career as a published novelist began impressively with *It Walks by Night* (1930), which introduced the saturnine French investigator, Henri Bencolin. Many of his books about Sir Henry Merrivale—another detective with a flair for solving impossible crimes—equal the Fell novels in terms of quality; a notable example is *The Judas Window* (1938). The Merrivale books were generally published as by Carter Dickson; he also wrote as Roger Fairbairn. After the Second World War, he turned increasingly to historical mysteries, and his final book, *The Hungry Goblin* (1972)—sadly not in the same league as his early masterpieces—features Wilkie Collins as a detective.

Chapter Six

Serpents in Eden

British crime writers have long recognised the potential of their green and apparently pleasant land as a backdrop for crime and mystery. Wilkie Collins' *The Moonstone* (1868) makes superbly atmospheric use of a country-house setting as well as an eerie rural locale; the Verinders' family seat in Yorkshire is close to the mysterious and dangerous Shivering Sands. In Conan Doyle's 'The Copper Beeches', Sherlock Holmes tells Watson: 'It is my belief, Watson, founded upon my experience, that the lowest and vilest alleys in London do not present a more dreadful record of sin than does the smiling and beautiful countryside…Think of the deeds of hellish cruelty, the hidden wickedness which may go on, year in, year out, in such places, and none the wiser.'

The rural idyll exerted a powerful appeal, not least for those who lived in towns and cities, although detectives escaping to the country or seaside in the hope of a little peace and quiet seldom found much respite from murder. In Christie's *The Murder of Roger Ackroyd* (1926), Hercule Poirot's retirement to King's Abbott to grow vegetable marrows proved short-lived. The story is narrated by the village doctor, as is Carter Dickson's *She Died a Lady* (1943), set in wartime Devon, where a scandalous liaison between a married woman and a young actor leads to an apparent suicide pact. Sir Henry Merrivale, conveniently convalescing in the vicinity, is on hand to solve an ingenious mystery.

Milward Kennedy was a leading exponent of the village mystery. In *The Murderer of Sleep* (1932), a mysterious stranger rowing along the river experiences a shocking introduction to a seemingly idyllic village, encountering 'the vicar of Sleep, sitting under a weeping-willow beside his own church-yard, strangled'. In *Poison in the Parish* (1935), the exhumed corpse of an elderly woman reveals that she was poisoned by arsenic. The book opens with a 'Prologue or Epilogue' which reveals the final act in the drama, and both murder motive and final twist are unusual and pleasing.

Among the deeds of hellish cruelty which became familiar elements in detective stories set in rural Britain was an outbreak of poison-pen letters. The neat plot of *The Moving Finger* (1942), a Miss Marple story set in a small market town, illustrates Christie's ability to exploit stereotypes about gender for the purpose of mystification. Poison-pen letters also feature in Carter Dickson's *Night at the Mocking Widow* (1950), Edmund Crispin's *The Long Divorce* (1951) and *Poison in the Pen* (1955) by Patricia Wentworth, which all appeared during the Fifties. Yet the three books belong in spirit to the Golden Age, when the faintest whiff of scandal could destroy a cherished reputation and lead to social ostracism.

The church stood at the heart of rural life, and a curate called Roger Cartwright assists in solving the murder of a village squire's unpopular wife in *The Bolt* (1929) by P.R. Shore, which the publisher, Methuen, equipped with an attractive endpapers map of Ringshall village and its neighbourhood. Cartwright's fellow amateur sleuth is the narrator, Marion Leslie, who is almost a younger version of Miss Marple. Shore was a pseudonym of Helen Madeline Leys, who wrote several books as Eleanor Scott, but only one other detective novel, *The Death Film* (1932).

Members of the clergy served as victims, suspects, detectives—and sometimes as detective novelists with a taste for crime in rural settings. James Reginald Spittal wrote three novels as

James Quince, including *Casual Slaughters* (1935), which starts and ends with a meeting of the Parochial Church Council. John Ferguson was a railway clerk who metamorphosed into a clergyman; his ministry took him to Guernsey, the setting for *Death Comes to Perigord* (1931). Cyril Argentine Alington, a royal chaplain who became Dean of Durham, produced a handful of detective novels, including *Crime on the Kennet* (1939). Canon Victor L. Whitechurch used a village pageant as a backdrop in *Murder at the Pageant* (1930), while in Father Ronald Knox's first detective novel, *The Viaduct Murder* (1925), a golfing foursome stumble across a body lying close to the fairway.

Golf and murder coincided regularly in the novels of Herbert Adams. Adams' titles played relentless variations on his favourite theme: *The Body in the Bunker* (1935), *Death off the Fairway* (1936) and *The Nineteenth Hole Mystery* (1939). *Death is No Sportsman* (1938) by Cyril Hare is an angling mystery, as are Ngaio Marsh's *Scales of Justice* (1935), and *Bleeding Hooks* (1940) by the less-celebrated Harriet Rutland, a pen-name used by Olive Shinwell for three quietly accomplished detective novels.

Shooting parties provided rather more obvious opportunities for homicide, and featured in novels such as J.J. Connington's *The Ha-Ha Case* (1934), Henry Wade's *The High Sheriff* (1937) and John Ferguson's *The Grouse Moor Mystery* (1934), a low-key impossible-crime story. Like Ferguson's novel, Cecil M. Wills' *Defeat of a Detective* (1936), in which the identification of firearms is central to the plot, was set in rural Scotland; the book had endpapers decorated with an attractive map of Craigalloch Forest, supposedly drawn by ex-Detective Inspector Boscobell. In Ianthe Jerrold's *Dead Man's Quarry* (1930), a cycling holiday is rudely interrupted by the discovery of Sir Charles Price's body in a quarry in the Welsh borders. Luckily John Christmas, a rich dilettante with a penchant for solving mysteries, is also vacationing in the area. As was a habit of Golden Age detectives, Christmas loves comparing himself to fellow sleuths, insisting: 'All great detectives have simple, rural tastes. Sherlock Holmes kept bees. Sergeant Cuff grew roses. I, when I retire, shall cultivate the simple aster.'

Even the humble walking tour was fraught with danger, as Harriet Vane discovered in Dorothy L. Sayers' *Have His Carcase*. While striding around the south-west coast of England, she comes across the body of a murder victim. The book was published in 1932, the same year as the mass trespass at Kinder Scout in Derbyshire. This was arguably one of the most successful instances of civil disobedience in British history, reflecting the anger and impatience of those committed to 'the right to roam', and their hostility towards restrictions imposed by landowners.

Such tensions spill into violence in *Death in a Little Town* (1935) by R.C. Woodthorpe; in the first chapter, local people take 'direct action' to tear down a fence erected by landowner Douglas Bonar, to block a public right of way. Bonar is soon found dead, apparently battered to death with a spade—a suitably bucolic end for a deeply unpleasant character. Ultimately, the culprit escapes the gallows, an outcome that is surprisingly common in Golden Age novels, despite the frequently made claim that the books are devoted to seeing the restoration of order to a society disrupted by murder. Woodthorpe, like Christie, Berkeley and many other writers of the period, was well aware that sometimes the legal system was an inadequate means of delivering true justice.

Living in rural Britain between the wars was often stressful. Mass unemployment caused many men without a job to roam the countryside, scavenging to survive; they cropped up in detective stories as 'passing tramps', often suspected of crime, but almost invariably proving to be innocent; their main function was to act as red herrings. Woodthorpe, skilled at social comedy, presented an appealing intellectual tramp in *The Shadow on the Downs* (1935), which again features a murder connected to the disturbance of rural life, this time the construction of a racetrack on the Sussex Downs.

The charm of Golden Age novels prompted W.H. Auden to confess in his essay 'The Guilty Vicarage' that he found it 'very difficult…to read [a detective story] that is not set in rural England'. Auden argued that: 'Nature should reflect its human inhabitants, *i.e.*, it should be the Great Good Place; for the more Eden-like it is, the greater the contradiction of murder. The country is preferable to the town …'

A generation later, Colin Watson, a crime writer rather less in sympathy with Golden Age fiction, coined the term 'Mayhem Parva' to convey a typical setting for traditional detective mysteries, a village that had 'an inn with reasonable accommodation for itinerant detectives, a village institute, a library, and shops—including a chemist's where weed-killer and hair dye might be conveniently bought…there would be a good bus service for the keeping of suspicious appointments in the nearby town …' For Watson, Mayhem Parva was 'a mythical kingdom…It was derived in part from the ways and values of a society that had begun to fade away from the very moment of the shots at Sarajevo.'

In modern times, writers as diverse as W.J. Burley (Cornwall), Ann Cleeves (Northumberland and Shetland) and Reginald Hill (Yorkshire and Cumbria) among others have made excellent use of rural backgrounds, successfully integrating those settings with their plots. Their work has reached large audiences when adapted for television, while achieving a level of realism seldom found in the Golden Age. In contrast, the body count in ITV's *Midsomer Murders* may have reached absurdly high levels over the course of one hundred episodes, but at the time of writing, there is no sign that the public appetite for the series is sated. The appeal of crime fiction set in the British countryside endures.

The Secret of High Eldersham
by Miles Burton (1930)

The sinister side of life in remote East Anglia is evoked in the second novel to appear under the name of Miles Burton. High Eldersham is a creepy place, 'saturated with local legend'. Late one night, the village constable drops in at the Rose and Crown, only to discover that the landlord, Samuel Whitehead, formerly a sergeant in the Metropolitan Police, has been stabbed to death.

The Chief Constable promptly calls in Scotland Yard, but Detective Inspector Young finds himself 'surrounded by impalpable forces beyond his power to combat'. After a promising early lead peters out, Young struggles to make headway with his investigation, and consults his friend, the wealthy and affable Desmond Merrion. Badly wounded during the war, Merrion had transferred to Naval Intelligence, becoming 'a living encyclopaedia upon all manner of obscure subjects which the ordinary person knew nothing about'.

On arriving in the village, Merrion encounters a war-time acquaintance, who hopes to marry the daughter of the local squire, Sir William Owerton. Merrion's eye is also caught by Mavis Owerton, who is as attractive as she is adventure-loving. But as he digs deeper into the mystery, he cannot help wondering if Mavis and her father are implicated in the strange and secretive goings-on in High Eldersham.

The story, also known as *The Mystery of High Eldersham*, combines a relatively straightforward detective plot with thriller-ish ingredients, but represents a considerable advance on the first Miles Burton book, *The Hardway Diamonds Mystery*, published earlier in the same year. Jacques Barzun and Wendell Hertig Taylor, authors of *A Catalogue of Crime* (1971, rev. ed. 1989), and for many years the most high-profile enthusiasts of traditional detective fiction, extolled Merrion's debut as 'a model in its class'. Today, the antics of the villagers seem tame, but Barzun and Taylor argued that Miles Burton was working in the Gothic tradition of Ann Radcliffe, author of *The Mysteries of Udolpho* (1794), and was the first of 'the moderns' to do so in the detective genre.

Merrion made such a favourable impression that, having married and settled down, in High Eldersham of all places, he became a long-running series character, although Young was soon replaced by Inspector Arnold as his main collaborator. Exceptionally, Arnold solves a complex puzzle—a locked-*bathroom* mystery—without Merrion's assistance in *Death Leaves No Card* (1939), one of the most ingenious Burton novels. Merrion's last appearances came as late as 1960, a year which saw the publication of both *Legacy of Death* and *Death Paints a Picture*. Even then, the real identity of Miles Burton remained a more closely guarded secret than that of High Eldersham. Only after the author's death did it emerge that the name was a pseudonym for Cecil John Street, better known as John Rhode, dozens of whose novels were set in the rural England that he loved.

Street had managed to put everyone off the scent for more than three decades; Burton's year of birth had been stated in reference works as much later than Rhode's, while different novels bearing an identical title—*Up the Garden Path*—appeared under both pseudonyms at different times. Street's flair for remaining a man of mystery was underlined when it was revealed by the Golden Age expert and researcher Tony Medawar, as late as 2003, that in the early Thirties he had also written four obscure mysteries under the name Cecil Waye, and featuring 'London's most famous private detective', Christopher Perrin.

Death Under Sail
by C.P. Snow (1932)

A cancer specialist, Roger Mills, takes a group of friends for a boating holiday on the Norfolk Broads, but is soon found dead at the tiller, having been shot in the heart. Ian Capel, the narrator, calls on his friend Finbow to help solve the crime, and acts as his Watson. Finbow, a wealthy Cambridge graduate and *bon viveur* who plays cricket and enjoys Chinese poetry, belongs to the Wimsey school of gentlemanly amateur sleuths. If anything, he makes a rather more plausible detective than the local sergeant, who is a comic figure.

Finbow's first name is never revealed: it is a curious feature of the genre that mystery surrounds the full names of so many of its detectives. In keeping with the Golden Age vogue for intertextual allusion, Snow makes passing mention of Dorothy L. Sayers and S.S. Van Dine's detective Philo Vance; in *Gaudy Night* (1935), Sayers returned the compliment by name-checking Snow's *The Search* (1934). Finbow also anticipates the plot of one of the most famous detective stories when he says: 'That's a splendid idea. Five people are suspected of murder. Who did it? Answer: everyone.'

On the dust-jacket copy of the first edition, an excited blurb writer claimed that: 'Few detective stories have ever been written under more extraordinary conditions than *Death Under Sail*. Dr C.P. Snow, a 26-year-old Cambridge "don", has been busily engaged in experiments which may well be of vital importance to the human race. He has already succeeded...in making and destroying vitamins by physical methods...Naturally work such as this has been a great strain to Dr Snow, and at one point during the proceedings he went for a short holiday on a friend's yacht on the Norfolk Broads. Here it was that he evolved an extraordinary form of mental recreation for a man engaged in work that may result in banishing famine from the world and bringing good health within the reach of all. He planned and began to write a "thriller"...he developed a plot as watertight as the yacht he sailed, and eventually created the cleverest possible solution to the murder of the Harley Street specialist who met his death with a smile upon his lips. *And they say scientists have no imagination!*

Famine remains to be conquered, but despite the hyperbole, the young academic was destined to achieve distinction in multiple fields. Detective fiction, unfortunately, was not among them. Charles Percy Snow was an expert in chemistry and physics who became a senior civil servant, and was also active in politics, ultimately becoming a life peer. He became a popular mainstream author, renowned for the sequence of novels known as *Strangers and Brothers*. For the title of one of the books, he coined the term 'the corridors of power', while 'The Two Cultures', his Reith Lectures of 1959, provoked widespread debate about the divergent interests of scientists and those interested in the arts. His wife Pamela Hansford Johnson was also an author; together with her first husband, a journalist called Neil Stewart, she wrote two light-hearted detective novels under the pen-name Nap Lombard.

Although Snow never had any intention of specialising in detective stories, his literary life came full circle with his last novel. *A Coat of Varnish* (1979) is a sombre crime novel rather than a whodunit. The subject is murder in Belgravia, but although the book is more ambitious than his debut, the result is less satisfying.

The Sussex Downs Murder
by John Bude (1936)

John Bude's third detective novel was set against a background of special significance to lovers of the genre. When his days as a consulting detective at 221b Baker Street were over, the great Sherlock Holmes had retired to the South Downs to take up bee-keeping. But given that Bude's first two mysteries, both published in 1935, were *The Cornish Coast Murder* and *The Lake District Murder*, it does not take a Sherlock to guess that Bude set his early mysteries in a variety of popular rural locations as a marketing ploy, at a time when authors commonly set rural mysteries in vaguely fictionalised counties called Downshire or Middleshire. Bude could scarcely have anticipated that his method would yield a dividend more than half a century after his death, when the British Library reprinted his countryside novels in paperbacks with attractive period cover artwork that far outsold the original editions.

The Sussex Downs Murder shows Bude's talent for depicting place, and offers a storyline more elaborate and compelling than in his apprentice works. The Rother family farmhouse, Chalklands, and the surrounding area are convincingly realised, and in keeping with Golden Age tradition, a map is supplied to help readers to follow the events of the story after John Rother goes missing, in circumstances which at first (but deceptively) seem reminiscent of the disappearance of Agatha Christie.

Bude's growing confidence as a detective novelist is demonstrated by a pleasing sequence of twists and turns. The cast list is limited, but suspicion neatly shifts from one character to another. A clever touch sees a significant clue planted at a very early stage in the story, while even the title of the book is significant.

The message which lures William Rother to Littlehampton General Hospital recalls the hoax at the heart of the legendary Wallace case, five years before the book was published. The mysterious message forms only one of a host of complications facing Inspector Meredith, introduced in *The Lake District Murder*, and relocated from Cumberland for the purposes of this story. Meredith is modelled on Freeman Wills Crofts' Inspector French, in his diligence, his contented home life, and his love of a good meal, but he possesses a sharper sense of humour. His son's amateur detective work makes a pleasing contribution to the storyline, while his innate humanity comes to the fore in the novel's closing stages.

Bude's real name was Ernest Carpenter Elmore. After publishing two weird and fantastic novels, he turned to fictional crime with enough success to become a full-time writer. On Guy Fawkes Night in 1953, he was among the handful of writers who joined with John Creasey to found the Crime Writers' Association at a meeting held in the National Liberal Club. Prior to his premature death, he adapted his technique of setting mysteries in attractive locales to the changing tastes of readers in post-war Britain, and allowed Meredith to venture across the English Channel in books such as *Death on the Riviera* (1952) and *A Telegram from Le Touquet* (1956).

Sinister Crag
by Newton Gayle (1938)

Rock-climbing offers ample scope for homicide, a possibility exploited by several authors, notably the mountaineer Frank Showell Styles, who used the pen-name Glyn Carr for a series of mysteries from the Fifties onwards. One of the most interesting cases of murder on the mountains, pre-dating Carr's work, was the last of five books to appear under the name Newton Gayle. Most of the action in *Sinister Crag* takes place in the fictional Lake District valley of Wannerdale. Three men have died while climbing the eponymous fell; did their deaths result from accident or murder?

Jim Greer, Gayle's series detective, suspects foul play, and spends much of the book climbing the fells along with his friend Robin Upwood, who narrates the story, and plays Watson to Greer's Holmes. They stay at the Herdwick Hotel, as do a number of potential suspects. Greer states the problem confronting him: 'Three men have been killed; but we don't know which of them was the intended victim…Except for their interest in mountaineering I doubt if there was a single common factor in their lives…This means that, in tackling the problem from the angle of motive, our difficulties are trebled.' Although thinly characterised, he is an efficient detective who at one point compiles an 'alibi chart'.

The Lake District, splendidly evoked, makes an ideal setting for crimes and misdemeanours. As Greer says: 'The whole place is a wilderness of gullies and cliffs. Even in clear weather you'd never find anybody who wanted to elude you.' There may be too much information about climbing to suit non-enthusiasts, but the world beyond the rural idyll is not forgotten: 'More wars and rumours of wars?' Upwood asks someone who has abandoned her newspaper in dismay. Mussolini is mentioned as an example of someone who suffered claustrophobia after spending time in prison.

The name of Newton Gayle concealed an unusual writing partnership, between Muna Lee and Maurice Guinness. Lee was an American poet and activist, and Guinness a British oil executive. Although they made an odd literary couple, their co-authored mysteries are distinctive. *Sinister Crag* is unique among Greer's recorded cases in taking place in Britain. The quality of writing was no doubt due to Lee, while Guinness was primarily responsible for supplying plot material—particularly in this book, where he made good use of his own enthusiasm for mountaineering. Lee spent many years living in Puerto Rico, which supplied the background for an unorthodox Newton Gayle novel, *Murder at 28:10* (1936), set at the time of a devastating hurricane. Lee later joined the US State Department as a cultural affairs specialist, while in the Sixties, Guinness wrote three thrillers under the name Mike Brewer.

Chapter Seven

Murder at the Manor

The success of *Trent's Last Case* (page 36), in which Sigsbee Manderson is murdered in the grounds of his country house, set a pattern for Golden Age detective novels. A tale about 'murder at the manor' offered authors the chance to create a closed circle of suspects, principally comprising house guests. The American detective novelist S.S. Van Dine went so far as to advance the snobbish argument that: 'Servants—such as butlers, footmen, valets, game-keepers, cooks, and the like—must not be chosen by the author as the culprit...It is a too easy solution...The culprit must be a decidedly worth-while person.' Detective stories in which 'the butler did it' were, contrary to popular belief, few and far between.

A country house invariably boasted a library, which sometimes became a crime scene, but more often, at the end of the book, a suitably august backdrop for the Great Detective's explanation of whodunit and why to those who had survived to the final chapter. It is no coincidence that the first recorded cases of Hercule Poirot, Albert Campion, Sir Clinton Driffield and Roderick Alleyn, among countless others, concerned murder in a manor. And when Anthony Berkeley bought a country estate, Linton Hills in Devon, he promptly made use of it as the setting for *The Second Shot* (1930).

Agatha Christie became familiar with country-house life as a result of staying with her sister and brother-in-law at Abney Hall in Cheshire. Abney may have been the model for Chimneys, the stately home which is the setting for her lively thrillers *The Secret of Chimneys* (1925) and *The Seven Dials Mystery* (1929), and there is no doubt that she fictionalised the house to supply the backdrop for *After the Funeral* (1953) and the title story in *The Adventure of the Christmas Pudding* (1960). Like Berkeley, Christie eventually acquired a country house of her own; Greenway, in Devon, is now in the care of the National Trust. In *Curtain* (an underestimated *tour de force* published in 1975, but written during the Second World War), Hercule Poirot ended his career where it had begun, at Styles Court. When a girl's corpse was discovered at Colonel and Mrs Bantry's home, Gossington Hall in St Mary Mead, Jane Marple was called in to investigate the mystery of *The Body in the Library* (1942). By the time murder, and Miss Marple, returned to Gossington Hall in the Sixties, the Bantrys were long gone, and the house had fallen into the ownership of a film star, Marina Gregg: *The Mirror Crack'd From Side to Side* (1962).

A Christmas party supplied a popular backdrop for 'murder at the manor' novels, including Mavis Doriel Hay's *The Santa Klaus Murder* (1936) and Christie's *Hercule Poirot's Christmas* (1938). *The Poisoner's Mistake* (1936), an early novel by G. Belton Cobb, offers a slight variation, with a New Year's Eve party culminating in the death of one of the guests. By the time Francis Duncan's *Murder for Christmas* appeared in 1949, the cost of running a country house was proving ruinous. Mordecai Tremaine, a retired tobacconist and amateur sleuth, reflects upon the sadness of 'a proud family coming slowly to oblivion'. The Duncan pseudonym concealed the identity of William Walter Frank Underhill, a former debt collector who became a lecturer in economics; his other novels included an 'inverted mystery', *They'll Never Find Out* (1944).

The popularity of country-house mysteries, and the possibility of gaining an inheritance by murder, meant that members of the aristocracy appeared in classic crime novels with disproportionate frequency, often as unmourned victims. Georgette Heyer devotes so many pages in *Penhallow* (1942) to establishing the odiousness of the eponymous lord of the manor that it is a relief when the inevitable finally happens.

Lady Cambers, the busybody strangled in E.R. Punshon's *Death Comes to Cambers* (1935) is another typical Golden Age murderee, who gives a large cast of suspects cause to wish her dead. Punshon's regular sleuth, Sergeant Bobby Owen, is conveniently on hand to solve the mystery; a grandson of Lady Hirlpool, he has been staying at Cambers, 'ostensibly to advise Lady Cambers on precautions to be taken against…burglary'. Punshon regularly included lords and ladies in his cast of characters; like P.G. Wodehouse, he enjoyed poking fun at those who owed their creature comforts to inherited wealth rather than their own efforts.

No detective novelist, not even Lord Gorell, had such first-hand insight into the country-house lifestyle as Henry Wade, the pen-name of Sir Henry Lancelot Aubrey-Fletcher, sixth baronet, CVO DSO, who served both as High Sheriff and as Lord Lieutenant of Buckinghamshire. Wade, unlike Punshon (and Gorell), was a conservative by both instinct and inclination, and he seized the opportunity to criticise punitive taxation in *No Friendly Drop* (1931), in which Inspector John Poole of Scotland Yard investigates the death by poisoning of Lord Grayle at the Grayle residence, Tassart Hall. The storyline reflects Wade's acute awareness that, following the First World War, the landed gentry were living on borrowed time.

The Hanging Captain (1933) supplies a plan of the ground floor of the scene of the crime in conventional fashion. Yet whereas Christie portrays Chimneys as a home full of life, as well as death, Wade makes clear that Ferris Court, like the family that owns it, is in a state of terminal decline: 'As for Ferris Court, the Tudor home of twelve generations of Sterrons…a glance at the garden was sufficient hint of the shadow which overhung the fine old house. Weed-encumbered beds and paths, untrimmed edges, overgrown shrubberies, told their tale of straitened means—or neglect sprung from a broken spirit.' Sir Herbert Sterron is a broken man long before he is found hanging by the neck from a curtain cord in his ancestral home.

Wade's deeply rooted pessimism about the future of the country estate was borne out after the Second World War, and reflected in Christie's *Dead Man's Folly* (1956). A 'murder hunt' at a summer fete held in the grounds of a country house with a *nouveau riche* owner results, inevitably, in an actual murder; luckily Hercule Poirot is on hand to see justice done.

Financial pressures and social change threatened a whole way of life, and the country-house mystery came to seem increasingly dated and irrelevant in the austere post-war era. Wade's continuing disdain for severe tax regimes is central to the plot of *Too Soon to Die* (1953), a notable 'inverted' mystery about the newly impoverished gentry. In the second chapter—grimly headed 'Estate Duties'—he recounts the misfortunes of the Jerrods of Brackton Manor, 'one of the oldest families in the county...Nobility in the form of title had never come their way, and distinction had stopped short at honourable and useful mediocrity...but they were Jerrods, and whatever extortions might be devised by successive Chancellors of the Exchequer, they would hold on to Brackton while life remained in their bodies.' When the family faces the prospect of financial catastrophe, the solution seems to lie in a cunningly devised fraud. But the Revenue's suspicious are aroused, and the family's hold on Brackton Manor is jeopardised once John Poole—now elevated to the rank of Chief Inspector—comes on to the scene.

The Crime at Diana's Pool
by Victor L. Whitechurch (1927)

Felix Nayland, a mysterious former diplomat, has returned to England after years abroad, and acquired a residence for himself and his unmarried sister in the heart of the countryside. The Pleasaunce nestles below the hills which flank one side of the village of Coppleswick, and stands in good-sized grounds with thick woods and a stream that has been dammed so that two natural hollows have become deep pools of water. Nayland decides to introduce himself to the local community by hosting a summer garden party, and the guests include Major Challow, the Chief Constable of the county, and Harry Westerham, a young clergyman.

Entertainment is supplied by The Green Albanian Band and Western Glee Singers, but, typical of an English summer, the fun is interrupted by a downpour. A member of the band is reported missing, and as Challow and Westerham stroll away from the gathering, they spot a man's body lying in a pool. The corpse belongs not to the bandsman, but to Nayland, who has been stabbed to death. The Pleasaunce soon becomes the setting not for a garden party, but a coroner's inquest.

Westerham's keen habit of observation makes him a useful ally to the police, whose first suspect, inevitably, is the missing foreigner. The plot involves the dead man's past in South America, and reflects Whitechurch's taste for blending a quintessentially

English country-house mystery with a touch of the exotic. The author, also a clergyman, surely speaks for himself as well as for Westerham when observing: 'Most people have the extraordinary notion that a parson is something different from an ordinary man, that he lives entirely apart from others in a theological atmosphere.' For good measure, he adds: 'the parson is rarely given credit for the many hours he spends in his study over a variety of matters which would puzzle many a business man'. Westerham is intelligent as well as amiable, and since he has 'some idea of writing', he may represent a portrayal of the author as a younger man.

In a preface, Victor Lorenzo Whitechurch explained that he adopted an approach that was at the time unorthodox: '... in reality, the solver of a problem in criminology has to begin at the beginning, without knowing the end, working it out from clues concerning which he does not recognise the full bearing at first... To begin with, I had no plot. When I had written the first chapter I did not know why the crime had been committed, who had done it or how it was done.' This was a daring method for an author seeking to set a puzzle, rather than to focus on evocation of character and setting, although it was not conducive to 'fair-play detection'. As Dorothy L. Sayers complained, he did not put the reader 'on an equal footing with the detective himself, as regards all clues and discoveries'. For her, this was a throwback to 'the naughty tradition', but she acknowledged that the novel was otherwise excellent.

Whitechurch earned election to the Detection Club, and contributed to *The Floating Admiral* (page 80). A former Chaplain to the Bishop of Oxford, he became honorary canon at Christ Church Cathedral, and rural dean of Aylesbury. He created two 'railway detectives', and his most highly regarded work in the crime genre was the collection *Thrilling Stories of the Railway* (1912). His final detective novel, *Murder at the College* (1932) was an early example of the Oxford crime story, although he calls his setting 'Exbridge'.

Some Must Watch
by Ethel Lina White (1933)

Helen, aged nineteen, takes a position quaintly described as a 'lady-help' with the Warren family at their lonely country house. The Summit is 'tucked away in a corner, on the border line between England and Wales' and 'looked strangely out of keeping with the savage landscape'. Its remoteness makes working there an unattractive proposition for anyone who is not desperate—but Helen is desperate.

She is a young woman of her time, a victim of the economic slump: 'Her one dread was being out of work…ladies were a drug in the market.' Her first job, at the age of fourteen, had been as a walker of the dogs of the rich; the dogs were better fed than she was. Fresh from the misery of unemployment, Helen is only too grateful to have board and lodging, and a worthwhile job, 'after weeks of stringent economy—since "starvation" is a word not found in a lady's vocabulary'. Far from ducking the realities of social conditions in the Thirties, Ethel Lina White makes them integral to the plot.

The new job seems almost too good to be true, and so it proves. At first, Helen finds the spookiness of the Summit enticing: 'danger…seemed to be everywhere—floating in the air—inside the house, as well as outside, in the dark tree-dripping valley'. But this is not a conventional country-house whodunit— a serial killer is at work in the vicinity. He has already killed four young women, and a fifth killing takes place uncomfortably close to the Summit. The unpleasant nurse to the invalid Lady Warren warns Helen about the murderer: 'Haven't you noticed that the murderer always chooses girls who earn their own living?... The country is crawling with women, like maggots, eating up all the jobs. And the men are starved out.' Ethel Lina White builds the tension with unobtrusive skill as a ruthless murderer closes in on Helen, before an ending which amounts to a form of poetic justice.

Some Must Watch was filmed in 1946 by Robert Siodmak, and Mel Dinelli's screenplay was adapted for the stage in 1962. The movie was remade in 1975 with Jacqueline Bissett as Helen, and again in 2000. Such longevity attests to White's flair for devising memorable 'woman in jeopardy' storylines, her speciality as a novelist and writer of short stories. The most famous film made from her work was *The Lady Vanishes*, Alfred Hitchcock's classic version of her 1936 novel *The Wheel Spins*, but the less-renowned *Midnight House*, aka *Her Heart in Her Throat* (1942), filmed as *The Unseen*, boasted a screenplay by Raymond Chandler.

Ethel Lina White came from Abergavenny, not far from the borderland setting of *Some Must Watch*. The daughter of a successful builder, she was one of a family of twelve raised by Welsh nursemaids. She worked in London for the Ministry of Pensions, but left the job 'on the strength of a ten-pound offer for a short story', and 'scratched a living on short stuff for quite a time before my first novel was published'. Her favourite form of relaxation was watching films, which perhaps accounts for her knack of writing vivid and suspenseful scenes.

Death by Request
by Romilly and Katherine John (1935)

This country-house whodunit is, like *The Murder at the Vicarage* (page 69), narrated by a member of the clergy. The Reverend Joseph Colchester has been vicar of Wampish for twenty-six years, and his distinctive, prissy voice supplies one of the book's incidental pleasures. The book opens with Colchester in reflective mood: 'It is not without a feeling of horror and reluctance that I take up my pen…Is it really serviceable to perpetuate the memory of so much guilt and wretchedness? I am shocked by the thought that my tale may be read by some as a diversion.' He proceeds to describe events that took place three years earlier at Friars Cross, the home of Matthew Barry, a friend of Colchester since they were at Oxford together.

The guests at Friars Cross include a girl called Phyllis Winter, the glamorous but enigmatic Mrs Anne Fairfax, Matthew's school friend Colonel Lawrence, and the libidinous young Lord Malvern. Over dinner, they discuss murder and the ethics of capital punishment; next morning, Malvern's body is found in his bedroom. He has been gassed, and it soon becomes clear that his death was the result of murder, rather than accident or suicide.

The dead man's son becomes a prime suspect, as does the butler Frampton, a socialist with a taste for blackmail. Colchester himself has 'considerable sympathy with the socialist movement', and this is not the only respect in which his personality and attitudes differ from the conventional Golden Age cleric. Inspector Lockitt, who leads the police investigation, focuses his attention on Edward, but the most energetic detective work is done by Nicholas Hatton, a young private investigator who collaborates with Mrs Fairfax. However, Mrs Fairfax, like many of those staying at Friars Cross, is nursing a secret of her own. A surprise 'solution' to the puzzle is followed by an entertaining, if not wholly original, twist in an epilogue. The Johns write wittily, and the Colonel's buffoonery is especially well done.

Romilly John, the seventh son of the celebrated artist Augustus John, described his unconventional upbringing in a memoir, *The Seventh Child* (1932). Despite his parents' lack of interest in formal education, Romilly went on to study at Cambridge, where he met his future wife, Katherine Tower; they married before either of them graduated. Katherine became a reviewer for the *Illustrated London News*, and a translator of Scandinavian books. Romilly served in the RAF during the war, spent a short time in the Civil Service, and wrote poetry as well as dabbling in physics. The couple never wrote another crime story, but *Death by Request* is written with such youthful exuberance that it is a shame that they failed to continue to play the game.

Birthday Party
by C.H.B. Kitchin (1938)

Astonishingly overlooked by historians of the genre, this is a country-house mystery with a difference. Kitchin's multiple narrators tell a quiet but compelling story in which clues to the truth are psychological rather than material. Four people connected to Carlice Abbey relate their versions of events; as the viewpoints shift, so does the reader's understanding of the relationships at the heart of the novel. The result is darkly ironic.

Isabel Carlice is a sharp-witted single woman devoted to the Abbey's garden, which she tends with loving care. But a past tragedy haunts the Abbey. Twelve years ago Isabel's brother, Claude Carlice, died in a mysterious gun-room accident. This was no murder, although it remains unclear whether he died of an accident or suicide. But if he killed himself, what was the reason? Claude's widow, Dora, continues to live at the Abbey, and her impoverished brother, Stephen, a failed novelist, pays a visit in the hope of saving himself from destitution. The tension mounts as the twenty-first birthday of Ronnie Carlice approaches. Oxford-educated, and an idealistic Communist, young Ronnie has his own ideas about what to do when he comes of age, and inherits Carlice Abbey. At the time the book was written, Ronnie's political views were fashionable. The detective novelist Margaret Cole was among those who travelled to Russia, as Ronnie does just prior to his birthday, to marvel at the success Stalin was making of his post-revolution society. The shadow of impending war looms over the people in the story, and the many subtle touches creating an atmosphere laden with doom provide a reminder that Kitchin was an accomplished author of literary fiction.

Clifford Henry Benn Kitchin was, as H.R.F. Keating said, 'born with a whole handful of silver spoons in his mouth'. After Oxford and training as a barrister, he increased his personal wealth through gambling at the Monte Carlo casino, at race-tracks (he bred greyhounds) and on the London Stock Exchange. A talented classicist, botanist and pianist, he published a book of poems in 1919, and an acclaimed novel, *Streamers Waving*, six years later, but his covert homosexuality and natural reserve meant that he never became a dominant establishment figure. His early books, including two detective novels, were published by the Hogarth Press, owned by Leonard and Virginia Woolf, who were intrigued by his experiments 'in the art of combining the emotions of every day with violent catastrophe'.

Death of My Aunt (1929) introduced Malcolm Warren, whose career as an amateur detective spanned twenty years but only four books. Warren is, like his creator, a stockbroker, and share-dealing and business skulduggery play a significant part in his second case, *Crime at Christmas* (1934). Kitchin made good use of the tropes of detective fiction, but tried to do something fresh with them. In an unusual coda to that novel, Warren muses that 'the real justification' of the detective story is that it provides 'a narrow but intensive view of ordinary life, the steady flow of which is felt more keenly through the very violence of its interruption'.

Julian Symons said in *Bloody Murder* that 'Kitchin brought nothing new to the crime story, although he has his place as a minor, amiable Farceur', which suggests that Symons never came across *Birthday Party*. This was rather the story of Kitchin's literary life: even in his heyday, his finest work received less attention than it deserved.

Chapter Eight

Capital Crimes

The immense popularity of Sherlock Holmes, and the atmospheric brilliance of Arthur Conan Doyle's writing, meant that by the start of the twentieth century, London had become the pre-eminent setting for detective fiction. G.K. Chesterton rhapsodised in 'A Defence of Detective Stories' about this phenomenon: 'No one can have failed to notice that in these stories the hero or the investigator crosses London with something of the loneliness and liberty of a prince in a tale of elfland...The lights of the city begin to glow with innumerable goblin eyes, since they are the guardians of some secret, however crude, which the writer knows and the reader does not...This realisation of the poetry of London is no small thing...The narrowest street possesses in every crook and twist of its intention, the soul of the man who built it, perhaps long in his grave.'

The lyrical tone and underlying theme of this passage are not so dissimilar from the more famous characterisation by Raymond Chandler, in his essay 'The Simple Art of Murder' (1944), of the lonely private eye as a sort of modern knight errant: 'down these mean streets a man must go who is not himself mean, who is neither tarnished nor afraid'. The phrase 'mean streets' itself recalls Arthur Morrison's *Tales of Mean Streets*, set in the East End of London and published in 1894, the year that Morrison in Kingsway where she had been employed, in *Murder Must Advertise* (1933). After being bullied by a fellow shop worker during the early stages of the Second World War, Christianna Brand found catharsis in murdering her adversary in *Death in High Heels* (1941), although she took the precaution of transforming the shop into a dressmaker's in Regent Street. Christopher St John Sprigg and R.C. Woodthorpe, both of whom spent time working as journalists, made fun of the Street of Shame in two books published in quick succession, *Fatality in Fleet Street* (1933) and *A Dagger in Fleet Street* (1934).

London was home to many 'gentlemen's clubs' which often provide a setting for scenes in detective stories, most notably in Sayers' *The Unpleasantness at the Bellona Club* (page 220). Richard Hull was a bachelor who gave his address as a club—the United Universities—and he set his second novel in a fictitious equivalent. *Keep it Quiet* (1935) concerns the death of a club member, apparently poisoned by the club cook, and the frantic efforts of the hapless secretary, assisted by a member who is a doctor, to cover up the calamity. The focus is not so much on whodunit as on whether the culprit will get away with it, and how many other members may be eliminated before the end of the story. Hull's neat variation on a familiar resolution improbably involves the laws of Latvia.

The heart of the city was a popular background for crime. Anthony Berkeley's ingenious *The Piccadilly Murder* (1929) opens with Ambrose Chitterwick taking tea with his formidable aunt at the opulent Piccadilly Palace Hotel, a venue which also features in the Detection Club's round-robin story *The Scoop* (1931) and Agatha Christie's *Lord Edgware Dies* (1933). Murder is committed at the Piccadilly Underground station in *Murder in Piccadilly* (1936) by Charles Kingston; this was a pen-name of Charles Kingston O'Mahony, an Irishman who wrote about true crime before turning to fiction. Kingston's book is a thriller, lively if stylistically a touch old-fashioned even by Golden Age standards; the same is true of *A Scream in Soho* (1940) by John G. Brandon, an exceptionally prolific writer whose mysteries included contributions to the long-running series featuring Baker Street's *other* Great Detective, Sexton Blake.

The eerie atmosphere of the black-out in London during the early stages of the 'phoney war' is caught in Brandon's book, and also in *A Deed Without a Name* (1940) by Dorothy Bowers, in which Archy Mitford is found hanged in a darkened room, with black-out curtains drawn. Although his death appears to be a case of suicide, three recent—and inexplicable—attempts on his life have been made. Dan Pardoe, the youngest Chief Inspector at Scotland Yard, suspects murder from the outset—'Men choose to die in the light'—and finds that Archy has left a cryptic 'dying message clue'. The author's commitment to fair play is emphasised by the proud boast emblazoned on the dust-jacket of the first edition: *Brilliant Detection—Absolutely No Cheating*. Bowers was a writer of distinction whose career of high promise ended prematurely as a result of the tuberculosis which plagued the later years of her life.

War-time London was also well evoked by Gladys Mitchell in *Sunset Over Soho* (1943) and in another book where the black-out is central to the plot, E.C.R. Lorac's *Murder by Matchlight* (1945), but perhaps no detective novelist of the Golden Age captured London's character in a more compelling manner than Margery Allingham. The endpapers of the first edition of *Death of a Ghost* (1934) boast a map of 'the Lafcadio House and Studios of Little Venice, Bayswater in London'. In the course of Albert Campion's investigation, he is tempted, in typical fashion, tempted to wonder 'why, with a murderer at large in Little Venice, Donna Beatrice should have escaped killing'. The plot is original, and the book among her best.

J.K. Rowling, an admirer of Sayers and Wimsey, has also heaped praise on Allingham, describing another of her London novels, *The Tiger in the Smoke* (1952), as 'phenomenal'. In creating the private investigator Cormoran Strike, whose office is in Denmark Street, Rowling has (writng under the name Robert Galbraith) ensured that, although Holmes, Wimsey, Poirot and Campion are long gone, the traditions of the London-based detective and the well-made detective novel live on.

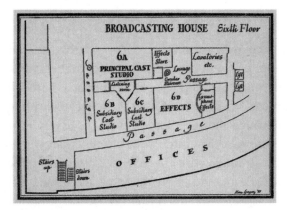

Death at Broadcasting House
by Val Gielgud and Holt Marvell (1934)

In 1932, the young British Broadcasting Corporation, having outgrown its premises at Savoy Hill in London, relocated to the purpose-built Broadcasting House in Portland Place. Val Gielgud, who was working for the BBC at the time as a producer, said in a memoir that, although some derided the new headquarters (critics mocked it as 'pretentious' and for having 'a queer shape'), it typified 'in steel and concrete...a new *professionalism*' about the Corporation's activities.

Gielgud and his colleague Eric Maschwitz realised that Broadcasting House would provide a perfect backdrop for a highly topical 'workplace mystery'. Both men were experienced actors and writers and had already collaborated on a detective novel, *Under London* (1933), with Maschwitz using the pseudonym Holt Marvell. Their BBC mystery is centred on the live broadcast of *The Scarlet Highwayman*, a radio play written by Rodney Fleming, and recorded in several studios, as was common at the time. After the broadcast, a member of the cast called Sidney Parsons is found strangled in studio 7C, and Julian Caird, the Dramatic Director, tells the Controller of the BBC, 'Do you realise that everyone who heard that play must have heard him die? That makes it pretty unique in the annals of crime.'

The police investigation is led by Inspector Spears, and the authors capture the tension that existed at the time between professional detectives and their superiors (such as the assistant commissioner, Major Cavendish), former soldiers who 'seemed to put discipline first and results, in comparison, nowhere'.

Three pages are devoted to floor plans of Broadcasting House, as a complicated plot unfolds. Dorothy L. Sayers admired the authors' writing, their commitment to fair play and the ingenuity of the plot, although with characteristic attention to detail, she quibbled that: 'it could hardly have taken a person 45 seconds to cross a passage and enter a room (a second is a much longer interval than one thinks, and in 45 seconds I can walk down 20 stairs, out through the back door, shutting it after me, and half-way down the garden)'.

Sayers was far from alone in enjoying the novel—known in the US as *London Calling!*—and Gielgud and Marvell felt that a film version of the story would be 'sure-fire', given that Broadcasting House was not only a modern building that was still newsworthy but 'rather a box of tricks'. After an initial struggle to find backers, *Death at Broadcasting House* was shot in twenty-nine days, not at Portland Place, but at a modestly sized studio in Wembley, with Gielgud playing the part of Caird.

The novel benefited from its highly topical setting—as many Golden Age mysteries did—yet it was not the first broadcasting mystery. A forerunner of the BBC had already supplied the title and background for *2LO* (1928) by Walter S. Masterman, an author of breezy thrillers who had gained first-hand insight into the criminal life as a result of serving a prison sentence for embezzling funds from the Board of Fisheries. 'The Broadcast Murder', by Grenville Robbins, was an enjoyable short story about a seemingly impossible crime—a murder during a live wireless broadcast, where the victim vanishes without trace.

Gielgud and Maschwitz each enjoyed a long and distinguished career in the media. Both men were of Polish descent, and colleagues in the BBC called them 'the Polish Corridor'. They wrote five novels together, and although Maschwitz is better remembered as lyricist for 'A Nightingale Sang in Berkeley Square' and 'These Foolish Things', Gielgud continued to write detective fiction, his final novel appearing as late as 1975. He collaborated successfully on radio plays with John Dickson Carr, collected more than sixty years after their first broadcast as *13 to the Gallows* (ed. Tony Medawar, 2008). He also formed a fruitful relationship with Sayers, producing radio adaptations of her novels as well as her highly successful cycle of radio plays *The Man Born to Be King* in 1941–2.

Bats in the Belfry
by E.C.R. Lorac (1937)

Anthony Fell, an Australian cousin of Bruce Attleton, has been killed in a motoring accident while visiting Britain. At the funeral gathering, Bruce's attractive young ward Elizabeth strives to lighten the mood by telling her fellow mourners about a form of 'murder game' she has been playing at her club. The challenge is: how best to dispose of a corpse? Bruce's wife Sybilla, a lovely but cold-hearted actress, suggests setting the body into the permanent fabric of the building.

Bruce is shaken by the death of his cousin, and the attentions paid to Sybilla by Thomas Burroughs, a wealthy stockbroker, are another cause for concern. In addition, his friend, the dramatist Neil Rockingham, tells young Robert Grenville that Bruce is being pestered—and perhaps blackmailed—by a mysterious individual called Debrette. Rockingham persuades Grenville to help him find out more about Debrette, who is based in Notting Hill. Grenville soon learns that Debrette claims to be a sculptor, and lives in a strange place known locally as 'the Morgue'.

The Morgue, once home to a religious sect, is properly known as the Belfry Studio, and proves to be 'a gaunt tower…lit by the reflections of neon lights in the West End'. Grenville describes it as 'the most lunatic jumble of Victorian Gothic mixed with Oriental detail and debased Byzantine embellishment'. He is driven away by Debrette, but returns to find Bruce Attleton's suitcase in the coal cellar of the building. When Debrette vanishes, and Attleton also goes missing, Rockingham raises the alarm with Scotland Yard.

Inspector Macdonald leads the hunt for the missing men, and eventually a body is discovered—but to whom does it belong? Good-humoured but tough and determined, Macdonald is a methodical policeman in the tradition of Inspector French, although unlike Freeman Wills Crofts' detective he is a bachelor. The plot is elaborate, the characterisation crisp and the atmosphere of the dark London streets well evoked.

E.C.R. Lorac was the principal pen-name of Edith Caroline Rive, who was known to friends and family as Carol Rivett; her pseudonymous surname is Carol spelt backwards. She introduced Inspector Macdonald in *The Murder on the Burrows* (1931), and he proceeded to investigate in no fewer than four dozen novels, the last published posthumously. She also wrote a long series featuring Chief Inspector Julian Rivers, under the name of Carol Carnac.

A native Londoner, she was an accomplished author whose work deserves to be better known. Early Lorac titles include *Murder in St John's Wood* and *Murder in Chelsea*, both published in 1934. The former novel, praised by the often severe American critics Barzun and Taylor, presents yet another example of that staple Golden Age situation, the murder of a financier. Dorothy L. Sayers lauded *The Organ Speaks* (1935), set in a music pavilion in Regent's Park, as 'entirely original, highly ingenious, and remarkable for atmospheric writing and convincing development of character'; the first edition boasted a 'diagram of the console of the four-manual organ in the Waldstein Hall'.

Lorac was elected to the Detection Club in the year *Bats in the Belfry* was published, and served as the Club's Secretary. A teacher by profession, she developed a passion for the Lune Valley and the surrounding area in the north-west of England, which provides the backdrop to several of her later books. At the time of her death, she was working on a non-series mystery novel, while another late stand-alone novel, *Two-Way Murder*, has not as yet been published.

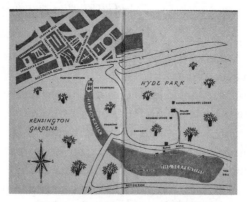

What Beckoning Ghost?
by Douglas G. Browne (1947)

The body of a man in his sixties is discovered in the Serpentine at Hyde Park. The deceased is Wally Whichcord, who had achieved notoriety seven years earlier as an independent witness to a sighting of 'the Hyde Park Ghost'. During an air raid in 1940, a bereaved mother whose son, Hugo Demarest, had died when his submarine was lost with all hands claimed to have encountered his ghost, wearing naval uniform, in Hyde Park. In her grief, Mrs Demarest had turned to spiritualism, and consulted a medium of questionable reputation, but her story was supported by a companion, as well as Whichcord, who was sleeping rough nearby. And shortly before his death, Whichcord claimed to have seen the ghost again.

In the wake of the tragedy, Harvey Tuke, a senior official with the Director of Public Prosecutions, accompanies his wife Yvette to a dinner party. The host and hostess, Clifford and Corinne Reaveley, live in an eccentrically designed home just across the road from the Park. The house once belonged to the late Mrs Demarest, and the only surviving person to have seen the Hyde Park Ghost is among those present. Tempers fray as the drink flows, and the night wears on. Eventually Corinne Reaveley flounces out, abandoning her guests, and leaving Tuke to speculate about the puzzling tensions he has detected during the evening as well as the mystery of Hugo Demarest's ghost.

When another body is found in the Serpentine, Tuke takes a personal as well as a professional interest. Formidable in appearance, and sharp in intellect, he forms an entertaining double-act with Sir Bruton Kames, the Director of Public Prosecutions, who is a larger-than-life character in the mould of the more renowned Sir Henry Merrivale, created by Carter Dickson. The duo's investigation takes them not only to Hyde Park and some of London's meaner streets, but also to the hidden world beneath the city's pavements. A series of lengthy set-piece scenes, notably an atmospheric subterranean chase, cunningly distract the reader's attention from an essentially straightforward plot which draws on Browne's knowledge of crime in real life.

Douglas Gordon Browne was the grandson of Hablot K. Browne, who as 'Phiz' provided illustrations for the work of Charles Dickens, alias 'Boz'. After leaving school, Browne studied art, and during the First World War, he was one of the first people to be trained to drive a tank. His interest in criminology led him to write several factual books, including a biography of the pathologist Sir Bernard Spilsbury, co-written with E.V. Tullett. He also published *The Rise of Scotland Yard* (1956), a book about fingerprints, and a life of the judge Sir Travers Humphreys. Of his novels, *Rustling End* (1948) draws on the Moat Farm murder at the start of the twentieth century, while *Death in Perpetuity* (1950) carries echoes of the Wallace case.

In 1934, the theologian and writer Charles Williams reviewed Browne's early thriller *Plan XVI* alongside Dashiell Hammett's *The Thin Man*, and Williams went so far as to bracket the authors together: 'Both Mr Hammett and Mr Browne, with different capacities, might, if they have the courage of imagination, quicken the forward movement of murder.' Time has proved kinder to Hammett's reputation than to Browne's, although Margery Allingham recorded in her diary that she sat up half the night reading *Plan XVI*, and at his best, the Englishman was an appealing writer. Major Maurice Hemyock, an archaeologist and amateur sleuth, appeared in books such as *The Looking-Glass Murders* (1935), which Dorothy L. Sayers praised for achieving 'an artistic unity of a very satisfactory kind', and *The May-Week Murders* (1937), set in Cambridge. Hemyock was later supplanted by Harvey Tuke, whose cases included *Too Many Cousins* (1946), an example of the 'who will be next?' murder mystery, in which a keen-eyed obituarist draws Tuke's attention to the fact that three members of the same family have succumbed to a sequence of fatal accidents in quick succession.

Chapter Nine

Resorting to Murder

Holidays offer an ideal opportunity to get away from it all, but the arrival of a Great Detective in any resort is invariably a harbinger of homicide. Crime writers have long favoured holiday locations as settings for their mysteries, in part thanks to inspiration gained from trips of their own. Holidays also offer endless scope in terms of plotting. Travellers in search of fresh experiences may find they lead to danger.

An early example of the holiday-based mystery is *Sudden Death* (1886) by Britiffe Constable Skottowe, in which crucial events occur during an extended visit to Homburg made by the wealthy narrator, Jack Buchanan. The foreign setting adds to the air of mystery that pervades an unorthodox novel boasting an ahead-of-its-time subtext about sexual ambiguity. Skottowe never wrote another crime story, although he was responsible for *A Short History of Parliament* (1887), as well as a book about Hanoverian kings.

Sherlock Holmes made his debut in *A Study in Scarlet* the year after Skottowe's book appeared. In 'The Devil's Foot', published in 1910 but set in 1897, Holmes is advised by a Harley Street doctor to 'lay aside all his cases and surrender himself to complete rest if he wished to avoid a complete nervous break-down'. He and Watson take a small cottage at the furthest extremity of the Cornish peninsula, but their holiday is soon interrupted by the local vicar, who brings news of 'the most extraordinary and tragic affair…We can only regard it as a special Providence that you should chance to be here at the time, for in all England you are the one man we need.' Naturally, the great consulting detective cannot resist the temptation to investigate the case of 'the Cornish horror'.

Crime writers often play variations on this theme. In *Murder in the Moor* (1929), a detective called Peregrine Clement Smith stumbles on a mystery during a walking tour on a thinly disguised version of Dartmoor. The wit and ingenuity of this novel have been praised by connoisseurs, yet little is known about the author, Thomas Kindon, except that he appears to have been, like Freeman Wills Crofts, John Rhode and Francis Everton, highly knowledgeable about engineering.

Agatha Christie was a skilful exponent of the holiday mystery. In *Peril at End House* (1932), Hercule Poirot and Captain Hastings arrive in St Loo, which Hastings says is 'well named the Queen of Watering Places…If only these weather conditions continued we should indeed have a perfect holiday.' Poirot turns down a commission from the Home Secretary, only to meet Nick Buckley, a young woman whose life appears to be in danger. Despite claiming to have solved his last case, he soon finds himself drawn into an elaborately plotted murder.

Poirot's attempt to relax on the beach at Smugglers' Island (a location modelled on Devon's Burgh Island) meets a similar fate in *Evil Under the Sun* (1941). In conversation with fellow residents of the Jolly Roger Hotel who are contentedly watching the sunbathers, Poirot argues that 'there is evil everywhere under the sun…Let us say you have an enemy. If you seek him out in his flat, in his office, in the street…you must account for yourself. But here at the seaside it is necessary for no one to account for himself.' Sure enough, glamorous, sun-loving Arlena Stuart is duly found stretched out on the beach; someone has strangled her.

Dorothy L. Sayers' *The Five Red Herrings* (1931) saw Lord Peter Wimsey taking a fishing holiday in Galloway, where the author and her husband had enjoyed several holidays. The area's landscapes have attracted a colony of artists, one of whom is found dead with a fractured skull, his painting half-finished. The story is Sayers' attempt to write a puzzle mystery with a closed circle of suspects, and the story turns on an alibi trick which elaborates on a plot device in J.J. Connington's *The Two Tickets Puzzle*, published the previous year.

In 1932, Sayers published a more compelling holiday mystery, *Have His Carcase*, in which Harriet Vane's coastal walking holiday is rudely interrupted by her discovery of a corpse with his throat cut. The question of 'howdunit', as often with Sayers, sparked her imagination, and the trimmings include an elaborate cipher which Lord Peter Wimsey manages to solve. The dead man was a foreigner who had been working at a nearby hotel, the Resplendent: 'one of those monster seaside palaces which look as though they had been designed by a German manufacturer of children's cardboard toys. Its glass porch was crowded with hothouse plants, and the lofty dome of its reception-hall was supported on gilt pilasters rising out of an ocean of blue plush.' And it proves to have been events in the Resplendent that sowed the seeds for the crime.

The calamitous impact of serial murders on a holiday resort dependent on tourism is evident when 'the Eastrepps Evil' strikes in Francis Beeding's *Death Walks in Eastrepps* (page 225). The murder of a philandering artist is the first of a sequence of deaths to plague the coastal town of Coldhithe in *And Being Dead* (1938), the first novel by Margaret Erskine, the pen-name of Margaret Wetherby Williams. Inspector Septimus Finch is told that the resort is 'the latest playground of Mayfair', but on arriving there concludes that it looks 'just the place for a murder'.

The dead man was involved in an unpopular scheme to develop Coldhithe, and a similar plan plays a part in E.R. Punshon's *Crossword Mystery* (1934): 'The idea was to build a big seaside golfing hotel...Suffby Cove itself would make a splendid swimming pool. Shooting rights were to be bought over land near, and there would be lots of fishing and boating, and, of course, a first-class jazz band...even an ice rink was thought of...it would be a gold mine.' Archibald Winterton opposes the development—but is found drowned in the Cove.

As flying, cruising and travelling long distances by rail became more commonplace, overseas holiday destinations saw an upsurge in fictional crime. Once again, Christie led the way. Foreign trips by train, plane and ship respectively formed the background for three of Hercule Poirot's principal cases, recorded in *Murder on the Orient Express* (1934), *Death in the Clouds* (1935) and *Death on the Nile* (1937).

Long after the era of classic crime, a stay in the luxurious Burgh Island Hotel remains on the wish-list of thousands of Christie fans, while tourist authorities everywhere recognise that successful crime stories set in an attractive location bring a welcome boost to the local economy. Ann Cleeves' recent novels about Detective Inspector Jimmy Perez, televised as *Shetland*, provide a striking example. The series' success has even led to the appearance of a profusely illustrated coffee-table book written by Cleeves and celebrating the bleak beauty of an archipelago where crime is rare—except in fiction.

The Red Redmaynes
by Eden Phillpotts (1922)

Mark Brendon, a highly regarded young Detective Inspector from London for a trout-fishing holiday on Dartmoor. A workaholic, he has reached a point in his life where his thoughts are turning to the future, and the possibility of marrying and raising a family. Heading from Princetown towards the deep pools of Foggintor Quarry, he has a brief encounter with a beautiful young woman; later, while fishing, he passes the time of day with a red-haired man. When murder interrupts Mark's holiday, both strangers play a central part in the investigation.

The young woman is Jenny Pendean, and it seems that her husband has been killed by her uncle—who proves to be the red-haired man, Captain Robert Redmayne. Jenny tells Brendon the story of the troubled Redmayne family, the 'peculiar will' left by her wealthy grandfather, and the tensions caused by her marriage to Michael Pendean, who had avoided fighting during the war. Robert Redmayne has gone missing, and Pendean's body cannot be found.

Brendon becomes increasingly obsessed with Jenny, but his pursuit of her is no more successful than the police's efforts to track down Robert Redmayne. He encounters a rival for Jenny's affections in the shape of Giuseppe Doria, a flamboyant Italian boatman who works for Robert's brother, Bendigo, and before long murder again strikes the Redmayne family. The story is told in leisurely fashion, but benefits from Phillpotts' lyrical descriptive writing, and a pleasing plot twist. Brendon makes a likeable protagonist, although in the later part of the book, he plays second fiddle to a snuff-taking Great Detective, a retired American policeman called Peter Ganns, who had a long friendship with another of Jenny's uncles, Albert Redmayne.

Eden Phillpotts worked as an insurance clerk before becoming a writer; early success enabled him to settle in his beloved Devon, which he seldom left thereafter; Phillpotts was shy and reticent, shunning interviews and only ever making one public appearance, at Exeter Cathedral, to unveil a memorial window to *Lorna Doone*'s author, R.D. Blackmore, who had encouraged him early in his career. Despite his reluctance to socialise, he became friendly with Agatha Christie's parents, who were neighbours, and he advised Christie on her first, unpublished, novel, introducing her to his literary agent. She said in her autobiography: 'I can hardly express the gratitude I feel to him.'

A renowned regional novelist, Phillpotts also wrote poetry and plays, two of them in collaboration with his daughter Adelaide. His detective fiction, written under his own name and as Harrington Hext, once much admired, was lauded in an essay by John Rowland, a crime writer who shared Phillpotts' enthusiasm for contriving impossible-crime scenarios. Rowland compared *The Red Redmaynes* to the work of Wilkie Collins, while Jorge Luis Borges ranked Phillpotts with Poe, Chesterton and Collins, and included *The Red Redmaynes* in his never-completed list of one hundred great works of literature. Barzun and Taylor ranked the novel 'only one cut below *Trent's Last Case*'. In the half-century after Phillpotts' long life came to an end, his reputation has faded, but his crime fiction is ripe for re-evaluation.

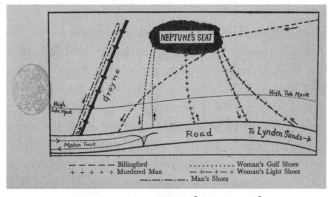

Mystery at Lynden Sands
by J.J. Connington (1928)

All Great Detectives were unrelenting in their quest for the truth about mysterious crimes, but the English legal system did not always satisfy their thirst for justice. Sometimes, they set themselves above the law. They might show compassion to those who were technically guilty, or impose their own punishment when the law proved impotent. It was not even unknown for them to commit murder themselves, while somehow managing to remain on the moral high ground. Sir Clinton Driffield, created by J.J. Connington, is a prime example of a sleuth with a cold-blooded streak; not for nothing was one of his recorded cases given the title in the US of *Grim Vengeance*.

Sir Clinton holds the office of Chief Constable, but the books in which he appears are not conventional police stories, and at one point he resigned in order to conduct unspecified intelligence work, although this proved short-lived. Connington was a professor of chemistry, and an admirer of R. Austin Freeman's detective fiction. *Mystery at Lynden Sands* typifies his work in emphasising scientific and technological know-how rather than the minutiae of police procedure.

Sir Clinton is much younger than the Chief Constables typically found in detective fiction of the inter-war years, most of whom are former military men. Aged about thirty-five, he has returned to England after holding a senior post with the police in South Africa. His friend Wendover, whom he nicknames 'Squire', is an affable country gentleman whose intellect is sharper than his hearty appearance might suggest.

Sir Clinton and Wendover are enjoying a golfing break at the seaside when an elderly man is found dead. Soon they are embroiled in a puzzle involving a missing heir, an unscrupulous trustee, unintentional bigamy, and blackmail. The Victorian case of the Tichborne Claimant supplied real-life inspiration for one strand of the narrative. Connington exploits the geography of Lynden Sands, using the beach, quicksand and unusual rock formations to supply crime scenes, and a dramatic climax. The book's tone is characteristically sardonic. Like Dupin, Holmes or Poirot teasing their luckless sidekicks, Sir Clinton chides Wendover: 'Masterly survey, Squire. Except that you've left out most of the points of importance.' And when a vicious criminal faces an agonising death, Sir Clinton is unsympathetic: 'This isn't a case where my humanitarian instincts are roused in the slightest.'

By the time this book appeared, T.S. Eliot, a crime-fiction enthusiast, had already placed its author in the first rank of detective novelists. J.J. Connington was the pen-name of Alfred Walter Stewart, a Glaswegian academic who published a well-received dystopian novel, *Nordenholt's Millions*, in 1923, before turning to detective fiction with a strong emphasis on fair-play clueing. Sir Clinton made his debut in *Murder in the Maze* (1927), a country-house murder mystery which the publishers boldly claimed was comparable with 'the half dozen great masterpieces of this delightful form of literature'.Once he has identified the culprit, Sir Clinton contrives to make the murderer 'his own executioner…my method was a stiffer one than mere hanging'. Admitting that his approach is unorthodox, he makes no apology: 'I can only say that my conscience is quite clear.' Great Detectives commonly dispensed their own brand of justice to malefactors, but nobody did so quite as ruthlessly as Sir Clinton Driffield.

Murder in Black and White
by Evelyn Elder (1931)

In this holiday mystery set in the south of France, the author—better known as Milward Kennedy—plays a game with his readers; the sporting theme is reinforced by the central role of real tennis in the storyline. The book is divided into four sections, and the author states in a prefatory note that: 'When the reader reaches the end of Part Three he is in possession of all the facts needed to reach the solution of the problem.' The first section is set at a cocktail party, attended by a young architect and amateur artist, Sam Horder, on his return from holiday in picturesque St André-sur-Mer at Carnival time. He breaks the news about the French equivalent of a country-house mystery—murder at the Chateau St Andre during a fancy-dress ball. Louis de Vigny, dressed in a black and white costume, has been murdered, shot by a rifle bullet 'practically under my eyes'. But the crime appears to be an impossibility.

Part Two reproduces six entries from Sam's sketchbook: a plan of the chateau where the crime took place; a sketch of a 'flying bridge'; a picture of the Tour Pantillon; four sketches of scenes in the old town; a view of the crime scene from the sea; and a picture of the chateau from above the seashore. The sketches contain visual clues to the solution of the mystery, a pleasing device adopted and modified by Francis Beeding in *The*

Norwich Victims (1935), a novel prefaced with photographs of the suspects which merit careful study.

The meat of the novel is contained in Part Three, in which Sam describes the events surrounding the murder. He concludes by summing up the problem if the police's theory about the crime is rejected: 'only one of three people could have fired the shot, and none of the three had a rifle, or could have concealed it.' Henry Evelyn acts as amateur sleuth, deducing what has happened on the basis of what Sam has told him, coupled with the sketches—which prompt him to make his own rough diagrams.

The combination of a 'challenge to the reader' with artistic clues was a clever innovation from a writer who seemed destined to become one of the major Golden Age novelists. The sketches were actually drawn by his friend Austin Blomfield, an architect and artist who went into practice with his father, a distinguished architect whose work included buildings at Lady Margaret Hall, Oxford. Kennedy swiftly produced a second novel under the Evelyn Elder pseudonym, the disappointing *Angel in the Case* (1932).

Milward Rodon Kennedy Burge became director of the London office of the International Labour Office from 1924, and started writing in his spare time. After co-writing with his friend A.G. Macdonell *The Bleston Mystery* (1928), a thriller published as by Robert Milward Kennedy, he started to write detective novels under his own steam as Milward Kennedy, and became a founder member of the Detection Club. His admiration for the books of Anthony Berkeley caused him to experiment with the genre, sometimes with intriguing results. But his desire to vary the formula with each book meant that he never created a successful series character, although Inspector Cornford appeared in a couple of books, as did the suave confidence tricksters Sir George and Lady Bull.

Chapter Ten

Making Fun of Murder

With *Trent's Last Case* (page 36), E.C. Bentley meant to satirise the supposed infallibility of great detectives. The book's most unexpected twist was that it laid down the template for the classic whodunit novel. The game-playing nature of the whodunit after the First World War created opportunities for humourists. It is no coincidence that regular contributors to *Punch* included several of the leading detective novelists to emerge in the Twenties. E.V. ('Evoe') Knox, the brother of Ronald, was editor of *Punch* for seventeen years, and wrote 'The Murder at the Towers', perhaps the wittiest short parody of the traditional whodunit.

The success of P.G. Wodehouse (a keen fan of detective fiction) influenced writers such as Anthony Berkeley and Agatha Christie. Berkeley's non-series mystery *Mr Priestley's Problem* (1927), in which a group of Bright Young Things play a 'murder hoax' on a meek little man similar to Berkeley's more famous character Ambrose Chitterwick, is a romp in the style of a novel by Wodehouse. Christie's early thrillers such as *The Secret of Chimneys* (1925) and *The Seven Dials Mystery* (1929) are equally playful. Humour was a recurrent, and routinely under-rated, feature of her writing, and *Partners in Crime* (1929), featuring her third-string sleuths Tommy and Tuppence Beresford, parodies the work of then-popular authors of detective fiction. The targets include such prominent figures as G.K. Chesterton, Edgar Wallace and Berkeley, as well as the now seldom-remembered American authors Isabel Ostrander and Clinton H. Stagg.

Humour, especially facetiousness, tends to date badly in fiction, while satire loses its bite once the satirist's target has faded from memory. The best Golden Age parodies nevertheless remain readable today. They include 'Greedy Night' by E.C. Bentley, a short story which, like *Gory Knight* (1937) by Margaret Rivers Larminie and Jane Langslow, took its title from Dorothy L. Sayers' 'novel of manners' set in Oxford, *Gaudy Night* (1935).

The most innovative and ambitious Golden Age parody was *Ask a Policeman* (1933). This was written in collaboration by six members of the Detection Club, four of whom exchanged detectives with each other. Their chosen murder victim was a newspaper baron, and among the suspects were an archbishop, a police commissioner and the government Chief Whip. The Home Secretary calls in four leading amateur sleuths, each of whom duly propounds a different solution to the mystery. The story was introduced by an exchange of letters between John Rhode and Milward Kennedy. Rhode wrote the book's long introductory section, while Kennedy had to fashion a logical outcome to what had gone before, a tricky challenge which he met at the expense of strict fair play.

Once Rhode had set the scene, Helen Simpson took over, with a chapter introducing Gladys Mitchell's Mrs Bradley. Mitchell returned the compliment in her contribution, which features Sir John Samaurez, the detective created by Simpson in collaboration with the novelist and playwright Clemence Dane. The highlight of the book is Anthony Berkeley's chapter featuring Lord Peter Wimsey; in contrast, Sayers' rendition of Berkeley's inquisitive amateur sleuth Roger Sheringham is competent but not wholly compelling. The book's sheer *joie de vivre* is appealing, but it is most impressive as a demonstration of the craftsmanship of writers at the peak of their powers.

Crime novels in which the humour stems from the characters or the situation are usually more successful than those where the sole purpose of the book is to be funny. Part of the problem is that murder in real life is an appalling crime which causes untold distress. Making fun of it without tastelessness requires more care and skill than merely making a game out of it. Sustaining a career as an author of funny detective novels is especially challenging. Alan Melville, for instance, built a considerable reputation as a wit, but despite producing a handful of amusing detective novels, he soon abandoned the genre in favour of a career as a broadcaster and playwright. Another journalist and broadcaster who wrote plays was Denzil Batchelor, who published *The Test Match Murder* (1936) early in his career. England's star batsman is poisoned by curare, administered via his batting glove, while walking out to the crease at Sydney. This light-hearted thriller, which features a pleasing caricature of the Great Detective, falters when Batchelor resorts to introducing a dope gang and even a mysterious Chinaman. A former secretary to the legendary cricketer C.B. Fry, Batchelor became better known as a sports writer than as a novelist.

After writing captions for newspaper cartoons together, Caryl Brahms and S.J. Simon experimented with a humorous mystery novel. The tone of *A Bullet in the Ballet* (1937) is set in the opening sentence: 'Since it is probable that any book flying a bullet in its title is going to produce a corpse sooner or later—here it is.' It was followed by two more books featuring the impresario Vladimir Stroganoff and Inspector Adam Quill. *Casino for Sale* (1938) includes a locked-room mystery, but the authors' speciality lay in amusing rather than baffling their readers. Caryl Brahms' real name was Doris Caroline Abrahams, while 'Skid' Simon, born Seca Jascha Skidelsky in Manchuria, was a champion bridge player whose early death ended a highly successful comic writing partnership.

Of the ironic writers inspired by Berkeley's work under the name Francis Iles, the most consistently amusing was Richard Hull. Hull's *The Murderers of Monty* (1937), for instance, begins enjoyably, with four professional men setting up a company which has the object of killing their eponymous friend, who is rather a bore. Why is the company called The Murderers of Monty Limited? Because it is limited to Monty, of course. The joke backfires when Monty Archer is found dead, and the novel suffers because the entertaining idea at its heart does not sustain a full-length book.

John Dickson Carr's books featuring Sir Henry Merrivale, and published as by Carter Dickson, utilise slapstick humour as a means of misdirecting the reader's attention from vital plot information. Carr's most high-spirited disciple was Edmund Crispin, who wrote detective novels with lashings of comedy as well as ingenuity. Rather like Alan Melville, however, Crispin ran out of steam all too soon.

In contrast, two long-serving employees of major banks sought escape from the sinister world of finance by leavening many of their detective stories with a touch of humour. Clifford Witting was a former clerk with Lloyds Bank; the first half of *Measure for Murder* (1941), set against the background of an amateur dramatic society's staging of *Measure for Measure*, is narrated by a former bank clerk. The book presents an interesting picture of English small-town life during the early stages of the Second World War. Also in 1941, George Bellairs made his debut with *Littlejohn on Leave*. In real life, Bellairs was Mancunian bank manager Harold Blundell, who published detective stories for almost forty years; the longevity of his career was probably due to the care he took to ensure that the crimes investigated by Inspector Littlejohn did not become submerged by comedy.

Writing a funny crime story that will stand the test of time is difficult. Julian Symons, as fiercely critical of his own books as he was of sub-standard work by others, concluded that his light-hearted debut *The Immaterial Murder Case* (1945) was so bad that it should never be republished. Symons' books became increasingly serious as he sought to reflect what he saw as an evolution in the genre from the detective story to the crime novel.

After the Second World War, Pamela Branch published *The Wooden Overcoat* (1951), an engaging story about a club for wrongly acquitted murderers, but she was another witty writer who lacked staying power, the last of her four books appearing in 1958. Joyce Porter was more prolific, but her early work featuring the lazy and repellent Chief Inspector Dover was by far her best.

Coffin, Scarcely Used (1958) by Colin Watson launched the Flaxborough Chronicles, a dozen novels set in and around a market town with an unexpectedly high level of homicide. The series was adapted for television in 1977 as *Murder Most English*; five years earlier, *Lonelyheart 4122* (1967) had become a TV movie, *The Crooked Hearts*. Watson was arguably the most successful British writer of comic crime to emerge in the second half of the twentieth century. A journalist by profession, he is also said to be the first person to have obtained libel compensation from the satirical magazine *Private Eye* after it described his writing as like Wodehouse, 'but without the jokes'; an unkind review can dull even the sharpest sense of humour.

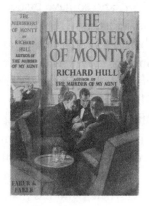

Quick Curtain
by Alan Melville (1934)

Quick Curtain opens with a first-night performance in front of a full house at the Grosvenor Theatre. The great and the good have come to see *Blue Music*, and so have Inspector Wilson of Scotland Yard and his journalist son. The show is a 'musical comedy operetta' produced by the legendary Douglas B. Douglas. Words and music come courtesy of Ivor Watcyns, who wrote the book 'between the grapefruit of one breakfast and the tomato juice of the lunch immediately following that breakfast'.

Douglas has 'a flair for picking legs, spotting personality, and persuading the public that something merely mediocre was something simply sensational'. The stars of his show are Brandon Baker, who has kept himself in trim as a 'juvenile lead' for nearly thirty years, and Gwen Astle, who has married six times, twice into the peerage, and has recently become engaged to the son of an American multi-millionaire. The thin storyline of *Blue Music* involves the shooting of the leading man, but Brandon Baker is killed by a real bullet. Within minutes, the presumed culprit is found dead in his dressing room, having apparently hanged himself, but the two Wilsons who form a comic equivalent of Holmes and Watson, discover that there is more to the case than meets the eye.

In a review for *The Sunday Times*, Dorothy L. Sayers said that Melville 'gets great enjoyment out of scarifying all the leading lights of the profession, from producer to dramatic critic', although she fretted that he 'blows the solemn structure of the detective novel sky-high'. He makes amusing use of his inside knowledge of backstage life, and Sayers said that his satire included 'several thinly veiled personal attacks'. In the twenty-first century, the pleasure of the story lies not in reading between the lines to detect the identity of Melville's targets, but in his witty portrayal of characteristic types. These include not only the producer and performers, but also James Amethyst, weary drama critic of the *Morning Herald*, who finds the musical comedies that he reviews so formulaic that he scarcely troubles to pay attention.

As Sayers said, Melville looks on 'all this detective business as a huge joke', but not only does he sustain the joke to the end of the book, his humour has also survived the passage of time. Melville, whose real name was William Melville Caverhill, was a versatile writer who worked as a scriptwriter and radio producer for the BBC, and dabbled in detection, as well as working as a lyricist and writing for the theatre.

He adapted his first mystery, *Week-end at Thrackley* (1934) into a play, which became *Hot Ice*, a film screened in 1952. In all, he produced six mysteries during the mid-Thirties before turning his attention elsewhere. During the television era, he became chairman of the Brains Trust, hosted a satiric revue series called *A–Z*, and was a panellist on *What's My Line?*. As an actor, his credits included parts in a Noel Coward's *The Vortex*, and in a costume drama, *By the Sword Divided*, which earned high audience ratings in the Eighties. By that point, his work as a detective novelist was long forgotten.

Case for Three Detectives
by Leo Bruce (1936)

It is no mean feat to combine an intricate locked room mystery with a successful parody of three Great Detectives, but Leo Bruce rose to the challenge in his first detective novel. The book introduces Sergeant Beef, an apparently uncouth, beer-drinking, darts-playing policeman whose skills as a detective are routinely underestimated, not least by Lionel Townsend, who narrates the story.

Townsend is among the guests at the country home of the amiable and seemingly inoffensive Dr and Mrs Thurston, when the conversation turns to the difference between murder in fact and fiction. Shortly afterwards, a woman's screams are heard, and Mrs Thurston is found dead in her locked bedroom with her throat cut. It cannot be suicide—but how, and by whom, has she been killed? The village bobby, Sergeant Beef, is summoned, but he is quickly usurped by three of 'those indefatigably brilliant private investigators who seem to be always handy when murder has been committed'.

Lord Simon Plimsoll, Amer Picon and Monsignor Smith are thinly disguised versions of Wimsey, Poirot and Father Brown, and the mannerisms, dialogue and methods of detection familiar from the originals are captured wittily and with considerable skill. Lord Simon's imperturbable sidekick Butterfield does his legwork, just as Mervyn Bunter does for Lord Peter; Picon talks in broken English; while little Smith makes Delphic utterances, and finds intriguing parallels between murderers and monks.

The closed circle of suspects includes a puritanical yet prurient vicar, a ne'er-do-well young man, a smug solicitor, a sinister butler, a feisty housemaid and a chauffeur with a criminal record. Is it conceivable that they are all in it together? Townsend acts as a self-appointed Watson to each of the great men, and is rewarded when each of them, in turn, comes up with a breathtakingly ingenious explanation for the crime. But it is Sergeant Beef who has the last laugh.

Beef and Townsend formed a pleasing double-act in seven further novels and a scattering of short stories. Bruce was as willing to experiment with the form and conventions of the detective story as Anthony Berkeley: *Case for Three Detectives* is a worthy successor to *The Poisoned Chocolates Case* (page 64) as an example of the mystery with multiple solutions. Bruce's *Case with Four Clowns* (1939) is, like Berkeley's *Murder in the Basement* (1932), an example of the 'whowasdunin', a story in which murder is pre-ordained, but the victim's identity is a mystery to be solved. To Townsend's astonishment, Beef sets up as a private investigator in *Case with No Conclusion* (1939), another novel which makes jokey references to the classic detective story, while *Case for Sergeant Beef* (1947) offers a clever spin on the concept of the inverted mystery.

Bruce was the pen-name of Rupert Croft-Cooke, a versatile and gifted writer who regarded his detective fiction as rather less important than his other work. This view was common among writers of his vintage, but with the passage of time it has become clear that they erred in underestimating the long-term appeal of the detective story. Croft-Cooke was widely travelled, and spent fifteen years living in Morocco following his release from prison; he had been convicted of homosexual offences in 1953 in a controversial case which helped to create pressure for liberalisation of the law. Following his time in jail, he never wrote another book about Beef, but his creative powers remained undimmed.

He quickly established a new series detective, the school-teacher Carolus Deene, and became a member of the select sub-group of crime novelists who wrote fiction with some success after a serving a prison term; Walter S. Masterman was another, while Robert Forsythe apparently started writing the first of his eight detective novels while serving time for his role as ringleader in a conspiracy to defraud Somerset House; the fact that he published under the name Robin Forsythe suggests that he was not adept at covering his tracks. As for Leo Bruce, he wrote no fewer than twenty-three books about Deene. The last of them, the trendily titled *Death of a Bovver Boy*, was published in 1974. However, although they are adroitly constructed, he never surpassed his delightful debut novel.

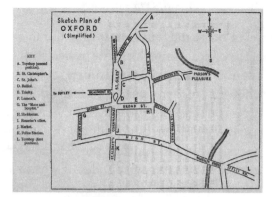

Sketch Plan of
OXFORD
(Simplified)

KEY

A. Toyshop (second position).
B. St. Christopher's.
C. St. John's.
D. Balliol.
E. Trinity.
F. Lennox's.
G. The "Mace and Sceptre."
H. Sheldonian.
I. Rosseter's office.
J. Market.
K. Police Station.
L. Toyshop (first position).

The Moving Toyshop
by Edmund Crispin (1946)

Few crime novels can match Edmund Crispin's most celebrated mystery for sheer exuberance. A teasing, seemingly impossible situation, a wonderfully evoked setting among the dreaming spires of Oxford, and an amateur sleuth in the finest tradition of great detectives, make up the ingredients of a much-loved novel. Published shortly after the Second World War ended, the storyline belongs in spirit to the between-the-wars Golden Age of detective fiction.

Richard Cadogan, a poet visiting Oxford, chances one night upon a toyshop on Iffley Road. Its awning has been left down and, finding the door open, he ventures inside. There he stumbles upon the dead body of an elderly woman, only to be hit on the head by an unknown assailant. After regaining consciousness, he hurries off to report the crime to the police, and accompanies them to the scene, but they discover that the toyshop has metamorphosed into a grocer's store. As the police are sceptical about Cadogan's story, he turns for help to Professor Gervase Fen of St Christopher's College, and a madcap investigation ensues.

Crispin enjoyed writing chase scenes, two of which feature in this novel. At one point, when facing a choice about which direction to take, Cadogan decides to turn left, allowing the author to poke fun at his socialist publisher: 'After all, Gollancz is publishing this book.' Like John Dickson Carr, Crispin was quite happy to break the fourth wall, and also to make fun of his publisher's political sympathies. The second chase culminates at Botley fairground, and an out-of-control roundabout; Alfred Hitchcock bought the right to use the scene for the film version of Patricia Highsmith's *Strangers on a Train*. A screenplay of *The Moving Toyshop* was written, but no film of the book was made, although a version for TV launched the BBC's much-admired series *Detective* in 1964 (many episodes of which, sadly, have not been preserved).

Crispin dedicated the book to his friend and fellow student at St John's College, the poet and detective-fiction fan Philip Larkin, who had sparked his imagination by telling him about an Oxford shop with a flapping awning. Richard Cadogan shares some attitudes with Larkin, and jokes about poetry abound. Larkin is even name-checked by Fen, and described as 'the most indefatigable searcher-out of pointless correspondence the world has ever known'.

Edmund Crispin was the pen-name of Bruce Montgomery, who was equally gifted as a composer and a novelist. His first detective novel, *The Case of the Gilded Fly* (1944), was written while he was an undergraduate, in a ten-day burst of activity during the Easter vacation when he should have been revising for Finals. His clever, frivolous mysteries rapidly earned a following. In *Buried for Pleasure* (1948), a village mystery in which Fen stands for Parliament as an Independent candidate, the sleuth meets a detective novelist who says: 'Characterisation seems to me a very over-rated element in fiction...It *limits* the form so.' No doubt he was speaking for Crispin.

Crispin became a pillar of the Detection Club, but after publishing eight novels and a collection of short stories within a decade, he ran out of creative juice as a crime writer. He struggled with writer's block, alcoholism and poor health, and his ninth and final novel about Gervase Fen, the underwhelming *The Glimpses of the Moon* (1977) did not appear until the year before his death.

Chapter Eleven
Education, Education, Education

In the years after the First World War, authors gradually began to recognise the possibilities of workplaces as settings for detective stories. One country house was much like another, but workplaces might also offer a suitably restricted circle of suspects in the event of murder being done, together with fresh and interesting background colour. But authors were limited to workplace backgrounds that they knew well, either as a result of personal experience or in-depth research. J.S. Fletcher, Dorothy L. Sayers and Freeman Wills Crofts, who had earned a living in journalism, advertising and railways respectively, made excellent use of their insight into those worlds in their fiction. The majority of crime writers, however, had little or no first-hand knowledge of the business environment. Life in an educational establishment was much more familiar. Many were university graduates, while some taught in schools or colleges.

This was a time when most crime writers came from London or the Home Counties. In 1939, a list of Detection Club members revealed that not a single one of them lived in the north of England, although Sir Hugh Walpole had a place in the Lake District as well as in Piccadilly. Similarly, their experience of school and university was not representative of the population as a whole. With relatively few exceptions, they came from well-to-do families, and were educated at public school; many went to Oxford or Cambridge. Of the first twenty-eight men and women admitted to Detection Club, no fewer than four— Ronald Knox, Douglas Cole, Lord Gorell and Edgar Jepson— had studied at Balliol. Sayers chose the same college as the *alma mater* of Lord Peter Wimsey (said to have been based on the college chaplain, although Gorell himself thought he was the original of Wimsey). R.C. Woodthorpe and John Dickson Carr, both elected to membership of the Club during the Thirties, also created detectives who were Balliol alumni: Nicholas Slade and the much more renowned Dr Gideon Fell respectively.

Theirs was, in many ways, a small and elitist world, and this helps to explain why classic crime novels often include phonetic renditions of the dialogue of working-class people which make modern readers cringe. Some of the attitudes evident and implicit in the books of highly educated authors, for instance as regards Jewish and gay people, would be unacceptable in fiction written in the twenty-first century. It is worth remembering that theirs was not only a tiny world, but also a very different one from ours, and one of the pleasures of reading classic crime fiction is that it affords an insight into the Britain of the past, a country in some respects scarcely recognisable today.

Christopher Bush, Nicholas Blake, R.C. Woodthorpe, F.J. Whaley and Gladys Mitchell all exploited their experience as teachers in giving their school-based mysteries a touch of authenticity. Francis John Whaley was the most obscure member of this quintet, but his debut novel, *Reduction of Staff* (1936) continues to be admired by connoisseurs. Mitchell spent a lifetime working in traditional schools, but was fascinated by the controversial educational views of A.S. Neill, founder of the progressive school Summerhill, and these influenced her presentation of the Hillmaston co-educational school in *Death at the Opera* (1934), also known as *Death in the Wet*.

Woodthorpe's debut, *The Public School Murder* (1932) was acclaimed by Dorothy L. Sayers: 'The gorgeous picture of life in the masters' common room made it the most brilliant and humorous detective story of its season.' Soon the novel gained startling notoriety. In September 1934, the Rev. Dr Elliott Speer, headmaster of Mount Hermon Preparatory School for Boys in Northfield, Massachusetts, was found murdered in circumstances uncannily similar to those in the book. He was shot one evening through the open window of his study. Curiously, Speer owned a copy of *The Public School Murder*, and it was said that he had recently lent it to Thomas E. Elder, the school's dean. Elder was a traditionalist hostile towards Speer, who had been liberalising the school's strict Presbyterian regime, but although circumstantial evidence hinted at his guilt, there was not enough to justify his arrest. Elder left the school, and six years later was tried for threatening a former colleague from Mount Hermon with a shotgun, but was acquitted. Speer's murder was never solved, and it remains a matter for a conjecture whether the killer borrowed his *modus operandi* from the novel.

Which Way Came Death? (1936) by Faith Wolseley, was a well-written novel in which the splendidly three-dimensional central character is the wife of the head of a public school. The author was married to the headmaster of Hurstpierpoint College, which may account for her decision to opt for a pseudonym: she had previously written under her own name, Stella Tower.

The Oxford Murders (1929) by Adam Broome was the first of many detective novels to take full advantage of the old university city as a setting, and in 1936, Broome—a pen-name of Godfrey Warden James—produced *The Cambridge Murders*. In 1945, Welsh-born archaeologist and Cambridge don Glyn Daniel also published a book called *The Cambridge Murders*, under the name Dilwyn Rees. *The Boat Race Murder* (1933) by R.E. Swartwout (who, three years before publishing the book, had been the first American to cox Cambridge to victory over Oxford in the Boat Race) and *The Punt Murder* (1934) by Aceituna Griffin, are Cambridge mysteries with a boating background.

Oxford was, however, a more frequent setting for classic crime fiction than its ancient rival, in part thanks to the influence of J.C. Masterman's *An Oxford Tragedy* (1933). Masterman was an

Oxford insider who eventually became Vice-Chancellor of the University, and his account of life in a senior common room carried a ring of truth. The academic bickering is briefly disrupted by the murder of an unpopular don in the rooms of the Dean, who has been foolish enough not only to leave a loaded gun there, but also to mention this fact at High Table.

Dermot Morrah's sole detective novel. *The Mummy Case* (1933), also known as *The Mummy Case Mystery* offers an appealing mix of Egyptology and detection, like R. Austin Freeman's *The Eye of Osiris* (page 28) more than two decades earlier. Jacques Barzun and Wendell Hertig Taylor, authors of *A Catalogue of Crime* and highly knowledgeable but habitually severe judges, ranked Masterman's book as a masterpiece, and Morrah's as a triumph.

Michael Innes was inspired by Masterman's success to turn to crime, and Innes in turn exerted an influence upon Edmund Crispin, creator of Gervase Fen, Professor of English Language and Literature at St Christopher's College, and a vigorous amateur sleuth in nine novels and two collections of short stories. By definition, undergraduates were never destined to become series characters, but a quartet of female students take centre stage in Mavis Doriel Hay's sole Oxford novel, *Death on the Cherwell* (1935), in which they investigate the killing of the much-disliked bursar of Persephone College.

Persephone, based on St Hilda's, where Hay had been a student, is a women-only college, and in the year that Hay's book appeared, Dorothy L. Sayers published *Gaudy Night*, set in a fictionalised version of her old college, Somerville, and regarded by many of her admirers as her finest achievement. Harriet Vane returns to Shrewsbury College after a gap of some years, rather as Sayers had gone back to Somerville as guest of honour at a reunion after a long absence. The Dean seeks Harriet's help in unmasking the person responsible for a series of poison-pen letters and for defacing a manuscript, but the element of mystery in the story is subordinate to Sayers' attempt to produce 'a detective novel of manners' and to integrate her plot with her chosen theme of intellectual integrity. As the book's subtitle, 'a love story with detective interruptions', implies, the primary focus is not on the crime or its solution. Sayers is preoccupied by the relationship between men and women in general, and between Harriet and Lord Peter Wimsey in particular. The novel continues to divide opinion, but as a love letter to Oxford in the guise of a detective story, it remains unsurpassed, despite the seemingly never-ending fictional crime wave among the dreaming spires.

Murder at School
by Glen Trevor (1931)

Colin Revell, still in his twenties, has had 'one of those "brilliant" careers at Oxford that are the despair alike of parents and prospective employers', enjoys a private income of four pounds a week, and has acquired a reputation as 'a neat solver of mysteries'. He has also found time to publish a novel: 'of course he had done *that*'. His expert assistance is sought by the headmaster of his old school, Oakington, after a pupil dies, apparently by accident, in the dormitory.

It seems clear that, despite the existence of a mysterious 'will' left by the dead boy, his death was an accident. A few months later, however, Revell learns that another pupil has died at Oakington, apparently having drowned by accident while foolishly swimming in the dark. An even more troubling coincidence is that the two dead boys were brothers. Their cousin, a housemaster, is now in line to inherit one hundred thousand pounds. Is it possible that he has contrived two ingenious murders? The account of Revell's hapless investigation into the deaths is flavoured with an irony reflecting the influence of Francis Iles, although the plot is scarcely in the same league as that of Iles' *Malice Aforethought* (page 259).

The novel was published by Ernest Benn in a yellow dust-jacket whose style bore a distinct similarity to that pioneered by Victor Gollancz, formerly managing director of Benn, who had set up his own publishing house with immediate success, poaching authors such as Sayers and J.J. Connington from his old firm. Gollancz, whose marketing flair was legendary, had made a mystery out of the identity of Francis Iles, prompting a great deal of wildly erroneous speculation, much to the amusement of the author himself.

Benn followed this lead. The jacket claimed 'special attention' for 'a thriller of exceptional ingenuity', while a competition on the rear flap offered a prize of ten pounds for the first correct solution to the mystery of Glen Trevor's identity, to be opened on New Year's Day 1932. The clue given was that his real name was 'known to the discerning as the Author of a number of novels distinguished for their penetrating observation in the drawing of character'. His most recent book had also been published by Benn.

The correct answer was James Hilton, whose earlier books included *Dawn of Reckoning* (1925), a mainstream novel which includes a trial for murder, and was later transformed into a crime film, *Rage in Heaven*, Hilton's father was headmaster of a school in Walthamstow, and Hilton put his understanding of school life to use again in *Goodbye, Mr Chips* (1934) a short and sentimental book that became a bestseller and a memorable film. In 1933, he published two novels that were filmed, *Knight without Armour* and the much better known *Lost Horizon*, set in idyllic Shangri-La. His gifts for visual writing and telling a good story took him to Hollywood, where he won an Academy Award for his contribution to the screenplay for *Mrs Miniver*. *Murder at School* enjoyed a new incarnation in the US as *Was it Murder?*, with Hilton credited as the author, but Colin Revell's first case, unlike Philip Trent's, was his last.

Murder at Cambridge
by Q. Patrick (1933)

Hilary Fenton, an undergraduate at All Saints College, Cambridge, is a native of Philadelphia who has come to England 'to polish off any odd corners that may have survived four years at Harvard.' A clever but sullen fellow student from the Orange Free State in South Africa, Julius Baumann, swears Hilary to secrecy before asking him to witness a document and giving him an envelope, to be posted in the event of Baumann suddenly leaving college. Shortly afterwards, during a thunderstorm, Baumann is found dead in his room. He has been shot, and lying on the floor close to his hand is a revolver.

Hilary, a likeable and enthusiastic narrator, decides that Baumann has been murdered, and leaps to the conclusion that the killer is a young woman with whom he is besotted. Believing he has spotted her lovely profile on a staircase in the vicinity of the crime scene, and that traces of her distinctive perfume have lingered in Baumann's study, he determines to protect her. A second murder occurs, and the puzzle of the two deaths is investigated by Hilary in tandem with Inspector Horrocks, who proves remarkably tolerant of the student's attempts to obstruct the course of justice.

This high-spirited mystery benefits from the energy and inside knowledge of an author not many years older than Hilary, who sprinkles his narratives with jokes about the Cambridge way of life. A light-hearted glossary provided for readers 'who have not sojourned long at Cambridge' describes a combination room as 'a mysterious chamber in which the fellows of the college assemble to drink port after Hall. No one has ever yet discovered what they talk about there, but the conversation is reputed to be very brilliant'. A proctor is defined as 'a don dressed up as a policeman'.

Somerset-born Richard Wilson Webb was well qualified to write this novel—also known as *Murder at the 'Varsity*—having studied at Clare College, Cambridge, and lived in France and South Africa prior to emigrating to the United States. He worked for a pharmaceutical business in Philadelphia, and his creative mind found an outlet through the invention of a pocket inhaler as well as by writing detective fiction. After producing two crime novels under the Q. Patrick pseudonym with Martha Mott Kelley, he retained the writing name when she left their literary partnership, and made use of his inside knowledge of Cambridge college life for this solo novel.

Following *Murder at Cambridge*, Webb wrote two more Q. Patrick books in collaboration with Mary Louise Aswell, including the excellent but very dark rural mystery, *The Grindle Nightmare* (1935). His publisher made a mystery of his identity without hinting at his collaborators' existence: 'Q. Patrick is not his name, America not his birthplace, writing is not his vocation...A Jekyll and Hyde is Q. Patrick—by day an important Eastern executive, by night a recorder of macabre crime!...Q. Patrick the author is an enigma! Q. Patrick is a riddle! Q. Patrick is a mystery!'

Under the same pseudonym, Webb proceeded to join forces with another Englishman, Hugh Wheeler. Wheeler and Webb also wrote under the name Jonathan Stagge and Patrick Quentin, and Wheeler continued to produce Quentin novels after Webb's retirement from writing in the Fifties, although he later became better known as the author of books to musicals such as *A Little Night Music* and *Sweeney Todd*.

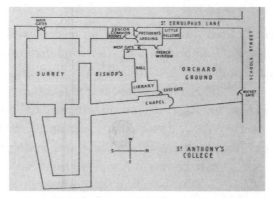

Death at the President's Lodging
by Michael Innes (1936)

'An academic life, Dr Johnson observed, puts one little in the way of extraordinary casualties. This was not the experience of the Fellows and scholars of St Anthony's College when they awoke one raw November morning to find their President, Josiah Umpleby, murdered in the night. The crime was at once intriguing and bizarre, efficient and theatrical. It was efficient, because nobody knew who had committed it. And it was theatrical because of a macabre and unnecessary act of fantasy with which the criminal, it was quickly rumoured, had accompanied his deed.'

Michael Innes announced his arrival as a detective novelist characteristically, with a quotation, a paradox, a baroque scenario and a touch of humour. Umpleby has been shot, little piles of human bones have been scattered around his corpse, and on the oak panels of his study, someone has chalked a couple of grinning death's heads.

The puzzle is too much for the capable but unimaginative local policeman, and Inspector John Appleby of New Scotland Yard is summoned. There is 'something more in Appleby than the intensely taught product of a modern police college. A contemplative habit and a tentative mind, poise as well as force, reserve rather than wariness—these were the tokens perhaps of some underlying more liberal education.' He prefers to solve problems 'on a human or psychological plane' rather than by focusing on the practicalities of 'doors and windows and purloined keys.' We are left in no doubt that Appleby is a 'gentleman', and suspicion shifts around a closed circle of college men (no woman plays a significant part in the story); in the US, to avoid any hint of infamy at the White House, the book was re-titled *Seven Suspects*. Although part of a fictitious university located at Bletchley, St Anthony's, the erudition, playfulness and petty jealousies of college life are evoked so well because the author was a consummate Oxford insider. Appleby finally reveals all in the suitable setting of the college common room, although naturally he waits until after port and sherry have circulated around the assembled Fellows.

Michael Innes was a pen-name taken by John Innes Mackintosh Stewart, who studied at Oriel College and later returned to Oxford to become a student (i.e. Fellow) at Christ Church. In the mid-Thirties, as he said in his memoir *Myself and Michael Innes* (1987), 'in one class of polite society, writing detective stories had superseded writing ghost stories as an acceptable relaxation', and he began the novel 'with the notion of its bringing in a little pocket-money'. In much the same spirit Cecil Day-Lewis, another Oxford man, had written his first detective story under the name Nicholas Blake to fund the repair of a leaky roof.

Appleby and his creator enjoyed long careers. Innes' work included several thrillers, and sometimes verged on the fantastic, as with *The Daffodil Affair* (1942), while he became equally prolific as a writer of 'straight' novels and non-fiction under his own name. Sounding a little defensive, he wrote that 'detective stories are purely recreational reading, after all, and needn't scorn the ambition to amuse as well as puzzle'. Appleby ultimately became Metropolitan Police Commissioner and earned a knighthood; his son Bobby also became a detective and featured in later books.

Chapter Twelve

Playing Politics

In traditional detective whodunits, politicians and financiers became murder victims almost as regularly as elderly relatives of impoverished people desperate for an inheritance. Members of all three groups supplied plenty of suspects with reasons to kill them. Bankers and members of political elites were no more popular in the first half of the last century than they are today. Readers of detective stories in the aftermath of the First World War, through the misery of the economic slump, and in the run-up to the Second World War, were looking for escapism, and writers were ready, willing and able to supply it. Nevertheless, both before and during the Golden Age, writers touched on political and economic concerns of the time more often than post-war critics have acknowledged.

Financial shenanigans keep cropping up in Freeman Wills Crofts' novels of the Thirties, as in *The End of Andrew Harrison* (1938), a locked-room mystery involving the apparent suicide of a rascally businessman. *The Times'* review of Crofts' book said that 'the barons of commerce are as much the stock in trade of many of the writers of thrillers as were the bold, bad baronets of our grandfathers' time', and the same column featured two further examples. In F.J. Whaley's *Southern Electric Murder*, 'motor car manufacturing firms are found using bribery and espionage in order to secure the market for themselves', while trade rivalry between competing owners of multiple stores lie at the heart of Basil Francis' *Slender Margin*.

Politicians fared even worse in detective stories than those barons of commerce, yet Stanley Baldwin and President Woodrow Wilson professed their enthusiasm for the genre, and the left-wing publisher Victor Gollancz masterminded an imprint known as 'The Prime Minister's Detective Library', one of his less-successful marketing ploys. During the Golden Age, several men and women prominent in political life tried their hand at detective fiction. Julian Symons claimed in *Bloody Murder* that 'It is safe to say that almost all the British writers of the twenties and thirties...were unquestionably right wing', but this confident assertion was quite wrong.

The long list of exceptions included the husband-and-wife team of G.D.H. and Margaret Cole, the former air minister Lord Gorell (who defected from the Liberals, only to be drummed out of the Labour Party because of his association with Ramsay MacDonald) and Ellen Wilkinson, who became a post-war Labour minister. Nicholas Blake (Cecil Day-Lewis) was a Marxist when he began his crime writing career, as was Cameron McCabe (Ernst Wilhelm Julius Bornemann), while Raymond Postgate was a founder member of the British Communist Party, and Christopher St John Sprigg met his death while fighting against Franco in the Spanish Civil War. Bruce Hamilton and his brother Patrick flirted with communism, R.C. Woodthorpe was a left-wing journalist working for the *Daily Herald*, while Anthony Wynne and E.R. Punshon both took pot-shots at capitalism in their novels, occasionally to the detriment of narrative pace.

Politicians dropped like flies in books such as *Murder of an M.P.!* (1927) by Robert Gore-Browne, who came from a family with a tradition of political service, *The Mystery of the House of Commons* (1929) by Fielding Hope (an early pen-name of Graham Montague Jeffries, who went on to enjoy a prolific career writing as Bruce Graeme), in which three members of the Socialist Party meet their end in quick succession, *Death of the*

Home Secretary (1933) by Alan Thomas, and Helen Simpson's *Vantage Striker* (1931).

Simpson's novel, alternatively and more bluntly titled *The Prime Minister is Dead* (1931), reflects a keen awareness of the menace of fascism, as did satiric work such as Ronald Knox's story 'The Fallen Idol', R.C. Woodthorpe's *Silence of a Purple Shirt* and Punshon's *Dictator's Way* (1938), a flawed yet interesting novel which also swiped at City financiers who funded the bully boys. In Stanley Casson's *Murder by Burial* (1938), an eccentric heritage association becomes a front for a crypto-fascist organisation.

The political attitudes articulated, or hinted at, in classic crime fiction were often unsophisticated, as in Agatha Christie's light-hearted early thrillers. Similarly, the political elements of Anthony Berkeley's *Death in the House* (1939) are unenlightening, and although he supplied an impossible crime committed in Parliament, together with a 'challenge to the reader', the puzzle lacked his usual flair. *We Shot an Arrow* (1939) by George Goodchild and Carl Bechhofer Roberts features a by-election, and the authors are even-handed in killing off both the Conservative and Labour candidates. The characters discuss the Munich Agreement and the looming threat of war, but the story's main interest lies in the authors' remarkable decision to present themselves as the central characters in the story, an experiment that, perhaps wisely, they never repeated.

Anthony Berkeley's non-fiction polemic, *O England!* (1934), published as by A.B. Cox, examined 'the causes of our present discontents, social and political: a book which affects every citizen personally', and referred to 'one great nation reverting to hooliganism and medieval Jew-baiting', but his book received much less attention than G.D.H. Cole's contributions to the Left Book Club, an imprint of Victor Gollancz. Berkeley's attitude towards politicians was, in essence, to say 'a plague on all your houses', but he was by instinct a conservative, and so were Agatha Christie and Dorothy L. Sayers. Even those authors whose work made clear their political sympathies usually concentrated on writing an entertaining mystery. Any consideration of crime novels that, whenever written, emphasise political didacticism tends to suggest that they were wise to do so.

The increasingly frightening international situation in the Thirties exerted a greater influence on traditional detective fiction than has been supposed. Crime writers have long been preoccupied with questions about the nature of justice, and an alarming number of Great Detectives, including Sherlock Holmes, Hercule Poirot and even Sir Clinton Driffield—a Chief Constable!—showed themselves willing, at one time or another in their long careers, to commit murder themselves if it was the only way to achieve true justice. In the Thirties, the circumstances in which murder could be morally justified were explored regularly by leading lights of the Detection Club, including not only long-forgotten figures such as Milward Kennedy and Helen Simpson, but also Christie, Berkeley, and John Dickson Carr. It was no accident that this upsurge of interest in 'altruistic crime' coincided with the rise and rise of Mussolini and Hitler.

Vantage Striker
by Helen Simpson (1931)

When this unusual novel was published in the United States, its title—a term taken from tennis—was changed to *The Prime Minister is Dead*. Although one of Helen Simpson's less-renowned books, it earned the admiration of the stringent American critics Jacques Barzun and Wendell Hertig Taylor, who called it: 'Not strictly detection, but a remarkable and witty story of politics, murder, English life and character. To say more would disclose the original theme—but watch that tennis game, and say whether suspense as now understood comes within miles of the quality generated there.'

The first chapter is set in Whitechapel, where Dermot Boyne and Lady Sarah Benedict watch a boxing match before Dermot himself becomes involved in a fracas. As Dermot, who works for the International Office, subsequently confides to his friend, a doctor called James Stringfellow, he suffered a head injury in the war which makes him susceptible to outbursts of violent rage. A keen sportsman, he confines himself to lawn tennis: 'there isn't that physical contact to set me off'.

Dermot is sent to deliver an urgent sealed despatch to the newly installed Prime Minister. Albert Edward Aspinall is a nonentity who has been elected in preference to the International Secretary, Julian Brazier, a brilliant but odious maverick. Brazier has made no secret of his hostility towards the new leader, shocking the House of Commons with a speech in which he proclaimed, 'No great nation wants Peace with Honour; it wants Aggrandisement with Safety.'

After Aspinall is found dead, apparently as a result of a blow to the head, Dermot's struggles with anger management make him a convenient scapegoat, even though the evidence is thin. Simpson's priority is to examine the complexities of human behaviour rather than to fashion a complex whodunit, and it is typical of this unorthodox story that, in the closing paragraphs, Stringfellow says: 'If you want to find the villains of the piece, look in the Home Office and at Scotland Yard.'

Helen de Guerry Simpson was born in Sydney but relocated to Europe, and studied briefly at Oxford before concentrating on a literary career, publishing verse, short stories, plays and a novel with criminous elements, *Acquittal* (1925). She married a prominent surgeon, Desmond Browne, who no doubt assisted with the medical elements of the plot of *Vantage Striker*. In the field of detective fiction she collaborated with Winifred Ashton, who was better known as the playwright and novelist Clemence Dane. Their first book, *Enter Sir John* (1928), introduced the actor-sleuth Sir John Saumarez, and was highly praised; in the US, Dashiell Hammett noted that the crime was 'interestingly devised'. The story was filmed by Alfred Hitchcock as *Murder!*. The authors credited their publisher, C.S. Evans, for the plot, but gratitude did not deter them from producing a follow-up novel, *Printer's Devil* (1930), in which a publisher is murdered. Sir John was a bit-part player in that book, but returned to centre stage in *Re-enter Sir John* (1932).

Both Simpson and Dane became founder members of the Detection Club, but their interests ranged far beyond the crime genre. Simpson earned fame with historical novels such as *Saraband for Dead Lovers* (1935) and *Under Capricorn* (1937), which were filmed by Basil Dearden and Alfred Hitchcock respectively. She maintained a strong interest in detective fiction, working with her friend Dorothy L. Sayers on a supposed history of Lord Peter Wimsey's family. Her enthusiasm for politics was reflected by her adoption as Liberal Party candidate for the Isle of Wight, but campaigning was interrupted by the outbreak of war, and shortly afterwards she succumbed to cancer.

Silence of a Purple Shirt
by R.C. Woodthorpe (1934)

Publication of this novel, known as *Death Wears a Purple Shirt* in the US, coincided almost precisely with a large rally at Olympia held by Oswald Mosley's British Union of Fascists, which resulted in a mass brawl between his black-shirted supporters and their left-wing opponents. R.C. Woodthorpe showed that witty detective fiction could highlight the absurd yet menacing nature of fascism more persuasively than chanting slogans or meeting violence with violence.

Woodthorpe satirised Mosley and his followers in the form of the odious Duke Benedict and his purple-shirted 'Make Britain Free' movement. Henry Truscott, one of Benedict's sidekicks, is bludgeoned to death during the course of a secret mission which takes him to the Dorset coast. The police arrest another fascist, Alan Ford, and Ford's estranged wife seeks help from her uncle, the novelist Nicholas Slade.

Politics are integral to the storyline and, in an acerbic tirade, Nicholas Slade tells Ford, '… in spite of the best efforts of you and your fellow harlequins, this is not yet Russia or Germany or Fascist Italy. Let us have no more of this nonsense.' Slade is 'not overmuch in love with the established order of things. Indeed, he had satirized it in many of his books.' But he prefers the status quo to the dismal prospect of a regimented life under the Purple Shirts.

Slade also dismisses a suggestion that Britain is 'a law-abiding country', saying 'I cannot remember a time, except, perhaps, during the war, when laws were not deliberately flouted in this country.' He refers to the Nonconformists, with their passive resistance, the Suffragettes and 'the army officers who mutinied in preference to coercing Ulster', as well as giving examples (dear to Berkeley's heart) of motorists who defy the speed limit and those who take part in illegal lotteries. This unconventional approach to the law and justice is reflected at the end of the book, when someone who had committed murder is not only allowed to remain unpunished, but to bask in public admiration.

Ralph Carter Woodthorpe exploited his experience as a schoolmaster in his first detective story, *The Public School Murder* (1932), having abandoned teaching for journalism in the Twenties. He spent three years on the staff of the *Daily Herald*, and wrote a daily humorous column, experience which informed his second detective novel, *A Dagger in Fleet Street* (1934). More interested in social comedy with a political edge than in plotting and detection, his personal favourite among his novels was the non-criminous *London is a Fine Town* (1932).

Nicholas Slade, in some respects a fictionalised version of his creator, started his literary career with a popular novel whose success came to haunt him, as his 'name was known to everybody, though his works, with one exception, were read by nobody'. Slade enjoys playing the amateur sleuth, while Woodthorpe was keen on solving crossword puzzles. The dust-jacket blurb of the American edition of the book forecast that Slade 'will inevitably come to occupy a niche in the gallery of immortal detectives of fiction'. Even by the standards of publishing hyperbole, this forecast proved wildly inaccurate. Slade appeared only once more, in *The Necessary Corpse* (1939), an indifferent thriller featuring American gangsters; as usual in Golden Age fiction, their presence was a clue to the inferiority of the story. Despite being elected to the Detection Club in 1935, Woodthorpe soon abandoned the genre to 'vegetate in Sussex', where he returned to teaching, and relaxed by playing in chess tournaments.

The Nursing Home Murder
by Ngaio Marsh and Henry Jellett (1935)

The experience of undergoing major surgery caused Ngaio Marsh to reflect on a patient's vulnerability. This reality lay at the heart of 'The Case of Lady Sannox', a horrific story written by Arthur Conan Doyle more than forty years earlier. Marsh adapted the scenario to the form of the classic whodunit, with the Home Secretary on the operating table, surrounded by people with cause to hate him. Sir Derek O'Callaghan duly succumbs to a lethal dose of hyoscine. But who administered it?

The novel opens in 10 Downing Street, with a Cabinet meeting at which O'Callaghan sponsors a Bill designed to impose drastic curbs on anarchists determined to bring down the government. Like Sir Philip Ramon in *The Four Just Men* (page 13), he is a target for political assassination, and when he collapses in the House of Commons, suffering from peritonitis, his enemies are presented with their opportunity. Nurse Banks, an unsympathetically portrayed 'Bolshie', launches a diatribe against the dead man: 'He's directly responsible for every death from under-nourishment that has occurred during the last ten months. He's the enemy of the proletariat.'

Chief Inspector Roderick Alleyn investigates, and he and his associates attend a late-night meeting at Lenin Hall, Blackfriars, improbably masquerading as communist sympathisers. Tall, handsome and impeccably polite, Alleyn does not escape

Nurse Banks' wrath: 'I know your type—the gentleman police-man—the latest development of the capitalist system. You've got where you are by influence…you'll go, and all others like you, when the Dawn breaks.'

Marsh undertook her one and only collaborative novel in partnership with a doctor. While undergoing surgery in her native New Zealand, she had been attended by Henry Jellett, an Irish gynaecologist who became a friend. She started work on the book during her convalescence, with Jellett supplying the necessary technical expertise. The pair adapted the story into a stage play, *Exit Sir Derek*, for the final act of which the doctor produced 'a startlingly realistic false abdomen with an incision and retractors'. Marsh later related that the luckless actor play-ing the patient was actually clamped by mistake, and lay in agony throughout the scene. She, Jellett and other friends also collaborated on a musical, *There She Goes*, but Jellett made no other contribution to the crime genre.

The Nursing Home Murder is a crisp, uncluttered mystery with a closed circle of suspects, but despite writing with a light touch, Marsh made it clear that her story took place in troubled times. Nurse Banks and a chemist called Sage see political upheaval as the only solution to society's ills, while another character is a passionate advocate of eugenics. The book helped to establish Marsh alongside Christie, Sayers and Margery Allingham as one of the new 'Queens of Crime' and, according to her biographer Margaret Lewis, it 'outstripped all her other titles in sales'. The concept of death on the operating table was later brilliantly exploited by Christianna Brand in *Green for Danger* (page 206).

Ngaio Marsh was born in Christchurch, New Zealand, and her lifelong devotion to the theatre is reflected in many of her detective novels; the truth about O'Callaghan's death strikes Alleyn once he appreciates the parallel between an operating theatre and a theatre for performance in front of an audience. Alleyn, known to the Press as 'the Handsome Sleuth', is the author of *Principles and Practice of Criminal Investigation*, and when he meets New Zealand police officers after becoming involved in a case of murder in a theatrical company in *Vintage Murder* (1937), the local cops assure him that 'We've all been trained on your book.' During *Artists in Crime* (1938), he meets Agatha Troy, a painter, whom he subsequently marries. Despite Nurse Banks' dire prediction, Alleyn survived to enjoy a career spanning almost half a century. After Marsh's death, *The Inspector Alleyn Mysteries* became a popular BBC TV series in the Nineties.

Chapter Thirteen
Scientific Enquiries

Science and technology play a crucial role in the detection of crime, as they do in mystery fiction. As the twenty-first century dawned, the leading forensic entomologist Zakaria Erzinçlioglu argued in *Maggots, Murder and Men* (2002) that Arthur Conan Doyle 'was a pioneer forensic scientist...His Sherlock Holmes stories, which emphasised the central importance of physical evidence in criminal investigations, were actually used as instruction manuals by the Chinese and Egyptian police forces for many years, and the French *Sûreté* named their great forensic laboratory at Lyon after him. He transformed the very way criminal investigators thought about their work.'

Doyle was a doctor, and he modelled Holmes' deductive methods on the work of Dr Joseph Bell, whose lectures emphasised the importance of close observation in making a diagnosis. L.T. Meade, previously known for her stories set in girls' schools, began to compete with Conan Doyle by writing 'medical mysteries' for the *Strand* magazine, and many of her best stories benefited from the technical know-how of that perennial collaborator, Robert Eustace. Eustace was another doctor, as were Richard Austin Freeman and John James Pitcairn, who co-authored two books under the name Clifford Ashdown at the start of the twentieth century. When he began to write on his own, Freeman created Dr John Thorndyke, often described as the greatest of scientific detectives.

The authenticity of the science in Freeman's work, a major part of the appeal of Thorndyke's cases, impressed Dorothy L. Sayers but was less influential on Agatha Christie; her focus was not on forensic detail, despite the inventive use she made of the knowledge of poisons acquired while working as a nurse in a dispensary during the First World War. C.E. Bechhofer Roberts sought technical guidance from an expert when creating the scientific genius A.B.C. Hawkes, but the A.B.C. stories emphasise entertainment rather than realism.

The British public developed an insatiable thirst for information about forensic science after the forensic pathologist Bernard Spilsbury came to public attention through giving evidence for the prosecution in the Crippen trial of 1910, a thirst that has not been quenched to this day. Sayers' fascination with forensic science is illustrated by the presence of Sir James Lubbock, a Home Office analyst, in both the Wimsey canon and in *The Documents in the Case*. In one of Sayers' novels, the presence of Thorndyke stories in the library of a suspect is a clue to guilt. The way in which arsenic poisoning works is central to *Strong Poison* (1930), while forensic dentistry plays a part in 'In the Teeth of the Evidence'.

J.J. Connington, who earned distinction as a chemistry professor long before he tried his hand at detective fiction, admired the Meade-Eustace stories as well as Freeman's, and his impressively varied expertise is demonstrated time and again in his work, for instance with a pre-Photoshop scheme to fake photographs in *The Sweepstake Murders* (1931) and love letters in a cipher created by a Braille-writing machine in *A Minor Operation* (1937). As Connington said in his memoirs, 'In scientific research, the Inquirer plays the part of the detective in real life.' Both a scientist and a detective novelist, he said, need to have a logical mind.

His later books continued to reflect changes in technology, and in *The Counsellor* (1939), he introduced a new investigator.

Mark Brand is a popular radio personality, broadcasting via Radio Ardennes, and operating from a suite of offices in Oxford Street. As 'the Counsellor', he answers listeners' problems ('social, financial, ethical medical, legal and sporting') with the help of a multi-talented support staff, including a struck-off solicitor, an expert in racing tips, and even an analytical chemist. In his first recorded case, he investigates the disappearance of a young woman, and uncovers a convoluted criminal conspiracy. As usual with Connington, technical expertise plays a crucial part in the solving of the mystery. At one point, Brand instructs his aides to 'arrange for the loan of a small epidiascope'; at another he explains how to commit murder by carbon monoxide poisoning. Connington was making a valiant attempt to keep up with the times, but Brand made only one more appearance, in the enjoyably complicated 'blazing car mystery' *The Four Defences* (1940), before Sir Clinton Driffield returned.

Freeman Wills Crofts and John Rhode regularly put their experience as engineers to effective use in devising ingenious means of murder, although their failure to pay comparable attention to creating in-depth characters was one of the factors which prompted Julian Symons to brand their writing as 'humdrum', a term which, like all labels, is helpful only up to a point. Developments in science and technology between the wars were chronicled with enthusiasm by crime writers on the look-out for new ideas, whether for murder motives, such as keeping the secret of a revolutionary invention or for means of committing murder. As the world shrank, Crofts and Rhode devised ingenious means of committing murder on trains and boats and planes in books such as *Death in the Tunnel* (published in 1936 by Rhode under his alias Miles Burton, and featuring a murder in a railway carriage staged to look like suicide); *Mystery in the Channel* (1931), an example of Inspector French's ability to deconstruct cunningly devised alibis; and *12.30 from Croydon* (1934), in which the murderer is not even present on the flight taken by his luckless victim.

Francis Everton was another engineer who became a crime writer. Although, perhaps because of the demands of his family business, he produced only a handful of novels, they display a touch of originality and flair that extends beyond the mechanics of committing murder. The same was true of Christopher St John Sprigg; he possessed a high level of technical know-how in the field of aeronautics, put to splendid use in *Death of an Airman* (page 190).

Science and technology still play a crucial role in crime fiction in the age of *CSI*, so much so that some writers have opted to concentrate on producing historical mysteries in which no complications arise as a result of DNA profiling, computer technology and so on. Forensics continue to fascinate writers, even if the reading public no longer thirsts as it once did for weird and wonderful methods of murder devised by imaginative doctors, scientists and engineers.

The Documents in the Case
by Dorothy L. Sayers and Robert Eustace
(1930)

The only Sayers novel not to feature Lord Peter Wimsey was also her sole collaborative mystery. The scientific concept at the heart of the 'howdunit' puzzle was contributed by Robert Eustace, whose technical know-how and enthusiasm for the genre led him to enjoy a lengthy career as a co-author of detective stories. But the writing was undertaken by Sayers, and her method of structuring the narrative betrays the influence of *The Moonstone* (1868) by Wilkie Collins, whose biography she was working on at the time, but never completed.

The story is introduced by a cryptic note from Paul Harrison, who asks Sir Gilbert Pugh to read an enclosed dossier of documents with an open mind in an effort to understand 'exactly what took place in my late father's household'. A sequence of letters supplemented by an occasional note provides insight into the passions swirling around suburbia. Margaret Harrison, attractive and impulsive, is finding married life with her staid older husband increasingly tedious. The Harrisons take in two lodgers, a poet called Jack Munting and an artist, Harwood Lathom, and before long, Margaret finds herself increasingly drawn to Lathom.

Sayers' starting point for the central situation in the novel was to fictionalise the key relationships in the Thompson–Bywaters case (Bywaters is even name-checked by Lathom when he pontificates about respectability in the suburbs), but the criminal *modus operandi* in the story, and its ultimate consequence, differ from those in the real-life case. A parallel is also drawn between the rashness of the killer in the story and that of Patrick Mahon, hanged in 1924 for the murder of his pregnant lover. Yet the 'true crime' elements form only one thread of an elaborately woven story.

Sayers utilises multiple viewpoints, notably those of Munting and the Harrisons' troubled 'lady-help', Agatha Milsom, to tackle subjects such as middle-class values, personal responsibility and the nature of relationships between men and women. Above all, she takes the bold step of integrating her detective plot with the question put by Munting towards the end of the book: 'What is Life?' He is taking part in an erudite dinner-party discussion with a parson, a curate, a physicist, a biologist and a chemist, during the course of which the truth about an ingenious plan to commit an apparently perfect crime emerges. As the curate says to Munting, the scientific means of detecting the truth is 'better than Crippen and the wireless'. But perhaps he reflects Sayers' anxiety about the complicated nature of the scheme when he adds: 'Only they'll have a bit of a job explaining it.'

Robert Eustace was the pen-name adopted by Eustace Robert Barton, a doctor who began to co-author crime fiction in the late nineteenth century, often in collaboration with L.T. Meade, although occasionally on his own. With Edgar Jepson, Eustace wrote a much-anthologised impossible-crime short story, 'The Tea Leaf', and he became a founder member of the Detection Club. The danger of tackling complex and unusual ideas in the guise of crime fiction was illustrated when *The Documents in the Case* was criticised for scientific inaccuracy, although further research satisfied Eustace that the complaint was itself mistaken. But the damage was done, and although he and Sayers had contemplated continuing to collaborate, she decided to go her own way, and Wimsey made a swift return to action.

The *Young Vanish*
by Francis Everton (1932)

This intriguing, eccentric story begins with a sequence of apparently unconnected deaths. The question for Inspector Allport is whether it was 'chance, and nothing but chance, that half a dozen prominent Trade Union officials, all of whom held moderate views, should have succumbed to one form of accident or another in the short space of a few weeks?'. At a time when 'a second general strike was brewing', is a right-wing serial killer responsible—or are sinister Russians to blame?

Everton's detective is one of the ugliest in fiction: 'from whatever angle you looked at Allport, he seemed to have met with an accident…Seen full face, his eyes bulged and the dimple in the middle of his chin created a grotesque impression. And the rear view was not much better…but nature had given him, in compensation, a first class brain.' His powers of deduction are further challenged following the discovery of the body of a man with his head inside a gas stove in a workman's house in Bermondsey. An inquest returns a verdict of suicide, but Allport is not satisfied with easy explanations.

The plot complications come thick and fast following the discovery of a charred corpse in a motor car; many of them are technical, and the clues include diagrams of marks made on three different matchboxes. Allport receives expert help from an engineering company called Sheepbridge Stokes Centrifugal

Castings. The company's technical director advises him about the 'metallurgical fingerprints' to be found on the cylinder blocks of internal combustion engines, and suggests 'that this is the first occasion on which metallurgical and spectrographic analysis has been called to the aid of the Law'.

The book takes its strange title from an inn in Glapwell, Derbyshire, which features in the story, and the author's insistence that it is not to be confused with a real-life inn with the same name in Glapwell seems like a case of protesting too much. Everton also notes that 'there really is a company registered under the name of The Sheepbridge Stokes Centrifugal Castings Co. Ltd.'. Given that the business was run by Everton's family, his cunning plan was presumably to use his detective novel as a form of commercial advertisement.

Francis Everton's real name was Francis William Stokes, and he studied engineering at Nottingham University, later becoming well known as an engineer with a creative turn of mind, who patented several inventions, and eventually became managing director of Sheepbridge Stokes. Allport was introduced in Everton's first novel, *The Dalehouse Murder* (1927), of which Arnold Bennett rhapsodised that it was 'at least as good as any detective story I have read since Conan Doyle and Gaston Leroux'. Everton exploited his technical know-how in books such as *The Hammer of Doom* (1928), set in a foundry, and *Insoluble* (1934), which involved industrial chemistry. Dorothy L. Sayers said the latter novel was 'intriguing and…full of life and movement', but after *Murder May Pass Unpunished* (1936), Everton abandoned the genre, presumably to devote his energies full-time to the mysterious world of centrifugal castings.

Death of an Airman
by Christopher St John Sprigg (1934)

Edwin Marriott, an Australian bishop on leave in England, wants to learn to fly from one end of his diocese to the other. He joins Baston Aero Club, managed by the vivacious Sally Sackbut, and is on hand when the aeroplane of flight instructor Major George Furnace plummets to the ground. At the inquest, a coroner's jury returns a verdict of death by misadventure, before the discovery of a letter sent by the dead man to society beauty Lady Laura Vanguard suggests that Furnace committed suicide. When an autopsy reveals a bullet in the dead man's brain, however, the Bishop becomes fascinated by the question of who shot him, why—and how. The Bishop and Inspector Bray of Scotland Yard, working in tandem, uncover a criminal racket, but in his quest for the truth, the Bishop eventually finds his own life in jeopardy.

The story 'bubbles over with zest and vitality', as Dorothy L. Sayers said in *The Sunday Times*; she applauded 'a most ingenious and exciting plot, full of good puzzles and discoveries and worked out among a varied cast of entertaining characters'. The atmosphere of life at the Aero Club is credibly evoked, although Sayers noted that the appeal of the mystery does not derive from fair-play detection. She did not, however, regard that as a major flaw: 'The solution depends upon certain flying technicalities which are outside the province of an ignorant critic like myself. Mr. Sprigg certainly gives the impression of being thoroughly at home in the air, and his buoyant and vigorous style carries us blithely through all the complications of the intrigue.'

As she surmised, Christopher St John Sprigg understood the world he describes in the novel. He and his brother inherited legacies from an aunt which enabled them to set up an aeronautics publishing business, Airways Publications Limited, which produced a journal called *Airways* as well as flying magazines. His early books included *The Airship: Its Design, History, Operation and Future* (1930) and *Fly with Me: An Elementary Textbook on the Art of Piloting* (1932), while *British Airways* (1934) illustrated his fascination with the potential for global connectivity brought about by international air travel.

The first of his seven detective novels, *Crime in Kensington* (*Pass the Body* in the US) appeared in 1933. After soaking himself in the work of Marx, Engels, Lenin and company with his habitual energy, Sprigg joined the British Communist Party. In 1935, he adopted his mother's surname when publishing as Christopher Caudwell *This My Hand*, a crime novel markedly different from his previous mysteries, all of which were rooted in the Golden Age tradition. As Caudwell, he concentrated on serious literary work, writing a Marxist critique of poetry, *Illusion and Reality* (1937); *Studies in a Dying Culture* (1938); and poems that have been much acclaimed. In December 1936, he enlisted with the International Brigade of the Spanish Loyalist Army, and trained as a machine gunner, but was killed in battle at Jarama the following February, having packed an extraordinary range of achievements into a restless life that lasted a little less than thirty years. The last of his lively mysteries, *The Six Queer Things*, appeared posthumously in 1937.

A.B.C. Solves Five
by C.E. Bechhofer Roberts (1937)

A.B.C. Hawkes, a sleuthing scientist, tackles five puzzles in this slender—and extremely rare—collection of stories. A.B.C. shares a cottage in Sussex with a Welsh 'Watson' called Johnstone, but the pair spend much of their time travelling the world in a floating laboratory of A.B.C.'s own design, the 600-ton yacht *Daedalus*. A.B.C.'s fame as 'the most distinguished living British scientist' is such that, even when they land at Batum in Bolshevist Russia, the man in charge of landing permits declares, in halting French, his pride at meeting the great man in the flesh.

The stories have an engagingly cosmopolitan flavour. A.B.C., multi-lingual and multi-talented, investigates the murder of a Hindu scientist in Berlin, rescues a bullfighter from death in Seville and foils a threat to world peace in Georgia. Returning to England, he saves the life of Muriel Panton, the glamorous tragic actress with whom he had previously had an extremely improbable romance.

A.B.C. seems to have made his first appearance in 'The Island under the Sea', which was published in the *Strand* magazine in 1925. Featuring an exotic female preserved in a 'huge slab of solid glass and crystal' and originating from Atlantis, this fantasy adventure was prefaced by a rather defensive author's note saying that the story was 'written in collaboration with a well-known Professor of Science so the reader may rest assured that nothing is related that could not actually have happened'. There is no mention of the un-named Professor in *A.B.C. Solves Five*. Bechhofer Roberts put A.B.C.'s scientific genius to work in the service of detecting crime, producing a series of short mystery stories, collected in two volumes, of which this is one, and *A.B.C.Investigates*, also published in 1937, is the other. A solitary novel, *A.B.C.'s Test Case* (1936), sees the great man investigating the death of a motor-racing baronet. The suspects include a psychologist who claims to be able to prove survival after death by means of word tests applied through a medium.

Born Carl Erich Bechhöfer, in London but of German heritage, Carl Erich Bechhofer Roberts started writing while still a student. Occasionally, he anglicised his name to Charles Brookfarmer; later, he removed the umlaut from his surname, and added the name Roberts. After enlisting as a trooper with the 9th Lancers in 1914, he became a military interpreter, and an expert on Russia.

He served as secretary to Lord Birkenhead, who practised at the Bar as F.E. Smith, and secured the acquittal of Crippen's mistress Ethel Le Neve at her trial for murder. In addition to writing Birkenhead's biography, he adopted the pen-name 'Ephesian', a play on F.E.'s initials. A meeting with the influential esotericist George Gurdjieff kindled an interest in spiritual teaching, but scepticism prevailed, and his scorn for fraudulent mediums is reflected in *Tidings of Joy* (1936). This was one of a handful of crime novels and plays co-authored with a more prolific writer of detective stories, George Goodchild, to whom *A.B.C. Solves Five* (in which he is given a teasing name-check by A.B.C. himself) is dedicated.

The Jury Disagree (1934) fictionalised the Wallace case, while *The Dear Old Gentleman* (1935) updated the Sandyford murder case of 1862. Both novels were collaborations with Goodchild, and reflect Bechhofer Roberts' enthusiasm for criminology. He was called to the Bar in 1941, and edited books of trials, including that of Helen Duncan, the last person in Britain to be imprisoned under the Witchcraft Act of 1735. He also collaborated with C.S. Forester on a play about Edith Cavell, and wrote biographies of Paul Verlaine and Conservative politicians (including the improbably titled *Stanley Baldwin: Man or Miracle?*). His light-hearted thriller about a gangster, *Don Chicago*, subtitled *Crime Don't Pay*, was filmed in 1945. Having survived a car crash caused by a drunk driver at Eze in France, he fictionalised the accident in *Tidings of Joy* (1936), co-authored with Goodchild, but his luck ran out in 1949 when he was killed after his car crashed into a refuge near Euston station.

Chapter Fourteen
The Long Arm of the Law

The police detective often cut a hapless figure in classic crime stories. Wilkie Collins and Charles Dickens created capable detectives in Sergeant Cuff and Inspector Bucket, both of whom had real-life models, but the Sherlock Holmes stories did nothing for the reputation of Scotland Yard. Arthur Conan Doyle hit on the idea of highlighting Sherlock Holmes' genius by contrasting his brilliance with the less than stellar work of Inspector Lestrade. Decades later, Agatha Christie adopted Doyle's method in her presentation of the relationship between Hercule Poirot and Inspector Japp—and, with a little variation, that between Jane Marple and Inspector Slack.

The first major British crime writer to create a gifted police detective who became a major series character was A.E.W. Mason, whose Inspector Hanaud had his own equivalent of Dr Watson in Julius Ricardo. Shortly afterwards, Frank Froest, who had acquired a larger-than-life reputation while climbing through the ranks of the Metropolitan Police, struck a blow for the professionals by publishing *The Grell Mystery* (page 199), which made clear his low opinion of 'story-book detectives'.

The First World War changed detective fiction as it changed much else. Freeman Wills Crofts decided that the time was ripe for a complicated and teasing mystery to be solved by a hard-working police officer's persistence and scrupulous attention to detail. Inspector Burnley's tireless work in *The Cask* (page 45) had none of the showmanship displayed by Hercule Poirot in *The Mysterious Affair at Styles* (page 53), but Crofts' approach was realistic and fresh. By the time he introduced Inspector French in his fifth novel, he was already regarded as one of the leading exponents of detective fiction.

His lead was followed by G.D.H. and Margaret Cole, who laboured under the misapprehension that, in presenting a professional detective, colourlessness was a virtue. Even when Superintendent Wilson resigned, and became the most highly regarded private detective in the country, he was no Sam Spade, and the Coles soon restored him to Scotland Yard. Nor was he the only the professional policeman who tried his luck in the private sector; Cecil M. Wills' Detective Inspector Geoffrey Boscobell, a rather more interesting character, left his job after the disappearance of his wife and son, and pursued his later investigations unconstrained by the bureaucracy and regulation of the Yard.

• • ● • •

Henry Wade, for whom Crofts was an early influence, had a close understanding of police work, and its internal politics, conveying the work of his detectives with realism but without sacrificing entertainment. As his confidence grew, Wade's accounts of the conduct of criminal investigations, skilfully integrated with whodunit plots, became increasingly compelling. He created a hard-working police constable, John Bragg, who appeared in short stories and a single novel, but his main series character was Inspector John Poole.

Like Ngaio Marsh's Roderick Alleyn, E.R. Punshon's Bobby Owen, Michael Innes' John Appleby and Margaret Erskine's Septimus Finch, all of whom came later, Poole was a 'gentleman cop'. In roughly the same mould was Francis Beeding's Inspector George Martin, described in *No Fury* (1937) as a member of 'the new school [of police detectives] which placed a premium on imagination and psychology'. Poole's ambition and quiet determination are plausible. So is Wade's depiction of rivalries and tensions within the police—typically between those, like Froest, who had risen from humble beginnings, and those whose education seemed, to some colleagues, to give them an unfair advantage.

Police numbers had been depleted by the First World War, and the Twenties saw increasing concern about their professionalism, as well as fears about corruption. Towards the end of that decade, the scandal surrounding Sergeant George Goddard, convicted for taking bribes from nightclub owners, made clear the need for change. At first, the Police Federation resisted proposals to introduce a new training regime, but the appointment of Lord Trenchard as Metropolitan Police Commissioner led to the establishment of a police college at Hendon. The Labour MP Aneurin Bevan denounced this as 'an entirely fascist development', and the *Police Review* claimed that Trenchard's reforms amounted to '"class" legislation with a vengeance'.

These tensions were not ignored in classic crime fiction. In *Comes a Stranger* (1938), E.R. Punshon employed his series policeman Bobby Owen, educated at Oxford, but not trained at Hendon, as a mouthpiece for his own views: 'Lord Trenchard thought the police only existed to protect society, and he only saw society as a society of the rich, so he thought he had to bring in chaps from the rich classes to keep the police loyal… The Trenchard result is that for the first time the police are split with class feeling…and none of them know quite where they are.' Agatha Christie also dropped a hint in *The ABC Murders* (page 231) that she was unconvinced by the Trenchard reforms, but a more positive view was presented by John Rhode in *Hendon's First Case* (page 204).

As time passed, links between police work and crime writing became more commonplace. Sir Basil Home Thomson, whose eventful life included spells as a prison governor, and as an Assistant Commissioner at Scotland Yard, wrote eight novels about a detective called Richardson who rose from police constable to Chief Constable almost in the blink of an eye. Thomson emphasises that effective police investigations depend upon team work, and are pioneering examples of the 'police procedural' story. The highly capable Richardson is no maverick loner, and in the last two books he takes a back seat as more junior officers do the legwork. Thomson was never elected to membership of the Detection Club, though that honour was granted in 1936 to Sir Norman Kendal (1880–1966), who was appointed Assistant Commissioner in 1928, seven years after Thomson's departure, but never wrote fiction.

The Detection Club also invited the recently retired Superintendent Cornish to take part in one of its collaborative books, *Six Against the Yard* (1936). The idea was that six writers, among them Dorothy L. Sayers, Margery Allingham and Ronald Knox, produced stories about a 'perfect crime', and then Cornish was tasked with explaining how the police would, in reality, bring the perpetrator to justice.

Detective novelists became increasingly interested in presenting police work realistically. Henry Wade led the way, and in the closing pages of *Lonely Magdalen* (1940), he combined a clever plot twist with a glance—all the more startling because it was unexpected—at police brutality.

After the Second World War, 'police procedural' novels such as those by Maurice Procter became increasingly popular. Unlike Froest and Sir Basil Thomson, Procter was a *serving* police officer, based in Yorkshire. His description of cops, criminals and everyday police work had a gritty authenticity that not even Wade could match. Although Procter soon resigned from the force in order to write full-time, his experience of front-line policing ensured that his later books remained credible as well as influential. Realism came to be regarded as a key requirement of an effective police procedural novel, although some novels featuring police officers, notably Colin Dexter's bestselling Inspector Morse series, continued to make a virtue of ingenious plotting rather than strict authenticity of investigative methods.

The Grell Mystery
by Frank Froest (1913)

Robert Grell is a daring explorer who has also enjoyed success in the worlds of finance and politics in the United States prior to settling in England as a gentleman of leisure. He spends his 'last night of bachelordom' prior to marrying the lovely Lady Eileen Meredith at his club. When he tells his friend Sir Ralph Fairfield that he needs to keep an appointment, his evasiveness about what he is doing puzzles Fairfield. Two hours later, 'a wild-eyed breathless servant' is reporting to the police that Grell has been found murdered in his study, and it emerges that another servant, a Russian called Ivan, has vanished. All is not, however, as it seems. The police quickly establish that the dead man is not Grell, but someone who bears him a close resemblance.

At the start of the second chapter, the author observes: 'When a man has passed thirty years in the service of the Criminal Investigation Department at New Scotland Yard his nerves are pretty well shock-proof. Few emergencies can shake him.' As a former policeman himself, Frank Froest was speaking from the heart. Similarly, when Heldon Foyle, Chief of the C.I.D., reflects that sometimes a police officer needs to 'put a blind eye to the telescope' and act in a 'technically illegal' way so as to do justice, there can be little doubt that this reflects Froest's own attitude. In real life, he was as unorthodox as many a fictional sleuth.

Frank Froest was born in Bristol, and joined the Metropolitan Police as a constable in 1879. He rose steadily through the ranks, becoming Superintendent in the C.I.D. in 1906, a post he held until his retirement six years later. A eulogistic obituary in *The Times* recorded that: 'He was quite unlike the popular idea of a detective, having all the appearance of a prosperous and ingenuous country gentleman, but he was a man of shrewdness and resource, and was highly esteemed for his professional ability, not only at home but also by his many friends among foreign detectives…He once had a desperate struggle with a captive while travelling in an express train. He managed to handcuff him, but was then nearly killed by a footwarmer which his prisoner contrived to hurl at him. He was particularly successful with "confidence" tricksters and with gangs of Continental swindlers.'

A capable linguist, Froest handled many cases with a foreign element, and was responsible for bringing the disgraced financier and former Liberal MP Jabez Balfour, who had fled the country, back from Argentina. When extradition proceedings dragged, Froest simply bundled his man into a train and later into a boat sailing for England. Described by one journalist as resembling 'a Prussian field-marshal' in appearance when in uniform, he was famed for his physical appearance, and known as 'the man with iron hands'. He received the King's Police Medal, and on his retirement in 1912, King George V gave a speech in his honour.

After leaving the Yard, Froest put his experience to good use in two novels, a collection of stories and a history of the Metropolitan Police. Generally, he acknowledged a journalist collaborator, George Dilnot, who may also have ghost-written *The Grell Mystery*. This novel and *The Rogues' Syndicate* (1916) were made into silent films, and Froest spent his final years in Somerset as a pillar of the community, becoming an alderman, and also a Justice of the Peace.

The Duke of York's Steps
by Henry Wade (1929)

After being involved in an apparently accidental collision on London's Duke of York Steps, Sir Garth Fratten, chairman of a bank, suffers a burst aneurism and dies. Inez Fratten, as shrewd as she is attractive, is not satisfied about the circumstances of her father's death, and shares her concerns with Sir Leward Marradine, the Assistant Commissioner in charge of the C.I.D. Chief Inspector Barrod regards the matter as a waste of time, and suggests that the newly promoted Inspector John Poole should look into it. Barrod has a low opinion of 'soft' university graduates like Poole, reckoning that 'a failure—or at any rate, a fiasco, would do him no harm'. But Marradine is wise enough to recognise Poole's potential as a detective.

Poole, the privately educated son of a country doctor, studied law at Oxford before becoming fascinated by crime, and earning election to the Criminologists' Club (perhaps a fictionalised version of the then embryonic Detection Club, of which Wade became a founder member). He is well aware that senior police posts 'usually went to soldiers and sailors, and even occasionally to barristers, though in some of the borough forces promotion through the ranks was becoming more common', but sets his heart on one day becoming the head of the C.I.D. himself.

As the investigation into Fratten's death becomes increasingly complex, Wade makes passing mention of the crime writer Robert Eustace, in connection with the stories he wrote with L.T. Meade. Poole is familiar with the detective work of Holmes, Poirot and Hanaud, but regards the approach of Freeman Wills Crofts' Inspector French as much more 'true to life'. Crofts' influence on Wade is reflected in the careful unravelling of an ingenious conspiracy, but even at this early stage in his career, Wade displays more interest than Crofts in bringing his characters to life. As his literary confidence increased, his writing became increasingly ambitious and impressive, but he did not sacrifice authenticity; in *Bury Him Darkly* (1936), in which the point is made that Poole (that is, his creator) had anticipated the Trenchard reforms, the realistic depiction of police work ensures that a Crofts-like quest to destroy an alibi, accompanied in the first edition by a fold-out map of roads and railways crucial to the plot, is never less than absorbing. *Heir Presumptive* (1935), a highly entertaining story in the tradition of *Israel Rank* (page 19) included two fold-out bonus extras: a family tree of the ill-fated Hendels, and a map of Captain David Hendel's deer-forest.

Henry Wade was the pen-name adopted by Henry Lancelot Aubrey-Fletcher when he turned to writing crime fiction. Aubrey-Fletcher was the son of a baronet, and educated at Eton and Oxford. He fought with the Grenadier Guards during the First World War, and when peace returned, he played cricket for Buckinghamshire, served on the county council, and became High Sheriff and Lord Lieutenant of the county. This book, like *The Missing Partners* (1928), demonstrates that Wade understood the practical world of business and finance better than many of his crime-writing contemporaries. An even more significant recurring element in his fiction is the impact of the First World War on individuals as well as on British society.

Wade's public appointments included a spell as a Justice of the Peace, and his stories display a fascination with the methods, and 'office politics', of the police. *Constable, Guard Thyself!*

(1934) is a clever whodunit about a murder of a chief constable inside a police station—floor plans are supplied. Poole solves the case, but Wade presents him subtly, as a human and fallible cop, rather than a superman. In *Bury Him Darkly* (1936) a naive lack of discretion on Poole's part is even responsible for the death of a colleague, and the novel ends on a note of tantalising uncertainty about the fate of one of the culprits. Wade's ambition as a writer is illustrated by books such as *Mist on the Saltings* (1933), a study of jealousy and suspicion with an atmospheric setting on the coast of Norfolk, and *Released for Death* (1938), which focuses on the misadventures of a former prisoner. His self-critical approach and determination to develop as a writer were key to the success of his books. In September 1946, he wrote to a friend that 'the last 6 or 7 chapters [of *Released for Death*] were thoroughly bad and when I was lying up last year with a bad leg I re-wrote them'. Regrettably, the revised ending never saw the light of day.

Poole made regular appearances in Wade's fiction for a quarter of a century, most memorably in *Lonely Magdalen* (1940), a poignant study of an investigation into the strangling of a prostitute on Hampstead Heath. The novel is memorable not only for the sophistication of the story but also for Wade's striking—given the period, and his position in the establishment—acknowledgement that the police were not always wonderful.

Hendon's First Case
by John Rhode (1935)

This ingenious poisoning mystery earned high praise from Dorothy L. Sayers, who judged the plot to be 'exceedingly good'. A chemist called Threlfall receives a menacing letter from his estranged wife, who is demanding a divorce. Before long, someone breaks in to the laboratory where Threlfall conducts research with a colleague called Harwood, there is an explosion in Threlfall's study, and Threlfall dies of ptomaine poisoning after dining in a restaurant with Harwood. Harwood shared the same meal, and is also poisoned, but recovers. The plot continues to thicken, not least with the discovery that Threlfall left with his solicitor a mysterious coded message.

Sayers considered the story in the context of a discussion about how writers of long series of novels might deal with the ageing of their detectives. One possibility is to prevent them from growing older; another is to allow them to age; a third is to 'hurl them over the Reichenbach Falls (at the risk, to be sure, of having to haul them painfully up again later) and let younger rivals step into their shoes'.

Rhode's solution to the dilemma was cunning. He had previously matched his brilliant, irascible Great Detective Dr Lancelot Priestley with an experienced Scotland Yard man, Superintendent Hanslet. In this book, he introduced a youthful new police officer, who works alongside the two older men as they search for the explanation of Threlfall's death.

Cambridge-educated Jimmy Waghorn is one of the first graduates of Hendon Police College, and has been appointed Junior Station Inspector. Hanslet, who had risen through the ranks in the time-honoured manner (rather as Frank Froest did), sees the merit of experimenting with a new regime, but fears that it will have an adverse effect upon morale—traditionally, the Metropolitan Police had not had an equivalent of the 'officer class' in the British Army.

Rhode's highly topical storyline was marred by failings characteristic of an author who wrote too much, too quickly. The discussion about ciphers becomes wearisome, and once Priestley decodes Threlfall's message, the mystery is wrapped up in perfunctory fashion. Yet the book presents an appealing trio of detectives with diverse skills. As Sayers put it, 'three ways of tackling a detective problem are fruitfully contrasted: the way of experience, the way of imagination, and the way of the scientific inquirer'. Jimmy Waghorn became a continuing character in Rhode's books, while Hanslet faded gradually into the background. Priestley also began to play a less active part in the stories—but Rhode refused to consign him to an English equivalent of the Reichenbach Falls.

Green for Danger
by Christianna Brand (1944)

'He looked rather a sweet little man,' Frederica Linley says, shortly after Inspector Cockrill takes charge of the investigation into the death of Joseph Higgins, while on the operating table at a military hospital. His nickname 'Cockie' is unlikely to inspire fear in a suspect. But in a detective story, appearances are invariably deceptive, and we are told that: 'Inspector Cockrill was anything but a sweet little man.' He has been described by Tony Medawar, introducing *The Spotted Cat and other Mysteries from Inspector Cockrill's Casebook* (2002), as 'one of the best loved "official" detectives in the whole of the crime and mystery genre'.

Higgins was a postman, and the first chapter sees him delivering letters in Heron's Park, Kent; seven other characters make an appearance, and we are told at the end of the chapter that one of them would die a year later, 'self-confessed a murderer'. This is a murder mystery with a closed circle of suspects, a form in which Brand specialised. Her ingeniously plotted detective fiction belonged in spirit to the Golden Age, even though she did not publish her first novel until 1941.

The frenetic atmosphere of rural England under attack by German doodlebugs is superbly evoked in a story combining an original murder method with a clever whodunit puzzle. Brand, like most Golden Age writers, had little interest in the minutiae of police procedure, and Cockrill is an unlikely cop, in part because, as Brand admitted: he was 'unique in being several inches below the minimum height for a British policeman…he does also seem to be a bit too old'. She acknowledged that Cockrill 'is not a great one for the physical details of an investigation', but he has the classic attributes of a successful fictional detective: 'acute powers of observation…a considerable understanding of human nature; a total integrity and commitment…Above all, he has patience.'

Crucially, he is an appealing character, a widower whose only child is dead; a man whose gruff manner conceals compassion, not least for the guilty. When he finally arrests the killer, he shows his humanity, saying: 'I'm sorry…This is a terrible thing for me to have to do.' Even at this late stage, with an unexpected motive for murder revealed, Brand still has time for a final ironic twist, and a poignant final paragraph.

Green for Danger was filmed in 1946 with the comic actor Alistair Sim cast as Cockrill. The result was one of the few examples of a highly successful movie version of an intricate whodunit novel, even though Sim plays the policeman for laughs. The book was only the third published by Mary Christianna Brand, but it confirmed her as a major crime writer, and she was elected to the Detection Club in 1946. In the same year she published *Suddenly at his Residence*, an accomplished impossible-crime story, and Cockrill's other cases included *Tour de Force* (1955), a very well-plotted 'holiday mystery'. His final case, *Jape du Chine* (another draft is called *Chinese Puzzle*) was written in 1963 but never published.

After a long break, during which she achieved prominence with her 'Nurse Matilda' stories for children, Brand resumed writing crime fiction in the Seventies, but her moment had passed. She did, however, provide a reminder of her virtuosity by conjuring up a fresh solution to the puzzle in *The Poisoned Chocolates Case* (page 64) when it was republished in the US in 1979, in tribute to her Detection Club colleague Anthony Berkeley, whom she once described as perhaps 'the cleverest of us all'.

Chapter Fifteen
The Justice Game

Fiction devoted to breaking the law inevitably raises innumerable questions about justice. A striking feature of detective stories is that it is not only criminals who are inclined to break the law. In 'The Abbey Grange', Sherlock Holmes confides in Watson that 'Once or twice in my career I feel that I have done more real harm by my discovery of the criminal than ever he had done by his crime…I had rather play tricks with the law of England than with my own conscience.' Every now and then in his illustrious career, Holmes turned a blind eye to criminal conduct, or even showed a willingness to break the law himself. His example was followed regularly by detectives in classic crime fiction.

A memorable example occurs in one of Agatha Christie's most famous whodunits, *Murder on the Orient Express* (1934), a story in which plot and theme both concern the question of how to impose justice when the law is helpless. Hercule Poirot propounds two very different explanations for the murder of a gangster called Ratchett, so as to allow the authorities an opportunity to arrive at an outcome which seems, as Christie assumed her readers would agree, morally right. A comparable theme runs through Christie's outstanding non-series novel, *And Then There Were None* (1939).

The notion of the 'altruistic crime' became a striking and recurrent element in much of the best detective fiction written during the Thirties. Authors were preoccupied by the thorny question of how to do justice, in moral terms, when the established legal process proved inadequate. This was more than an idle academic debating point. At a time of growing international tension, when dictators such as Hitler and Mussolini were expanding their power base in the most ruthless fashion, there were powerful reasons why the instinctively law-abiding wrestled with the question of when one person can justify killing another.

The shortcomings of the legal process are anatomised time and again in classic crime fiction. Sydney Fowler's *The King Against Anne Bickerton* (1930), built around extended accounts of an inquest and a murder trial, is interesting primarily as an extended diatribe against the perceived iniquities of the legal establishment. Fowler's full name was Sydney Fowler Wright, and he worked as an accountant before going bankrupt, a misfortune which may have sharpened his distaste for the law. He became a well-regarded author of science fiction.

The proceedings of inquests were often recounted in detail, and Milward Kennedy's *Death to the Rescue* (page 271) fictionalised a murder case in which the questioning of the prime suspect Philip Yale Drew was so brutal as to amount to 'trial by coroner'. The unreliability of coroners' juries, in an era when the law permitted them to name a person they believed guilty of murder, is wittily illustrated by Christie in *Death in the Clouds* (1935). At the inquest into the murder on an aeroplane of a blackmailer, the jurors' xenophobia tempts them to point the finger of guilt at Hercule Poirot.

Real-life miscarriages of justice inspired books such as F. Tennyson Jesse's *A Pin to See the Peepshow* (page 273), while the race against time to avert the execution of an innocent person accused of murder, a trope of the genre, crops up in books as different as *Clouds of Witness* (page 55) and *Trial and Error* (page 212). The trial scenes in both novels, as in Henry Wade's *The Verdict of You All* (1926) and *Malice Aforethought* (page 259) are described with flair and insight, although none of the authors were trained lawyers.

Courtroom drama is a staple of the genre, and in the original version of *The Mysterious Affair at Styles* (page 53) Poirot revealed the solution to the puzzle from the witness box. Christie borrowed this scenario from Gaston Leroux's *The Mystery of the Yellow Room* (1908), but her publishers regarded it as implausible. She agreed to rewrite the scene, and the result was a drawing-room denouement of the kind for which she became famous. *Sad Cypress* (1940), built around the trial of Elinor Carlilse for the murder of her wealthy aunt, is a soundly plotted Poirot novel, but Christie's most famous courtroom story is 'The Witness for the Prosecution'. The story first appeared in an American magazine in 1925 under the title 'Traitor Hands', was collected in *The Hound of Death* (1933), and has been adapted for the stage radio, television, and film, the most memorable version being Billy Wilder's 1957 film starring Charles Laughton and Marlene Dietrich.

Except for a prologue and an epilogue, the action of Eden Phillpotts' *The Jury* (1927), an overlooked story with a neat finale, takes place in the jury room of an assize court in the west country. Gerald Bullett, a versatile man of letters skilled in the art of characterisation, used the same title eight years later for a better known book; his *The Jury* (1935) concerns the trial of Roderick Strood on a charge of murdering his wife. Bullett adapted the story in his screenplay for the 1956 film *The Last Man to Hang?*.

Lawyers in crime fiction prove as fallible as the law itself. Solicitors embezzle funds in *The Blotting Book* and *Antidote to Venom* (pages 21 and 247), and although Baroness Orczy's Patrick Mulligan strives to achieve a just outcome for his clients, his methods verge on the unscrupulous. The same is true of H.C. Bailey's second-string detective, Joshua Clunk, a shrewd but sanctimonious, hymn-singing solicitor who preaches 'the Larger Hope, when business allowed'. John Dickson Carr's Sir Henry Merrivale is a barrister and brilliant amateur sleuth who defends Jimmy Answell on a charge of murder in an outstanding locked-room novel, *The Judas Window* (1938), published as by Carter Dickson. The difficulty confronting Merrivale is that his client seems to be the only person who could possibly have killed his prospective father-in-law.

Novelists ranging from Wilkie Collins to Lord Gorell trained as barristers, and Collins made repeated use of his knowledge of the law's quirks and failings, as in *The Law and the Lady* (1875). It was rare, however, for authors of classic crime fiction to combine their writing with full-time legal practice. Two exceptions stand out. The barrister Cyril Hare is said to have learned the news that his first novel, *Tenant for Death* (1937) had been accepted for publication while in the midst of conducting a case. His portrayal of the unlucky barrister Francis Pettigrew had the ring of truth, although Pettigrew developed into a more conventional series character as the years passed.

The solicitor Michael Gilbert, also distinguished in his branch of the profession, was in the early stages of his literary career as the twentieth century reached its mid-point. Over the decades, many of his novels and short stories benefited from his close understanding of the law and those who practise it, but for witty insights into legal life, *Smallbone Deceased* (page 218) remains unsurpassed.

Trial and Error
by Anthony Berkeley (1937)

Golden Age detective novelists often approached the concept of the 'altruistic crime' obliquely. With his customary effrontery, Anthony Berkeley tackled it head-on in *Trial and Error*. Typically, he sets the tone in the first line: 'The sanctity of human life has been much exaggerated.' At the age of fifty-one, a mild-mannered bachelor called Lawrence Todhunter learns from his doctor that he is suffering from an aortic aneurism, and must not expect to live for more than a few months. His nature is to make himself useful, and at first he decides that the most valuable service he can render humanity is to carry out a political assassination: 'There was certainly no lack of suitable candidates. Whether it came to rubbing out Hitler or bumping off Mussolini or even putting Stalin on the spot, the progress of humanity would receive an equal jolt forward.' He takes soundings from friends, but receives the bleak advice that a dictator's successor may be even worse: 'Hitlerism wouldn't collapse if Hitler were killed.'

As a result, he decides to eliminate the most obnoxious individual he can find, and settles on Jean Norwood, a deeply unpleasant actress-manager. Unfortunately, Todhunter proves to be too successful as a murderer. After Jean Norwood is found dead, someone else is charged with the crime, and when Todhunter insists that he is guilty, nobody believes him. Berkeley presents the legal tangle with dry wit, showing a mastery of the plot twist matched only by Agatha Christie. His occasional sleuth Ambrose Chitterwick plays an important part in the story, not least in the closing pages, which culminate in a piece of Berkeley's characteristic sleight-of-hand.

Trial and Error is no less cynical about crime than *Malice Aforethought* (page 259), and might have appeared under the Francis Iles name but for the presence of Chitterwick, who had previously appeared in two Berkeley novels. Despite the book's excellence, its author stopped publishing crime novels after 1939. In that year, a final novel appeared under the Berkeley name—the disappointing impossible-crime story *Death in the House*—along with an under-appreciated Iles novel, *As for the Woman*.

Berkeley's presentation of the legal technicalities in *Trial and Error* prompted questions, which he answered in an introductory note to a later edition. Explaining that he had based one part of the plot on the complications that ensued following a murder committed in a London pub in 1864, he said: 'There were…two men in prison at the same time, each of whom had separately been found guilty of the death of the same man, and the authorities clearly did not know what to do about it.' In the circumstances, he argued, it was reasonable for his story to feature a private prosecution, but if not, 'I am very, very sorry.' Berkeley's scepticism about the workings of the law and the machinery of justice was never more evident than in this unpredictable and highly entertaining novel.

Verdict of Twelve
by Raymond Postgate (1940)

An epigraph from Karl Marx ('It is not the consciousness of men that determines their existence, but on the contrary their social existence determines their consciousness') supplies an early clue that *Verdict of Twelve* is no conventional crime novel. Yet despite Raymond Postgate's unrelenting focus on the haphazard workings of the English justice system, he also fashions a fascinating story that combines exploration of human nature with a teasing mystery.

The first and longest of the book's four sections presents studies of the twelve members of a jury convened for a murder trial. The jurors are a varied bunch, and one of them has got away with committing a murder. Their personal backstories play a key part in their attitude to the evidence presented by prosecution and defence. The events leading up to the trial are recounted in a lengthy flashback. The main characters are an eleven-year-old boy, Philip, and his unpleasant aunt, Mrs Rosalie Van Beer, who have grown to loathe each other.

The third part of the book, 'Trial and Verdict', is notable for Postgate's description of the shifting attitudes of the jurors, once they have retired to decide whether or not the accused is guilty, which are illustrated visually with 'recording dials' summarising what is in each juror's mind. True originality is extraordinarily difficult to achieve in a crime novel, and the inner workings of a jury had previously been explored in Eden Phillpotts' *The Jury*, in *The Jury Disagree*, by George Goodchild and C.E. Bechhofer Roberts (1934), and in one of Richard Hull's finest mysteries, *Excellent Intentions* (1938). Yet Postgate's treatment of the jury's deliberations is distinctive. A brief final section adds a suitably ironic and dark flourish.

Verdict of Twelve was first published in Britain early in the war, 'in conditions hardly favourable for the success of a new novel', as a later edition put it; nonetheless, the American edition was swiftly acclaimed in the *New Yorker* as probably 'the best mystery of this year and many years to come', and by Raymond Chandler in his essay 'The Simple Art of Murder'.

Raymond William Postgate came from a wealthy family, and studied at Oxford before becoming a pacifist, and serving a short term of imprisonment for refusing to be conscripted. Briefly a member of the fledgling British Communist Party, he defected to the Labour Party, which was led by his father-in-law, George Lansbury, from 1932–1935.

Postgate's sister Margaret shared his political outlook, and married the left-wing economist G.D.H. Cole. The Coles were prolific detective novelists, although none of their books compares in quality (or social insight) with *Verdict of Twelve*. Postgate occasionally reviewed detective fiction, and was responsible for an enjoyable anthology, *Detective Stories of To-day* (1940) *Somebody at the Door* (1943), like *Verdict of Twelve*, explored the ways in which a person's background influences their behaviour, and can lead to crime; the sombre nature of life during the Second World War is well-evoked, and the culprit's *modus operandi* is uniquely dependent on war-time conditions. Postgate founded the Good Food Club, compiling the first edition of *The Good Food Guide* in 1951, but after producing a third crime novel, *The Ledger is Kept* (1953), which again inevitably failed to surpass the brilliance of his debut, his appetite for the genre was sated.

Tragedy at Law
by Cyril Hare (1942)

For this unorthodox variation on the concept of a crime novel set in a realistically evoked working environment, Cyril Hare drew on his own experience. Fifteen years spent practising at the Bar, and a spell as a judge's marshal, meant that he was ideally suited to describing life on a judicial circuit.

The book's characterisation is as credible as its milieu. Francis Pettigrew, who acts as amateur sleuth, is a disillusioned barrister, moderately successful and acutely aware of his own shortcomings, in a manner unthinkable in Great Detectives, and perhaps even in some members of his own profession. He recognises that he lacks some subtle quality that 'was neither character nor intellect nor luck, but without which none of these gifts would avail to carry their possessor to the front'. There is something rather modern about Pettigrew, not least his passionate opposition to capital punishment. His attitudes are not shared by Sir William Hereward Barber, a severe High Court judge, who advocates extending the death penalty. Pettigrew calls this 'stretching the stretching', which can perhaps be described as gallows humour.

As Mr Justice Barber travels from town to town, dispensing justice in his austere manner, he becomes involved in a sequence of bizarre incidents. He receives a threatening note, and someone evidently wishes him ill. To a seasoned reader of detective stories, the judge seems destined for victimhood. Yet his wife (another lawyer, with whom Pettigrew had once been in love) saves him from an apparent attempt on his life. Murder does not occur until a very late stage of the book—in the twenty-first of twenty-four chapters.

Pettigrew collaborates with Hare's usual investigator, Inspector Mallett, in solving the mystery, which turns upon an obscure (but fairly clued) point of law. Unlike those amateurs who involved themselves in murder cases for their own amusement, however, he is a reluctant detective. He cannot treat murder in the raw as a game, because he is too sensitive to the pain that it leaves in its wake. Sceptical about the nature of justice, he wonders 'whether his client would be hanged merely because the Judge had a down on his counsel'. And the bitterly ironic twist at the end of the story is as brilliant and unusual as anything in the Iles canon.

Cyril Hare's real name was Alfred Alexander Gordon Clark. His first crime novel, *Tenant for Death* (1937), introduced the shrewd Mallett, who investigated the murder of a crooked financier. Pettigrew returned to appear in four later novels, continuing to exploit his legal expertise in helping to solve mysteries. He began to enjoy better fortune, marrying a young woman he met while working in a government department during war-time in *With a Bare Bodkin* (1946) and acting as a deputy judge in *That Yew Tree's Shade* (1954). In spirit, Hare's fiction—especially his Christmas mystery, *An English Murder* (1951)—belongs to the Golden Age, but in portraying Pettigrew, he anticipated crime novelists of a later generation by creating a character of flesh and blood.

Smallbone Deceased
by Michael Gilbert (1950)

Just as Cyril Hare made superb use of his understanding of the world of judges and barristers in his detective stories, so his friend Michael Gilbert exploited his knowledge of life in a solicitors' practice to witty effect in one of the finest workplace-based detective novels. The tranquillity of the respectable Lincoln's Inn firm of Horniman, Birley and Craine is rudely disturbed by when a deed box is opened to reveal a corpse. It belongs to Marcus Smallbone, who had been co-trustee of the valuable Ichabod Trust with the firm's recently deceased senior partner.

The investigation is led by Chief Inspector Hazlerigg, who made regular appearances in Gilbert's early novels and short stories, but as so often in classic crime novels, the professional detective's enquiries are supplemented by the work of a talented amateur. When Henry Bohun, a young solicitor, explains why he discounted one suspect—'No-one who sings Bach like that could kill a man with a piece of picture-wire'—the older man is tolerant: 'You'd get on well with our modern school…They think that all detection should be a combination of analysis and hypnosis.' Highly readable, the book is packed with incidental pleasures.

Gilbert had been rudely interrupted while working on his first detective story by the Second World War, and *Close Quarters* did not appear until 1947. Set in a cathedral close, this accomplished debut was firmly in the Golden Age tradition, complete with three diagrams, a seemingly impossible murder and a crossword puzzle to solve. Gilbert soon took unique advantage of his experience as a prisoner of war in Italy to write an outstanding example of the impossible crime story, *Death in Captivity* (1952), which was filmed as *Danger Within*.

Michael Francis Gilbert had a knack of time management which enabled him to pursue twin careers, and rise to the heights in both. As a solicitor, his client list included Raymond Chandler and the government of Bahrain, and he became second senior partner of a leading London firm. As an author, he wrote an extraordinarily diverse range of crime novels, as well as scores of short stories, and plays for radio, television and the stage; his honours included the CWA Cartier Diamond Dagger for sustained achievement. When author and critic H.R.F. Keating chided him for being content to be regarded solely as an entertainer, Gilbert responded: 'What is a writer to do if he is not allowed to entertain?' Years later, writing Gilbert's obituary, Keating acknowledged his friend's modesty, and praised him for 'invariably illuminating sharply aspects of British life and, on occasion, digging deep into the human psyche so as to point to an unwavering moral'.

In addition to producing spy thrillers, adventure stories and police procedurals, he returned from time to time to the legal profession, notably in *Death Has Deep Roots* (1951), *Flash Point* (1974) and the undeservedly overlooked late novel *The Queen Against Karl Mullen* (1991). *Stay of Execution and Other Stories of Legal Practice* (1971) illustrates his mastery of the short form. The appealing Bohun featured in a handful of stories, but only the one novel; while regrettable, this reflects Gilbert's determination never to write the same book twice.

Chapter Sixteen
Multiplying Murders

Jack the Ripper remains the most notorious of all serial killers, but he was by no means the first. He was not even the first whose crimes sparked imaginative literature. The Ratcliffe Highway murders committed in London in 1811, for instance, inspired Thomas de Quincey's 'On Murder Considered as One of the Fine Arts'. William Palmer's audacious series of murders in the mid-nineteenth century are referenced in Arthur Conan Doyle's 'The Speckled Band' and Dorothy L. Sayers' *The Unpleasantness at the Bellona Club* (1928), and also supplied background elements of plot and character for Francis Iles' *Before the Fact* (1932) and Donald Henderson's little-known but excellent *Murderer at Large* (1936).

Yet it was the Ripper case in 1888 which opened the floodgates as regards sensational literature concerning serial killings. An early example from 1897 was the serialised story 'A Mystery of the Underground' by William Arthur Dunkerley, writing as John Oxenham, in which a killer terrorises passengers on the Tube. The early scenes are gripping, although the climactic revelations fail to match their quality.

In the early years of the twentieth century, *Israel Rank* (page 19) charted the homicidal career of a rationally motivated criminal, while *The Lodger* (page 30) achieved its success through the build-up of suspense, rather than by creating a mystery about the identity of the culprit. With the dawning of the Golden Age of detective fiction, the question was whether there was any place for serial killers in an ingenious whodunit.

The elaborate games played between Golden Age writers and their readers might seem to preclude a story about a deranged psychopath such as the Ripper. But writers soon discovered that there were two ways in which the whodunit form might accommodate serial killings. One option was for the killer's madness to be concealed beneath an apparently civilised exterior. Another was for the murderer to have a rational motive—financial gain, for instance, as with William Palmer—for the crimes, as well as sufficient ingenuity to pull the wool over the police's eyes. 1928 proved to be a breakthrough year, with no fewer than three notable British serial-killer mysteries.

In Anthony Berkeley's *The Silk Stockings Murders*, Roger Sheringham and Chief Inspector Moresby both investigate the strangling of four young women. The different crimes have varying motives, an over-elaboration which weakens a characteristically innovative book, albeit far from the author's best. In the United States, S.S. Van Dine (the pseudonym of Willard Huntington Wright) had his hugely popular, yet famously insufferable, detective Philo Vance solve *The Greene Murder Case*, in which members of the eponymous family are eliminated one by one; the killer uses a handbook on murder as his template, a device that has been re-worked countless times. John Rhode's *The Murders in Praed Street* added two additional elements to the mix—extreme ingenuity in murder methods, and a murder motive that was, at the time, pleasingly original, although subsequently it was borrowed so often that it came to seem hackneyed.

Soon, a host of detective novelists, including Neil Gordon (a pen-name of A.G. Macdonell, better known for his humorous writing) and Gladys Mitchell in Britain, and Ellery Queen and Q. Patrick in the United States, were trying their hand at this type of crime novel. Their work demonstrated that in a mystery featuring a series of linked murders, speculating about 'who will be next?' is often as tantalising as trying to deduce 'whodunit'.

J.J. Connington teased his readers with both questions in *The Sweepstake Murders* (1931). Nine members of a gambling syndicate win a fortune, but when one of them dies, litigation delays the pay-out. The survivors agree that the winnings should be divided between those who are alive at the time of payment, but the folly of this arrangement becomes evident when two more syndicate members meet an untimely end, apparently as a result of accidents. Unsurprisingly, the suspicions of the police are aroused, and their attention focuses on the survivors who will benefit from the deaths. One of them happens to be 'Squire' Wendover, the affable countryman who often acts as a sidekick to Connington's series detective, Sir Clinton Driffield. Wendover is an unlikely murderer—but might he become the next victim?

Agatha Christie's *And Then There Were None* (1939) remains the supreme 'who will be next?' story. A series of murders, patterned on a nursery rhyme, takes place among a closed circle of ten people who have been lured to a small island under false pretences. As one death follows another, the tension mounts relentlessly. The novel has been adapted for stage, radio, television and film, and is an undisputed classic of traditional detective fiction. The term 'serial killer' had yet to be coined when Christie published her masterpiece shortly after the outbreak of war, but the novel of multiple murder had already become a permanent feature of the detective fiction landscape.

The Perfect Murder Case
by Christopher Bush (1929)

A key element in the Jack the Ripper case, and the mythology surrounding it, was the correspondence purportedly sent by the killer to taunt Scotland Yard, most famously the 'Dear Boss' and 'From Hell' letters. Opinion remains divided as to whether the letters were hoaxes, but the concept of letters sent by a serial killer to tease an investigator on his trial fitted perfectly with the notion of the game-playing nature of classic detective fiction. Christopher Bush uses the device to build tension with considerable skill in his most renowned novel.

The press and New Scotland Yard receive a letter from someone calling himself 'Marius', which opens: 'I am going to commit a murder.' The fair-play ethos underpins his announcement: 'by giving the law its sporting chance I raise the affair from the brutal to the human'. Marius reveals the date when the murder will take place, 'in a district of London north of the Thames', and describes his proposed crime as 'the Perfect Murder'.

Two further letters give additional clues to the location of the killing, and cause a popular sensation: 'Flapperdom arranged murder parties at hotels. The Ragamuffin Club had a special dance gala and a gallows scene painted for it…medical students organised a gigantic rag. An enormous fortune must have been laid in bets…what Marius had intended to be the sublime was likely to become the gorblimey.'

Despite the advance warning, the authorities fail to save Harold Richleigh from being knifed to death in his own home. John Franklin, a former intelligence officer and policeman, investigates on behalf of an enquiry agency run by the Durangos conglomerate. He is assisted by Ludovic Travers, the company's financial wizard and author of *Economics of a Spendthrift*, widely regarded as 'a dilettante with economics as a passionate hobby' but also a formidable sleuth. The police struggle to make progress, but Franklin crosses the Channel in search of the answer, and dramatic climax takes place on a French island.

Travers plays second fiddle to Franklin here, but proceeded to enjoy a crime-solving career of remarkable longevity, during which he developed a speciality in breaking seemingly cast-iron alibis, rather like a private-sector equivalent of Freeman Wills Crofts' Inspector French. Over the years, as Bush strove to keep up with the times, Travers evolved into a comparatively conventional private eye, making his sixty-third and final appearance as late as 1968. If not quite a Great Detective, he was one of the most resilient.

Charlie Christmas Bush, known as Christopher Bush, came from a family of modest means; his father supplemented his income through poaching. Bush worked as a schoolteacher before becoming a full-time author. He earned election to membership of the Detection Club in 1937, and Dorothy L. Sayers captured his strengths (and, implicitly, his limitations) when she said in a review that his work was 'always workmanlike and pleasant to read'. Even more enthusiastic was Anthony Shaffer, a detective novelist himself before he found fame as a playwright, who said, 'A Bush in the hand is worth two of any other bird'.

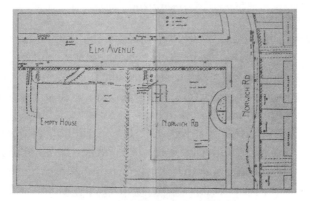

Death Walks in Eastrepps
by Francis Beeding (1931)

Robert Eldridge takes a train from London to Norfolk. He is heading for the coastal resort of Eastrepps, home of his married mistress Margaret. Eldridge is besotted with Margaret, who is reluctant to seek a divorce if it entails losing custody of her young daughter. The affair is not Eldridge's only secret. He is one of those villainous financiers who were as common in Golden Age detective fiction as they have been in the real world of twenty-first century commerce. His real name is James Selby, and sixteen years earlier, the crash of his company called Anaconda Ltd ruined many innocent investors—some of whom happen to live in Eastrepps. After years spent hiding in South America, he has re-established himself in Britain under a new identity. Although he has prospered, his victims have never been compensated.

On the day that Eldridge visits Eastrepps, one of the residents is stabbed to death. Before Inspector Protheroe and his rather more intelligent sidekick Sergeant Ruddock can progress their enquiries, a young woman called Helen Taplow is also killed. Chief Inspector Wilkins of Scotland Yard is called in to lead the investigation, but more deaths occur in quick succession. A man is arrested, but proves to be innocent. The effect of multiple murders upon the local community, and in particular the mounting tension created by 'the Eastrepps Evil' are succinctly yet atmospherically conveyed.

Eventually another arrest is made, and a trial takes place at the Old Bailey. That is not, however, the end of the story. The book is notable for a pleasing and original murder motive for the serial crimes, and the critic Vincent Starrett went so far as to say it was one of the ten finest detective stories ever written. Even in the early Thirties, that was slightly hyperbolic, but the tale is fast-paced, clever, and told in a stylish and entertaining manner.

Francis Beeding was the best-known pseudonym used by a writing duo, John Leslie Palmer and Hilary Aidan St George Saunders; they also collaborated under the names David Pilgrim and John Somers. Both men studied at Balliol College, but were not contemporaries at Oxford; they met while working for the League of Nations in Geneva, and their insight into the international situation lent strength to the long series of thrillers that they wrote together, as well to as a clever whodunit, *He Could Not Have Slipped* (1939).

Their regrettably infrequent detective stories included *The House of Dr Edwardes* (1927), memorably filmed by Alfred Hitchcock as *Spellbound*, and *The Norwich Victims* (1935), notable for the inclusion of photographs of the main characters, a gimmick which supplies a subtle clue to the central mystery. *Murder Intended* (1932) reverses a familiar Golden Age template, as a rich old miser eliminates her impecunious heirs. After Palmer's death, Saunders produced *The Sleeping Bacchus* (1951) under his own name. The book was interesting not only as an impossible-crime story, but also as an updated version of Pierre Boileau's *Le Repos de Bacchus*, published fifteen years earlier.

X v. Rex
by Martin Porlock (1933)

Despite his success with relatively orthodox detective novels about the cases of Colonel Anthony Gethryn, Philip MacDonald strove to avoid formula, and to use story-telling techniques designed to thrill as well as to challenge the intellect. Recognising the potential of the serial-killer novel for generating excitement, in 1931 he published the fast-moving *Murder Gone Mad*.

Two years later, under the cover of his occasional pseudonym Martin Porlock, he returned to serial killings. As with the earlier book, the events of *X v. Rex* move at breakneck speed. MacDonald keeps shifting viewpoint, making effective use of very short scenes and plenty of incident. MacDonald also supplies occasional witty asides, notably when a kaleidoscopic picture of what is going on in Britain at the time of the murders includes mention that the publisher, Victor Gollancz, 'denies that Francis Iles is the pseudonym of Mr Martin Porlock'.

An alternative title given to this book in the US is *The Mystery of the Dead Police*, which lacks subtlety but at least gives a clear indication of the link between the crimes. An unknown murderer is eliminating police officers in London and its environs with considerable ingenuity—in one instance, by concealing a gun under a sandwich board. The central character is the mysterious Nicholas Revel, a suave rogue who assists the police with their investigation, but is also a prime suspect.

The culprit confides in a journal, which gives some insight into his motivation, although the subtleties of criminal psychology were not MacDonald's forte. This structural device is an attempt to address a flaw in *Murder Gone Mad*, where the deranged killer's mindset was not satisfactorily conveyed, and has been borrowed many times.

MacDonald's vivid story-telling meant that he was ideally suited to writing cinematic screenplays, and a move to Hollywood soon reduced his productivity as a novelist. The year after the book appeared, he was responsible for adapting it as *The Mystery of Mr X*, with Robert Montgomery as Revel. In 1952, the film was re-made as *The Hour of 13*, with Peter Lawford playing Revel, and the events of the story moved back in time to the Victorian era.

Several of MacDonald's novels were filmed, although he did not always write the screenplays himself. He was not responsible, for instance, for the script for either the original film version of *The Nursemaid Who Disappeared*, based on his 1938 novel of the same name, or *23 Paces to Baker Street*, the better-known re-make. His lasting fame as a screenplay writer is owed rather to his contribution to two films that rank in most lists of all-time classics, Alfred Hitchcock's *Rebecca* and the sci-fi movie *Forbidden Planet*.

The Z Murders
by J. Jefferson Farjeon (1932)

When Richard Temperley arrives at Euston Station following a trip to the Lake District, he decides that before moving on to his next destination, he will take refuge in a nearby hotel. An elderly and rather disagreeable fellow passenger, who had snored his way through the train journey, follows suit. Within minutes the other man is shot while sleeping in an armchair, and Temperley has had a brief encounter with a beautiful young woman who promptly flees the scene. When the police arrive, Detective Inspector James questions Temperley, and then shows him a token that has been discovered at the crime scene: 'a small piece of enamelled metal. Its colour was crimson, and it was in the shape of the letter Z.'

Fascinated by the woman, Temperley discovers that her name is Sylvia Wynne and that she lives in Chelsea. Instinct convinces him that, whatever she may have to hide, she is not a murderer. He goes in search of her, with the police (whose treatment of him throughout seems remarkably good-natured in the circumstances) in hot pursuit. On arriving at her studio, however, he discovers another crimson Z, lying on the carpet.

The villain is apparently some kind of 'signature killer' (although that term had yet to be invented) but Sylvia's terrified refusal to tell Temperley what she knows, and her habit of disappearing from sight before he can make sure of saving her from whatever fate awaits, lead to further complications. The pair take part in a bizarre cross-country chase, first by train and later by taxi, before Farjeon finally reveals the truth, and unmasks one of the most sinister culprits in Golden Age fiction.

A passage shortly before the climactic scenes captures the appeal of the puzzle set in this kind of story: 'There was not even any theory to work upon. The murders…occurred, apparently, at any time and at any place. They appeared to be motiveless and purposeless, and to form no settled scheme. Within thirty hours three tragedies had occurred, known already as "the Z Murders" in thousands of homes, and countless anxious lips were voicing the questions, "How many more?" "Where will the next occur?" and "Who will the next victim be?"

By compressing the action into a day and a half, Farjeon ensures that he never loses his grip on the reader's attention. The plotting is melodramatic, and the portrayal of the principal villain lurid, while there are regular cliff-hangers similar to those in the stories of Francis Durbridge. But whereas Durbridge's approach to writing was strictly functional, Farjeon cared about his prose, and liked to spice his mysteries with dashes of humour and romance. Time and again, imaginative literary flourishes lift the writing out of the mundanity commonplace in thrillers of this period.

Joseph Jefferson Farjeon came from a distinguished literary family. His series character Detective X. Crook, a reformed criminal who becomes a private detective, appeared in many short stories, and after his first novel appeared in 1924, Farjeon became a popular novelist of whose best books Dorothy L. Sayers said 'every word is entertaining'. His reputation faded after his death, but *Mystery in White* (1937), a characteristically atmospheric Christmas crime story, became an unexpected best-seller when republished in 2014.

The ABC Murders
by Agatha Christie (1936)

Captain Arthur Hastings OBE, the narrator of many of Hercule Poirot's early cases, says in a foreword that the ABC case presented his friend with 'a problem entirely unlike any which had previously come his way', and that the little Belgian showed 'real genius' in solving it. This novel is one of Christie's masterpieces, and has been much flattered by imitation, although elements of the brilliant central plot idea were borrowed by Christie herself, for instance from a short story by G.K. Chesterton, "The Sign of the Broken Sword".

On returning to England from his ranch in South America, Hastings learns that Poirot has received a letter signed 'ABC' telling him to 'look out for Andover on the 21st of the month'. On the appointed day, a woman called A. Ascher, who keeps a tobacconist's, is bludgeoned to death in her shop. The crime appears to be motiveless, and a railway guide, also known as an ABC, is found at the scene. Poirot receives a second letter from ABC, drawing his attention to Bexhill-on-Sea on the 25th. On that day, a waitress called Elizabeth (or 'Betty') Barnard is found on a beach; she has been strangled with a belt, and again an ABC is discovered under her corpse. Poirot receives a third ABC letter, warning him of a crime at Churston on the 30th, but it arrives too late to prevent the murder of retired throat specialist Sir Carmichael Clarke.

Hastings' narrative is interspersed with short scenes featuring Alexander Bonaparte Cust, a commercial traveller dealing in silk stockings. An insignificant man who has suffered fits since sustaining a head wound during the war, Cust proves to have been in the vicinity of each of the crimes. Is he the murderer—and if so, what is his motive?

Christie blends a rich mix of ingredients into an exceptionally gripping whodunit. Cust's initials, and his line of business, are nods to Anthony Berkeley Cox, and *The Silk Stockings Murders* (1928), while the murderer's correspondence with Poirot calls to mind the Marius letters in *The Perfect Murder Case* (page 223). Killings linked by the alphabet previously occurred in *The Z Murders* (page 229), and the circumstances of the first murder are reminiscent of the (still officially unsolved) real-life case that inspired Milward Kennedy's *Death to the Rescue* (page 271).

Christie touches on a favourite theme, the horror of living in an atmosphere of suspicion, and pokes gentle fun at both the 'famous alienist', Dr Thompson, who is called in to assist Scotland Yard, and the well-educated smart-alec police officer, a product of the reforms of Lord Trenchard, who oversaw the establishment of Hendon Police College. At the climax of the story, she even demonstrates how the murderer's xenophobia contributed to the window-dressing of the crimes. All this is done with quite brilliant economy.

Poirot tells a (distinctly unimpressed) Hastings that he never ceases to be fascinated by 'the permutations and combinations of life', and he was no doubt speaking for Christie. Just as Miss Marple spots parallels between apparently mundane village life and the melodramatic events of a murder case, so the Belgian detective's understanding of human nature is the key to his success. And it is Christie's acute insight into the way people the world over behave—including victims, suspects, murderers, and detectives—that helps to explain the enduring popularity of her fiction.

Chapter Seventeen

The Psychology of Crime

Is Fyodor Dostoyevsky's *Crime and Punishment* (1866) an example of crime fiction? Raskolnikov's crime and its consequences are at the heart of the story, and Thomas Mann claimed that it was 'the greatest detective novel of all time', while Patricia Highsmith argued that it could be read as novel of suspense. Yet as Julian Symons said in *Bloody Murder*, while Dostoyevsky's work reveals an interest in mystery and sensation, it was for him 'only the means through which he expressed concerns far outside the interests of the crime novelist'.

For W.H. Auden, *Crime and Punishment* is 'a work of art which deals with murder', compelling in the reader 'an identification with the murderer which he would prefer not to recognise'. Similarly, Auden contrasted traditional detective stories involving the solving of a crime that has been committed, which he saw as escapist fantasies, with Franz Kafka's *The Trial* (1925), in which Josef K. is deemed to be guilty, even though the cause of his guilt is not clear. Auden, writing in the Forties, saw Josef K. as 'a portrait of the kind of person who reads detective stories for escape'.

A precise and truly satisfactory definition of the crime-fiction genre continues to prove elusive, but it is safe to say that it encompasses stories in which the focus is not on the detective or on the process of detection but rather on the behaviour and psychology of the criminal. Talented novelists uninterested in concocting intellectual puzzles for their readers to solve have long explored the mental state, not only of murderers. Such writers have in common with Dostoyesky and Kafka at least an interest in examining the effect of guilt upon their protagonists, and their work is often as deeply serious and thought-provoking as it is entertaining. In some cases their focus has been on the psychology of the victim, rather than of the perpetrator. Like authors of traditional detective stories, they often draw on material from real-life crimes, sometimes making radical changes to the facts of the case, sometimes using their imagination and a range of literary techniques (such as telling the tale by way of multiple viewpoints) to come up with fresh 'explanations' of mysterious unsolved crimes.

In the Edwardian era, *Israel Rank* (page 19) was the outstanding book of this kind, while Marie Belloc Lowndes' *The Chink in the Armour* (1912), inspired by the Goold murder case in Monte Carlo in 1907, builds suspense effectively as the danger facing the heroine becomes ever more apparent. After the First World War, A.P. Herbert's *The House by the River* and C.S. Forester's *Payment Deferred* (pages 238 and 240) were short, sharply written and rather cynical books which teased readers not with the question 'whodunit?' but rather by asking 'will he get away with it?' Herbert and Forester soon turned their attention elsewhere, and the same was true of Joanna Cannan after one fine novel in a similar vein, but interest in the work of Sigmund Freud (himself a detective fiction fan) was growing, and crime writers addressed psychology of crime with increasing zest and insight.

Herbert had hit on a means of telling a crime story that would be adapted and developed in countless different ways by writers as gifted as Patricia Highsmith and Ruth Rendell. This makes it all the more surprising that *The House by the River* has received relatively little attention in histories of the genre.

Anthony Berkeley, in a much-quoted dedicatory preface to *The Second Shot* (1930), argued that the future of the detective story lay either in experimentation with the manner of telling the story, or in an emphasis on character and atmosphere. He suggested that the detective story was already 'developing into the novel with a detective or crime interest, holding its reader less by mathematical than by psychological ties. The puzzle element will no doubt remain, but it will become a puzzle of character rather than a puzzle of time, place, motive and opportunity.'

The Second Shot was, Berkeley said, 'the story of a murder rather than the story of the detection of a murder'; despite this, it boasted the trappings of a conventional detective story, including a map of the scene of the crime (which highlighted the locations of key characters at a crucial time) and an idiosyncratic sleuth, Roger Sheringham. Adopting the pseudonym Francis Iles, Berkeley dispensed with these elements in *Malice Aforethought* (page 259) and *Before the Fact* (1932). The storylines in both novels were influenced by real-life cases, and the focus was on psychology: of the murderer in the first novel, and on the mindset of a born victim in the second.

The Francis Iles books were highly influential. Detective novelists who had started out in the late Twenties, such as Anthony Gilbert, Lynn Brock and Milward Kennedy, tried their hand at psychological crime fiction, as did newcomers to the genre in the Thirties such as C.E. Vulliamy, Richard Hull and Bruce Hamilton. In *Hue and Cry* (1931), Hamilton recounted the misadventures of a man who kills by accident and then flees justice. *Hue and Cry* is surely the only Golden Age novel to open at a football match, or to be set partly in a working-class railway town, apparently an amalgam of Crewe and Derby. While drunk, Tom Payton murders a wealthy director of the football club he plays for, and spends the rest of the story trying to escape justice. Hamilton creates a rounded character and describes with empathy the quiet desperation of ordinary people at the time of an economic slump.

Donald Henderson's *Mr Bowling Buys a Newspaper* (1943), a study of the misadventures of a wife-killer who embarks on a murder spree, was much admired by Raymond Chandler, who praised its 'tragic-comic idealisation of the murderer' in his essay 'The Simple Art of Murder'. Henderson adapted the novel for the stage, and it was televised by the BBC in 1956. *Goodbye to Murder* (1946), in which Thelma Winterton's quest for happiness leads to homicide, mined the same vein of quirky black humour, but lung cancer cut short the author's promising career. Henderson was an actor turned scriptwriter who, under various names, published seventeen novels, including *His Lordship the Judge* (1936) as by D.H. Landels. Henderson's eventful life included periods of extreme poverty (with several months spent living in a tent in the run-up to the war), work as a film extra and for the BBC and being buried under the wreckage of a bombed house in 1941. Had death not intervened, he might have built more extensively on the literary foundations laid by Iles.

In the Fifties, crime writers on both sides of the Atlantic, such as Shelley Smith, Julian Symons, Patricia Highsmith, Helen McCloy and Margaret Millar, took the genre further, with assured novels casting light on dark corners of the human psyche. Sometimes they utilised tricky plot devices, but primarily as a means of exploring human behaviour. A comparison of Roger East's *Murder Rehearsal* (1933) with *The Last of Philip Banter* (1947), published by the American John Franklin Bardin fourteen years later, shows how much had changed. In the earlier novel, a detective novelist's admiring secretary notices parallels between his work-in-progress and three recent and apparently unconnected deaths; what follows is a lively story with a neat late twist. In Bardin's book, a troubled advertising man discovers a manuscript which he may or may not have typed, and which seems to foretell events in real life, but the emphasis is on a study in psychological disintegration rather than whodunit or whydunit. East's story is entertaining, and he made sporadic but enjoyable contributions to the genre; his real name was Roger d'Este Burford and he was one of the few people to have pursued careers both as a diplomat and as a screenwriter. Bardin's novel, however, is the more memorable of the two.

The lead given by the post-war generation of writers was in turn followed by Ruth Rendell, who in the course of a career lasting just over fifty years took the psychological mystery to new heights in books such as *A Judgement in Stone* (1977) and *A Fatal Inversion* (1987); the latter was one of a string of outstanding novels published under the name Barbara Vine. But she was also responsible for the highly popular 'Kingsmarkham Chronicles' featuring Chief Inspector Reginald Wexford, a long series of whodunits. It is sometimes suggested that the psychological mystery supplanted the classic form of detective story, but that view is simplistic. The two kinds of crime fiction have co-existed for a century, and continue to do so. It is closer to the truth to say that modern writers such as Rendell in her later Wexford books have demonstrated, just as Dorothy L. Sayers did in the Thirties, that it is possible for a skilled author to say something of interest about society, and human nature, in a novel which in its essentials follows the classic form.

The House by the River
by A.P. Herbert (1920)

Hammerton Chase is 'a short half-mile of old and dignified houses, clustered irregularly in all shapes and sizes along the sunny side of the Thames…it had a unique, incomparable character of its own'. A couple called the Whittakers host a regular social evening, and those attending include Stephen Byrne, a handsome young poet, his pregnant wife Margery, their friend and neighbour, John Egerton, and pretty Muriel Tarrant, 'the sole unmarried and still marriageable maiden in the Chase'. On returning home that night, Stephen exchanges a smile with the Byrnes' attractive new maid, Emily Gaunt.

One evening shortly afterwards, while his wife is out of the house, Stephen makes a clumsy attempt to kiss Emily, and when she resists his overtures and screams, he puts his hands around her throat to keep her quiet. But he squeezes too hard, and strangles her. His comfortable life, and everything he has striven for, is suddenly at risk as a result of his momentary folly. As her body lies in front of him on the floor, someone comes to the front door. It is not Margery Byrne, but John Egerton, and Stephen persuades the startled young civil servant to help him dispose of Emily's corpse in the river.

After her body is found, an inquest is held, but the outcome is that the finger of suspicion points at John, rather than at Stephen. Stephen behaves disingenuously, and with supreme selfishness, while John's loyalty prevents him from telling the truth. Soon, the wretched young civil servant becomes a social pariah, quite unable to win over the woman he adores, Muriel Tarrant. Meanwhile Stephen becomes a father for the second time; increasingly daring and ambitious with his poetry, he also pursues his own interest in Muriel. The Thames, alternately attractive and menacing, plays a central role in the story's events as the tension mounts.

Herbert's brisk, yet at times lyrical, narrative benefits from a series of ironic vignettes, such as the witty portrayal of the verbose lawyer, Mr Dimple, but the main focus is on Stephen and John, and the ramifications of their doomed friendship. The reader knows the truth about the crime, but remains uncertain as to whether justice will be done or denied—and, if it is done, by what means.

Alan Patrick Herbert was a man of many parts. His most famous novel, *The Water Gypsies* (1930), again manifested his love of the Thames, while his *Misleading Cases*, first published in *Punch*, satirised the innumerable failings of the legal system; he had trained as a barrister, but never practised. When *Misleading Cases* was adapted for BBC TV in the Sixties, the screenwriters included Herbert, Alan Melville and Michael Gilbert. Herbert campaigned for reform of the divorce laws, among other causes, and sat as independent MP for Oxford University for fifteen years; he was knighted in 1945.

Today *The House by the River* is best remembered as a 1950 film directed by Fritz Lang, and judged by some critics an underrated example of 'Gothic noir'. The music for the film was written by George Antheil, an American renowned for his avant-garde compositions; under the name Stacey Bishop, he was also the author of an extravagant detective novel in the classic tradition of the locked-room mystery, *Death in the Dark* (1930), edited for Faber by T.S. Eliot.

Payment Deferred
by C.S. Forester (1926)

William Marble is a middle-aged bank clerk with a stupid, spendthrift wife, two children and a host of debts. He is at his wits' end when an unexpected visitor calls at the Marbles' little house in Dulwich. This is Jim Medland, Marble's nephew, who has just arrived in England and does not know a soul in the country. Jim has inherited money, and makes the mistake of letting his uncle see that his wallet is crammed with notes. The two men talk about investments, but Jim is unwilling to help out his uncle financially. Marble makes a swift decision, and after sending his wife off to bed, he poisons Jim's whisky, and buries his body in the garden.

Annie Marble suspects nothing, and Marble's luck seems to have turned. He persuades a bookmaker to collaborate with him on a speculation on the fortunes of the franc which proves so profitable that suddenly, he has more money than he can cope with. He starts drinking heavily, and becomes involved with a gold-digging dressmaker, while remaining grimly aware that he can never risk moving away from the scene of his crime. Marble is haunted by fear that his secret will be discovered, and Forester charts his disintegration in sharp, disdainful prose. *Payment Deferred* is a short but striking book; despite the young author's inexperience, it remains a compelling read.

Cecil Scott Forester was a successful novelist who remains well regarded, but his contribution to the crime genre has long been undervalued. This was partly because Forester, whose real name was Cecil Louis Troughton Smith, became celebrated as the author of books such as *The African Queen* (1938), together with the series of historical seafaring tales featuring Horatio Hornblower. Forester regarded *Payment Deferred* as a 'straight', realistic novel; because there is no detection, he did not see it as belonging to the same tradition as the mysteries of Poe and Collins, Doyle and Chesterton.

Payment Deferred was adapted for the stage, and filmed with Charles Laughton, and Forester continued for a few years to dabble in studies of criminal psychology. *Plain Murder* (1930) is one of the earliest crime novels where the action revolves around office life; set in an advertising agency, it pre-dates by three years Sayers' more famous *Murder Must Advertise*. Astonishingly, Forester's third crime novel, *The Pursued*, was lost, and not published until 2011. By the standards of 1935, when the book was written, Forester's frankness about the sexual relations between a suburban housewife and her violent husband is daring. As in Forester's earlier studies of crime, his dark and compelling evocation of the claustrophobic, financially straitened nature of life in lower middle-class England between the wars provides a vivid reminder that those years were far from a 'Golden Age' for millions of people. Small wonder that so many of them sought solace and escape in detective fiction.

No Walls of Jasper
by Joanna Cannan (1930)

Joanna Cannan, like C.S. Forester, enjoyed a long and successful literary career, but *No Walls of Jasper* never matched the success of *Payment Deferred*, although both books concern weak men who commit crime because of their desperate yearning for a better life. Perhaps Cannan was unwise to give her novel a title which failed to offer a clue to the story's nature or quality. 'No walls of jasper' is a phrase from a poem by Humbert Wolfe, in his heyday an admired writer, but now remembered only for a pithier verse: 'You cannot hope to bribe or twist/thank God! The/ British journalist/But seeing what the man will do/Unbribed, there's/No occasion to.'

Cannan demonstrates how the tedium of middle-class life can create the conditions in which an outwardly conventional member of society begins to contemplate committing the ultimate crime. Julian Prebble is married to a likeable wife, the downtrodden Phyl, and the couple have two sons. Julian works for a publishing firm, but does not earn enough to achieve the financial security and respectable place in society for which he yearns. Matters come to a head after he falls for a charming woman historical novelist on his list of authors.

The writer in question is Cynthia Bechler, who bears some similarity to a real-life novelist, Georgette Heyer. Heyer was best known as an author of immensely successful historical romances, although her detective novels, such as the locked-room mystery *Envious Casca* (1941), were also popular. She and Cannan had become friends during the First World War, and *No Walls of Jasper* is dedicated to her. Cynthia is not presented in a favourable light, but Heyer, who admired the book, was wise enough not to be offended by her fictional counterpart, who differed from Heyer in at least as many respects as she resembled her.

Julian's father is rich and disagreeable, and it is the destiny of rich and disagreeable characters in classic crime novels to provide murder victims. When the idea occurs to Julian that his father's death might solve all his problems, the older man's fate is sealed. Inevitably, however, Julian's plans go awry.

Joanna Cannan was the daughter of the dean of Trinity College, Oxford. Her husband was badly injured during the war, and she became the main breadwinner in the family; today she is best remembered as an author of children's books about ponies. She turned to detective fiction in 1939, introducing Inspector Guy Northeast of Scotland Yard in *They Rang Up the Police*. Northeast reappeared only once before the Second World War interrupted Cannan's crime-writing career. She later created a new detective, the deeply unappealing Inspector Price; his first case, recorded in *Murder Included* (1950), remains her most widely read crime novel. All her four children became writers, and one of them, Josephine Pullein-Thompson, wrote both pony novels and detective fiction.

Nightmare
by Lynn Brock (1932)

Nightmare represented a major departure for Lynn Brock, who had established himself as a specialist in highly convoluted detective stories, with a series detective, Colonel Gore, who was faintly reminiscent of Philip MacDonald's Colonel Gethryn. An ambitious novel, clearly intended as a 'break-out' book, *Nightmare* was described by the publisher, Collins, as 'an entirely original novel, which will arouse great interest and discussion. It is really a character study of a normal man turned murderer, a most fascinating study in psychology…We think *Nightmare* is one of the most remarkable books we have ever published.'

Confident words. Unfortunately for Brock and for Collins, *Nightmare* made little or no impression on the reading public, and was the first of Brock's crime novels to fail to achieve publication in the United States. From a marketing perspective, it might have been wiser to 'brand' the book uniquely, as with Francis Iles' *Malice Aforethought* (page 259), by giving the author a fresh pseudonym. Any reader expecting a cerebral whodunit similar to those featuring Brock's series detective, Colonel Gore, would have been startled and perplexed by this dark and disturbing story.

Simon Whalley, an Irish writer, and his attractive wife Elsa, are tormented by malicious neighbours. The interplay of the characters is credible and effective, and Brock conveys the febrile spirit of the times in the country as a whole, without distract-ing from the narrative flow. After Elsa becomes ill and dies, her husband vows revenge on those who have ruined his life.

Sexual undercurrents pervade the book; two of Elsa Whalley's middle-aged neighbours lust after her in secret, and in a strange and troubling passage, Marjory Prossip, one of Whalley's tormen-tors, is subjected to an attempted rape by a middle-aged man after conversations about 'Freud and birth control and homo-sexualism and totemism and infinity and things of that sort'.

Nightmare offers a striking combination of melancholy worldview and revenge tragedy, but Brock's experiment lacked the wit and strong finale that helped to make *Malice Aforethought* a success. Discouraged, Brock went back to writing more con-ventional books, and eventually resorted to resurrecting Colonel Gore in his final novel, *The Stoat*, subtitled *Colonel Gore's Queerest Case* (1940).

Lynn Brock was a pen-name for Alister McAllister, who also wrote as Anthony Wharton and Henry Alexander. Born in Dublin, and educated at the National University of Ireland, where he subsequently worked as Chief Clerk, McAllister became a playwright before joining the British Army in 1914. He was wounded while serving in the machine gun corps, and also worked in British Intelligence. In 1925, he turned to detective fiction, introducing Colonel Gore, at first an amateur sleuth and later a private investigator. T.S. Eliot admired Brock's novels, while regretting their excessively convoluted plots; he also expressed reservations about Colonel Gore's occasional 'stupidity', a characteristic which Brock probably intended as a refreshing change from the omniscience of the Great Detectives.

Chapter Eighteen
Inverted Mysteries

An 'inverted' or 'back-to-front' mystery cross-fertilises a study of criminal behaviour with a detective story. The first significant exponent of this type of crime writing was Richard Austin Freeman, the creator of Dr John Thorndyke. In a preface to a collection of stories called *The Singing Bone* (1912), he said that he regarded the focus of a detective story on the question of 'who did it?' as a mistake: 'In real life, the identity of the criminal is a question of supreme importance for practical reasons; but in fiction, where no such reasons exist, I conceive the interest of the reader to be engaged chiefly by the demonstration of unexpected consequences of simple actions, of unsuspected causal connections, and by the evolution of an ordered train of evidence from a mass of facts apparently incoherent and unrelated. The reader's curiosity is concerned…with the question "How was the discovery achieved?"…the ingenious reader is interested more in the intermediate action than in the ultimate result.'

Freeman asked himself if it would be possible to take the reader into his confidence, making them an actual witness of the crime, and furnished with every fact that could possibly be used in its detection: 'Would there be any story left when the reader had all the facts?' He decided that the answer was yes, and wrote an experimental story to prove his point. 'The Case of Oscar Brodski' is a rare example of a Freeman story based on a real-life case, which dated back more than forty years—the murder of Henry Raynor, a Nottingham rent-collector. The first half of the story follows the actions of his fictional killer, and is called 'The Mechanism of Crime'. Silas Hickler steals a packet of diamonds from his victim, Brodski, and lays the corpse across a railway track shortly before a freight train is due, so as to give the impression that the man died as a result of suicide or an accident. Hickler makes the mistake of leaving Brodski's felt hat at home, but later burns it in the fireplace. In the second half of the story, 'The Mechanism of Detection', Thorndyke comes on to the scene, and overcomes the scepticism of a local police inspector ('I don't see any significance in the diet of a man who has had his head cut off') to solve the puzzle thanks to his usual meticulous scientific detective work.

The Singing Bone was widely admired, but in 1928, Dorothy L. Sayers remarked in a long and insightful essay about the development of crime fiction that Freeman had 'had few followers and appears to have himself abandoned the formula, which is rather a pity'. In fact, he had recently expanded one of his inverted short stories 'The Dead Hand', into a novel, *The Shadow of the Wolf* (1925), and Sayers' words probably encouraged him to produce *Mr Pottermack's Oversight* in 1930. *When Rogues Fall Out* (1932) is also, in part, an inverted mystery.

Sayers' comments may also have persuaded other writers to adopt and adapt Freeman's method. They included Francis Beeding, author of the pleasingly unorthodox *Murder Intended* (1932), G.D.H. and Margaret Cole, and above all Freeman Wills Crofts, who took to the inverted form with gusto, publishing two novels of this type in 1934. *The 12.30 from Croydon* was a soundly constructed example of the form, which he rapidly improved upon with *Mystery on Southampton Water*, aka *Crime on the Solent*, with an unusual setting in a cement-manufacturing business. Crofts' *Antidote to Venom* (1938) is an especially ambitious book, combining an inverted mystery with a central theme, inspired by his deeply held religious convictions, about the redeeming power of faith in God. George Sturridge, the director of the country's second-largest zoo, is comfortably off and well respected. But nobody has it all, and George loathes his wife Clarissa, who is independently wealthy, but selfish and mean. To make matters worse, he has become addicted to gambling, and run up heavy losses. His expenses mount further when he begins an affair with a pleasant and lonely widow. There is one ray of light: an elderly aunt in poor health has already promised that he will inherit her estate. The stage appears to be set for her to meet an untimely end at George's hands, but Crofts confounds the reader's expectations in his most innovative novel. When, eventually, murder is committed, the *modus operandi* is so cunning and original that diagrams are supplied in order that the reader can understand howdunit.

The danger of repeating the narrative techniques of the inverted mystery is that the stories can become formulaic. Significantly, some of the best inverted mysteries are stand-alones rather than entries in series. A notable example is *Dial M for Murder*, by Frederick Knott, which began life as a television play before being successfully adapted for the stage, and then filmed by Alfred Hitchcock in 1954 (and re-made in 1998 as *A Perfect Murder*) Much less well-known, but equally watchable, is Vernon Sewell's 1957 film *Rogue's Yarn*, with a screenplay by Sewell and Ernie Bradford The popularity of the long-running American television series *Columbo*, with Peter Falk as the eponymous detective, and more recently episodes of *Luther*, starring Idris Elba, demonstrate that a well-told inverted mystery can attract large audiences.

Two of the finest post-war inverted mysteries were written by Presidents of the Detection Club. Arthur Brownjohn, the protagonist of Julian Symons' *The Man Who Killed Himself* (1967) is a character reminiscent of Dr Bickleigh in *Malice Aforethought* (page 259). Brownjohn, a henpecked husband, finds an outlet for his earthier side by creating an alter ego, Major Easonby Mellon. The early chapters are funny, but the mood darkens once Brownjohn starts to plan the murder of his domineering wife. *A Shock to the System* (1984), one of the few non-series mysteries published by Simon Brett, is equally gripping. The book was filmed in 1990 with a screenplay written by a fellow crime novelist, the American Andrew Klavan.

End of an Ancient Mariner
by G.D.H. and M. Cole (1933)

The Blakeaways own a large house overlooking Hampstead Heath, and as their chauffeur whisks Hilda Blakeaway and her daughter off in a long, black Packard to their country residence near Lambourn, her husband Philip reflects on his good fortune: 'rich, happily married, in good health, and conscious of his own charm and of a bounding capacity for making friends'. A year earlier, he had been an unsuccessful exporter, but marriage to the slim and gracious widow of a successful architect had transformed his fortunes. True, his step-children are not fond of him, but Philip has scarcely another care in the world.

Everything changes when Captain John Jay, an elderly seafarer, recognises him from the past. Philip, who believed the old man to be on the other side of the Atlantic, knows that with Jay in the neighbourhood, he will never know a moment's peace. When Jay turns up at his home, Philip resolves to take decisive action, and packs the butler and his wife out of the way.

The old man is duly found dead—shot, according to Philip, while attempting to burgle his house. At first, Philip's story seems plausible, and likely to be accepted by the authorities. Unfortunately, the butler becomes suspicious, while the dead man's daughter—who is unaware of his fate—tries to track down her father. Philip comes under increasing pressure, and the tension is ratcheted up once Superintendent Wilson of Scotland Yard comes on to the scene.

The Coles enliven the story with occasional satiric touches— 'the BBC cherishes an ineradicable hope that if it persistently addresses the public in good English with a cultured accent, by and by it will be as if the entire population of Great Britain had been educated at Winchester, and what nobler ideal can democracy set itself than that?' Politics gets a passing mention, and the authors have Philip deny sharing their socialist beliefs ('I'm far too fond of my own comfort') despite being on good terms with his chauffeur.

For George Douglas Howard Cole and his wife Margaret, writing detective stories was a sideline, inconsequential in comparison to their academic and political work. Margaret dismissed their novels with brevity in her autobiography, and in her biography of her husband. Douglas Cole was a distinguished economist and lecturer whose pupils included two future leaders of the Labour Party, Hugh Gaitskell and Harold Wilson. He married Margaret in 1918, and they worked together at the Fabian Society before moving to Oxford, the setting for their locked-room novella *Disgrace to the College* (1937).

An admirer of Freeman Wills Crofts' detective stories, Douglas published *The Brooklyn Murders* in 1923, but all the Coles' later books appeared under their joint names. Their fiction has been described as 'humdrum', an impression strengthened by Superintendent Wilson's dullness. Many of the books were written in haste, and a lack of care often shows. Nevertheless, the Coles indulged in an occasional interesting experiment, as with their two-volume Pendexter Saga, comprising *Dr Tancred Begins* (1935) and *Last Will and Testament* (1936), two linked novels about crimes separated by a quarter of a century. The books introduced a new detective, Dr Benjamin Tancred, although he was scarcely more memorable than Wilson. *End of an Ancient Mariner*, conversely, is good enough to make it a pity that the Coles did not devote more time and effort to developing the inverted form of detective novel.

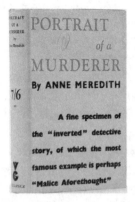

Portrait of a Murderer
by Anne Meredith (1933)

The opening paragraph of Anne Meredith's first book reveals that Adrian Gray was murdered by one of his own children at Christmas, and that the crime was 'instantaneous and unpremeditated'. Depriving herself of the opportunity to engage readers through a complex whodunit puzzle or an elaborate police investigation, Meredith concentrates on exploring the psychology of her characters, and incisive social comment. The Grays, members of the squeezed middle class, are much less happy than those both poorer and richer than they are: 'the Grays were solemn, because they did not desire to identify themselves with the uncontrolled lower orders, and were not sufficiently sure of themselves to be immune from criticism'.

Each member of the family is described in turn before the identity of the murderer is revealed through an extract from his private journal. Thinking quickly, he contrives to throw suspicion on his brother-in-law, a financier. An inquest jury returns a verdict of wilful murder against the scapegoat, and although a young lawyer who has married into the family begins to have doubts about the accused man's guilt, Meredith skilfully maintains suspense about whether there will be a miscarriage of justice.

Dorothy L. Sayers bracketed the book with R. Austin Freeman's ground-breaking inverted stories. She felt that Meredith offered a compelling portrayal of the killer's 'hard core of egotism…an egotism more for his work than for himself…and [it] possesses a sort of brutal grandeur which is almost its own justification. He knows his own genius to be better worth preserving than the lives of his disagreeable relatives…Because he is what he is, we can understand that callous determination, just as we understand his final act…He combines meanness and magnanimity, both in a heroic degree …The book is powerful and impressive, and there is a fine inevitability to the plot-structure which gives it true tragic quality.'

Anne Meredith was a pseudonym of Lucy Beatrice Malleson, who had previously published detective fiction as J. Kilmeny Keith, a number of whose books featured a politician-detective called Scott Egerton, and also under the name Anthony Gilbert. Having abandoned an attempt at a thriller, she resolved to venture upmarket and adopt a fresh literary identity for a novel influenced as much by Dostoevsky as by Francis Iles. Yet despite the praise accorded to *Portrait of a Murderer*, she recognised that 'the effects of the slump were unlikely to be permanently offset by books modelled, be it ever so faintly, on the works of Russian genius'. She continued to use the Meredith name, not least for her memoir, *Three-a-Penny* (1940), but ultimately achieved more success as Anthony Gilbert.

Gilbert's *Murder by Experts* (1936) introduced the beer-drinking solicitor Arthur Crook, who became a long-running series character, his final appearance coming as late as 1974. His cases included *The Woman in Red* (1941), but Crook was eliminated from both the 1945 film version of the story, *My Name is Julia Ross,* and an effective but drastically altered re-make, *The Dead of Winter*, directed by Arthur Penn in 1987.

The Department of Dead Ends
by Roy Vickers (1949)

In 'The Rubber Trumpet', the first story about Scotland Yard's Department of Dead Ends, Roy Vickers explains that the Department 'came into existence in the spacious days of King Edward VII and it took everything that other departments rejected...The one passport to the Department was a written statement by the senior officer in charge of the case that the information offered was absurd. Judged by the standards of reason and common sense, its files were mines of misinformation. It proceeded largely by guesswork. On one occasion, it hanged a murderer by accidentally punning on his name.'

This quirky scenario is a world away from the scrupulous technical correctness of R. Austin Freeman's inverted mysteries. Vickers makes clear that this is deliberate: 'It was the function of the Department to connect persons and things that had no logical connection. In short, it stood for the antithesis of scientific detection.' Yet the Dead Ends stories, ten of which were brought together in this book, rank alongside Freeman's ground-breaking collection as the best short inverted mysteries. Introducing the collection, Ellery Queen acknowledged that Vickers' stories were not as 'deductively conceived' as those in Freeman's *The Singing Bone*, and that 'the nature of the evidence is not as scientific or irrefutable'; chance plays a significant part. However he argued that Vickers' stories were more gripping and suspenseful.

The Department, presided over by the likeable but low-key Detective Inspector Rason, 'played always for a lucky fluke'. Sometimes this pays off, as in the case of George Muncey and the rubber trumpet, where the detectives 'arrived at the correct answer by wrong reasoning'. Vickers makes a virtue out of this, skilfully enticing the reader to turn the pages: 'the rubber trumpet had nothing logically to do with George Muncey, nor the woman he murdered, nor the circumstances in which he murdered her'.

In 'The Man Who Murdered in Public', the same facility for piquing the reader's interest is demonstrated in the opening sentence: 'How little do you know about a man if you only know that he has committed four murders?' This story was inspired by the case of the 'Brides of the Bath', while Alfred Cummarten, the protagonist of 'The Henpecked Murderer', is based on Hawley Harvey Crippen. But we are told at the outset that 'Cummarten made most of Crippen's minor mistakes. He was not as anxious… that no-one else should suffer for his sins—a moral defect which brought its own penalty.'

The thirty-seven Dead Ends stories written from 1934 onwards by William Edward Vickers (known as Roy) secured his reputation as an imaginative and highly readable author. Yet they represent a tiny fraction of his output under several names. Because he was so prolific, some of his stories, especially those published early in his career when he was short of money, are slapdash. At his best, however, Vickers wrote vividly, and with feeling—especially about his pet hate, social snobbery, a subject which crops up in the Dead Ends story 'The Case of the Social Climber', as well as in novels such as *Murder of a Snob* (1949).

Chapter Nineteen

The Ironists

The ironic finale of C.S. Forester's *Payment Deferred* (page 240) was echoed by the ending of Francis Iles' *Malice Aforethought* (page 259). Forester's book was successful enough to be adapted for stage and film, but Iles' novel made an even greater impression. Forester's portrayal of the consequences of murder was downbeat in mood, whereas Iles' story was not only well plotted but also shot through with the author's characteristically cynical humour.

As Anthony Berkeley, Anthony Berkeley Cox devised tricky puzzles based on true crimes, notably in *The Wychford Poisoning Case* (1926), which fictionalises the mysterious and controversial death of James Maybrick, a Liverpool cotton broker, in 1889. As Francis Iles, he went much further, presenting his readers with insight into the mindset of criminals and their victims, and relieving the darkness of his vision with flashes of cynical wit. A keen student of criminal trials, he was deeply troubled by the apparently unjust hanging of Edith Thompson for the murder of her husband in 1922, and he concluded that she had been 'executed for adultery'. For him, irony was the perfect tool for expressing his belief that the legal machine sometimes malfunctioned with catastrophic results.

The success of *Malice Aforethought* encouraged other authors to give stories about crime an ironic twist. One or two of them even deployed irony in order to make political points. An example was Bruce Hamilton, who joined the Communist Party during the Thirties. He infused his plots with a socio-political dimension, not least in a strange and highly original novel published in 1937, *Rex v. Rhodes: The Brighton Murder Trial.* The book is presented in the style of an entry in the then-popular series of 'famous trials'. In the guise of editor, Hamilton makes it clear that the story is set a few years in the future, when there is conflict between the forces of the left and the extreme right, with the Communists destined to prevail. The man on trial, Rhodes, is a Communist accused of killing a leader of the Brighton branch of a right-wing group. The main evidence against him—which seems damning—comes from two young, and possibly thuggish, men who worked for the victim. The focus of the story is not on what has actually happened, but on whether Rhodes will survive the trial process.

Sic Transit Gloria (1936) was an experimental novel by Milward Kennedy. The storyline reflects the troubled mood of British society in the shadow of looming international conflict. James Southern determines to find out whether Gloria Day killed herself or was murdered, and ultimately finds himself reflecting on the morality of murder for political purposes, and playing 'the part of justice…A jury could only have secured injustice. What did the law matter—if the law could not have secured justice? People talked of judicial murder: was not judicial failure to secure the just punishment of a murderer just as bad?' This question about the justifiability of murder—could the crime, in some cases, amount to an act of altruism?—became a recurrent element in Golden Age fiction, cropping up in novels written by Agatha Christie and John Dickson Carr, and especially evident in the work of ironists such as Iles and his disciples.

Like the bitingly ironic *Verdict of Twelve* (page 214), Richard Hull's *Excellent Intentions* (1938) also focused on the deliberations of jurors, although none of Hull's work had a political dimension. Hull's stories focus on individuals rather than society at large or the class system. Making use of irony, unreliable narrators and tricky story structures, he explored the misadventures of the malevolent with formidable inventiveness. Arguably, he never surpassed the success of his first crime novel, *The Murder of My Aunt* (1934), but several of his later books are witty and off-beat studies of criminal behaviour which deserve to be better known.

It is no coincidence that *Verdict of Twelve*, *Excellent Intentions* and Anthony Berkeley's *Trial and Error* (page 212) addressed the fallibility of the legal system. This was a recurrent theme in the Thirties, an age of anxiety during which the plots of two of the finest detective novels ever written, Agatha Christie's *Murder on the Orient Express* (1934) and *And Then There Were None* (1939) reflected similar dissatisfaction with the limitations of conventional justice.

In the hands of novelists determined to explore the paradox of a system of justice that too often delivered injustice, irony was more than a literary tool; it became a weapon. The master of the ironic twist never published another book after 1939, either as Berkeley or Iles, and inevitably his influence faded. But it is evident in James Ronald's *This Way Out* (1940), a fictionalisation of the Crippen case featuring a man goaded into murder, which was filmed with Charles Laughton as *The Suspect*, and in a superb novel published by a barrister in 1952. Edward Grierson's *Reputation for a Song* charts the ruthless destruction of a man's good name: far from preventing injustice, the law is manipulated so as to achieve it. The Ironists may, as Julian Symons argued, have lacked staying power, but the sardonic originality of their best work remains compelling.

Malice Aforethought
by Francis Iles (1931)

The first book published by Anthony Berkeley Cox under the name of Francis Iles was set deep in the Devon countryside, in a village brimming with as many petty rivalries and as much gossip as Agatha Christie's St Mary Mead. But *Malice Aforethought* is nothing like *The Murder at the Vicarage*. The gulf between Miss Marple's debut and Iles' is reflected by the tone of the very first paragraph: 'It was not until several weeks after he had decided to murder his wife that Dr. Bickleigh took active steps in the matter. Murder is a serious business. The slightest step may be disastrous. Dr. Bickleigh had no intention of risking disaster.'

Outwardly a pillar of the community, Bickleigh is an unhappily married fantasist whose meekness conceals a sadistic streak. He falls for another woman, and concludes that his future happiness depends on his disposing of his domineering wife. Bickleigh's crime is reminiscent of the poisoning in the case of Herbert Rowse Armstrong, the only British solicitor ever to be hanged for murder, and the final plot twist owes something to *Payment Deferred* (page 240). But what set *Malice Aforethought* apart was the cool wit of the story-telling, which makes the book compulsive reading despite the shortage of characters with whom readers would wish to identify. It was entirely in keeping with the ironic tone of the book that it was dedicated to the author's wife, from whom he became divorced less than a year later. For good measure, he endowed Bickleigh with some of his own personality traits.

Malice Aforethought received a rapturous reception from critics, and was followed in 1932 by another ambitious and extraordinary Iles novel, which drew on aspects of the real-life case of Dr William Palmer. *Before the Fact* begins in equally arresting fashion: 'Some women give birth to murderers, some go to bed with them, and some marry them. Lina Aysgarth had lived with her husband for nearly eight years before she realised that she was married to a murderer.' Although the reader is thus let in on the secret right from the outset, the urge to see what—if anything—will happen to the pleasant but desperately naive Lina is irresistible. The closing pages are dark and memorable; the ending of Alfred Hitchcock's 1941 film version, *Suspicion*, was very different, and much less powerful.

The title of the third and final Iles book, *As for the Woman* (1939), was taken from a dismissive remark of the judge who presided over the Thompson–Bywaters trial in 1922. This novel, again remarkable for the lack of sympathetic characters, explores how murder might be committed by accident, and suggests that guilt or innocence are as much matters of luck as of moral rectitude or turpitude. Iles' publishers, oddly, described the book as 'a love story', a misreading of the story that, in a suitably ironic twist, may have contributed to the author's despair. *As for the Woman* was supposed to be the first volume of a trilogy, but Iles never published another novel.

Family Matters
by Anthony Rolls (1933)

One of the first crime novelists to follow in the footsteps of Francis Iles was another talented writer who disguised his identity with a pseudonym. C.E. Vulliamy adopted the name Anthony Rolls for his first novel, *The Vicar's Experiments* (1932), which traces the misadventures of a homicidal clergyman. *Lobelia Grove*, about two murders in a garden suburb, appeared in the same year.

Family Matters soon followed, earning a rapturous review from Dorothy L. Sayers in *The Sunday Times*: 'The characters are quite extraordinarily living, and the atmosphere of the horrid household creeps over one like a miasma.' The story, she explained, 'concerns the efforts of various members and friends of the Kewdingham family to get rid…of one of the most futile and exasperating men who ever, by his character and habits, asked to be murdered'.

At the time the book was written, the effects of financial crisis, with the Wall Street Crash, followed by the economic slump, were being felt far and wide. The conventional wisdom is that Golden Age fiction never addressed the economic realities of the Thirties, but that assessment is overly simplistic. Detective novelists of the period usually avoided dwelling on the hardships suffered by millions of people in Britain and elsewhere, because their main objective was to offer their readers escapism, but inevitably their storylines and characters were influenced by what was happening in the world at large.

Robert Kewdingham has become one of the long-term unemployed. When he seeks refuge in a fantasy world, his young and pretty wife Bertha is driven to despair. Given that two men find her attractive, motives for murder abound, but attempts to poison Kewdingham soon go awry, creating what Sayers described as 'a most original and grimly farcical situation'. Although Sayers had no idea whether the medical aspects of the plot were technically correct, she declared herself 'quite ready to accept anything that is told me by so convincing an author' and admired an 'ironic surprise-ending, pregnant with poetical injustice', which was firmly in the Francis Iles tradition.

Colwyn Edward Vulliamy studied art, and published *Charles Kingsley and Christian Socialism* in 1914. While serving in the Middle East during the war, he developed an interest in archaeology, which was reflected in his fourth crime novel as by Anthony Rolls, *Scarweather* (1934), as well as in his non-fiction. Throughout his literary career, he displayed a gift for satire that strengthens his novels, and compensates for a recurrent failure to create plots strong enough to fulfil the promise of his opening chapters.

After a long period of parole, Vulliamy returned to a life of crime in the Fifties, producing half a dozen further mysteries, this time under his own name. The first and most successful of these post-war novels was *Don Among the Dead Men* (1952). The story follows a similar pattern to *The Vicar's Experiments*, and was filmed in 1964 as *A Jolly Bad Fellow*. Unfortunately, not even an excellent cast, a script by the author of the screenplay for *Kind Hearts and Coronets* and a soundtrack by John Barry enabled it to make a lasting impression.

Middle Class Murder
by Bruce Hamilton (1936)

Middle Class Murder, also known as *Dead Reckoning*, betrays the influence of *Malice Aforethought*, whose author is given a subtle hat-tip by the inclusion in the story of the names Berkeley and Cox. But whereas Anthony Berkeley Cox, alias Francis Iles, was a disgruntled Conservative, Bruce Hamilton flirted with communism, and gave his portrait of a wife-killer a socio-political context.

The book opens memorably, with Tim Kennedy drafting a fake suicide note from his wife Esther, who has been disabled and disfigured in an accident. Kennedy is a successful dentist in an affluent Sussex village, superficially likeable and charming, but wholly self-centred. Hamilton's account of how he 'graduated into homicide from the school of arm-chair murderers' is laced with irony: 'this class of people, nearly always recruited from the middle station of life, is habitually taken with so little seriousness as a potential menace to society that it is considered safe to indulge and even pamper it. It is given fairy-tales in the form of the detective story…The middle class, taken as a whole, lacks the toughness required for murder. It is frequently strong in imagination, but fearful of any action that has not the sanction of class-tradition. Besides, it is squeamish about hanging…In the last issue, they know their musings for what they are—the poetry of the respectable.'

He contrasts this with the rare exception: '… who will regard the most dreadful of crimes as preferable to the loss of conventional good opinion and the economic consequences it entails. Then you get the true middle-class murderer, a figure of awful menace and awful fascination.'

Kennedy is vain, proud and obstinate, but his charm disguises these flaws, and nobody guesses at his monstrous selfishness: 'He was incapable of any real feeling for others.' Yet, as with Crippen, a real-life middle-class murderer of an earlier generation, 'You could not help liking him.' When poor, damaged Esther tries to re-kindle their sex-life, Kennedy feels a disgust sharpened by his infatuation with a younger woman.

Although forced to abandon a plan to disguise Esther's death as suicide, he successfully contrives a fatal accident. In an ironic passage typical of Francis Iles' followers, the coroner notes that he was 'a devoted husband, full of the most tender concern for his wife's health and welfare'. But Kennedy's pursuit of Alma Shepherd is complicated not only by increasing money and business troubles, but also by the ultimate indignity for a middle-class professional man—he falls victim to a blackmailer. Hamilton charts his decline and fall with chilly cynicism.

Arthur Douglas Bruce Hamilton, a godson of Arthur Conan Doyle, seems destined to be remembered mainly as the elder brother of the more gifted Patrick Hamilton, whose biography he published in 1972. A talented novelist in his own right, Bruce published an excellent first novel, *To Be Hanged*, in 1930 (for which Conan Doyle supplied an admiring quote), and tried something different with each succeeding book. His final novel, *Too Much of Water*, was set on board a passenger ship bound for the West Indies. A high-calibre closed-circle whodunit, it was rather typical of Hamilton's career as a literary 'nearly man'. He published it as late as 1958, by which time the vogue was for bleaker books focusing on criminal psychology, of the kind he had written more than twenty years earlier.

My Own Murderer
by Richard Hull (1940)

A specialist in unreliable narrators, and a crime writer with a
taste for ironic twists matched only by Francis Iles, Richard
Hull surpassed himself in this book by giving his own real name
(Richard Henry Sampson) to the amoral solicitor who tells the
story. The opening paragraph is characteristic of Hull, and sets
the tone in the best Iles tradition: 'Even before he murdered
Baynes I never was really much attracted by Alan Renwick,
which in a way makes it odd that I did so much for him...the
relations between solicitor and client are very seldom subject to
the stress to which they were put in this case.'

Renwick has killed a valet who tried to blackmail him over
his liaison with a married woman called Anita Kilner. Renwick
pressures Sampson into sheltering him in his London flat, and
a complicated scheme is devised to enable him to escape justice.
Predictably, the plan goes awry, and soon Sampson finds himself
pursued by the determined Inspector Westhall.

Sampson's boundless capacity for self-deception, in particular
his belief that he is keeping one step ahead of his enemies, is
central to the book's appeal. His naivety is reminiscent of Edward
Powell's in *The Murder of My Aunt* (1934), Hull's first novel,
about the hapless attempts of a fat and greasy young man to
dispose of his rather more intelligent Aunt Mildred. Like Francis
Iles, Hull specialised in odious characters, and explained to the

American critic Howard Haycraft that there was more to say about unpleasant people, whom he found more amusing. Hull continued to try to find new ways to present the darker side of human nature in a wry and innovative manner. He liked to experiment with structure, sometimes by ringing variations on the theme of the 'inverted' mystery. *Excellent Intentions* (1938), admired by Jorge Luis Borges, opens at the start of a trial for murder, but the identity of the accused is concealed from the reader. The victim was a deeply repellent individual: in such a case, how can justice best be done? *Murder Isn't Easy* (1936), an ingenious example of unreliable narration, is set in an advertising business, and prompted Nicholas Blake to say in a review that Hull had 'a great gift for character'.

Like Iles, Hull guarded his privacy, saying with typical dry wit that he was convinced that a publicity photograph would be detrimental to his sales. Despite the success his work enjoyed in the Thirties, little is known about his personal life, other than that he was a chartered accountant, and a bachelor who gave his address as a gentlemen's club in London. Elected to the Detection Club in 1946, he later became its Secretary.

After the war, he continued to come up with clever ideas that were rich in irony, but realising their full potential proved an increasing challenge. *Last First* (1947) was dedicated to people who read the end of a detective novel first, and opens with the final chapter, while preserving the mystery, but the book as a whole does not do justice to the splendid concept. *A Matter of Nerves* (1950) is narrated by a murderer whose identity is withheld from the reader, but again the execution of the concept does not fulfil its promise.

Chapter Twenty

Fiction from Fact

Crime writers have always found inspiration in real-life cases, although they have usually seasoned fact with a liberal helping of imagination. 'The Mystery of Marie Roget', Edgar Allan Poe's second tale chronicling the detective exploits of Chevalier C. Auguste Dupin, fictionalised the killing of a young woman called Mary Rogers, and shifted the events across the Atlantic to France. Wilkie Collins' *The Moonstone* (1868) adapts incidents from 'the Road case', in which Inspector Whicher of Scotland Yard arrested Constance Kent, suspected of murdering her young half-brother. Arthur Conan Doyle, who investigated a number of crimes himself, most notably the Edalji case, probably drew on the criminal career of the arch-villain Adam Worth when creating Sherlock Holmes' adversary Professor Moriarty.

To this day, crime novelists make frequent and effective use of actual cases in building their stories, but perhaps this technique was most prevalent during the Golden Age of detective fiction, a period which overlapped with an equally notable, if much longer, era of real-life crime. In his essay 'Decline of the English Murder', George Orwell argued that: 'Our great period in murder...seems to have been between roughly 1850 and 1925, and the murderers whose reputation has stood the test of time are the following: Dr. Palmer of Rugeley, Jack the Ripper, Neill

Cream, Mrs. Maybrick, Dr. Crippen, Seddon, Joseph Smith, Armstrong, and Bywaters and Thompson.'

These cases attracted the attention of leading crime novelists. The Palmer, Armstrong, and Bywaters and Thompson cases, for instance, were all plundered by Francis Iles. Jack the Ripper's exploits inspired Thomas Burke's chilling short story 'The Hands of Mr Ottermole', as well as *The Lodger* (page 30) by Marie Belloc Lowndes, another keen student of true crime.

Orwell pointed out that, leaving aside the Ripper killings, six of the eight cases he highlighted were 'poisoning cases, and eight of the ten criminals belonged to the middle class...sex was a powerful motive in all but two cases, and in at least four cases respectability—the desire to gain a secure position in life, or not to forfeit one's social position by some scandal such as a divorce—was one of the main reasons for committing murder. In more than half the cases, the object was to get hold of a certain known sum of money such as a legacy or an insurance policy, but the amount involved was nearly always small.'

These psychological components suited the cases to adaptation into Golden Age mysteries with a domestic milieu and a restricted circle of suspects. Reviewing Alan Brock's *Further Evidence* (1934), Dorothy L. Sayers (whose own desire for respectability led her to conceal the fact that she had given birth to an illegitimate child) argued that 'of all motives for crime, respectability—the least emphasised in fiction—is one of the most powerful in fact, and is the root cause of a long series of irregularities, ranging from murder itself to the queerest and most eccentric misdemeanours.' This preoccupation with respectability, noted by Orwell, is a striking feature of classic crime fiction. As a suburban doctor tells a friend in Anthony Rolls' *Lobelia Grove* (1932): 'You don't understand the importance of respectability in a place like this. Respectability is the ideal, the religion, the cruel god of these little men.'

A keen student of true crime, Sayers was conscious that: 'The usual fault of novels "based on" real life cases is a curious baldness of style, hovering between the two-dimensional outlines of a police-court report and the child-like brightness of one of Mr. Punch's "Simple Stories".' She admired novels which overcame this difficulty, such as Catherine Meadows' *Henbane* (1934), based on the Crippen case: 'a fine novel of human passion and suffering, neither more nor less convincing because it happens to be a transcript of actual facts'. Meadows' only other novel, *Friday Market* (1938), fictionalised the same case as *Malice Aforethought*, the story of Herbert Rowse Armstrong, the only solicitor to be hanged for murder.

The trial of William Herbert Wallace in 1931 post-dated the murder cases cited by Orwell, but was equally remarkable. *The Jury Disagree* (1934) by George Goodchild and C. Bechhofer Roberts was among the novels inspired by William Herbert Wallace's trial, but, as Sayers said, the duo's story was not 'a re-interpretation of the case…for the incidents have been altered and fresh material added, so as to produce an entirely different situation'. The possibilities for mystification offered by the evidence inspired not one book by the industrious John Rhode, but two. In *Vegetable Duck* (1944)—the title refers to a marrow stuffed with mince, a delicacy whose preparation also supplies an opportunity to commit an ingenious crime—Inspector Jimmy Waghorn opines that 'if Wallace indeed murdered his wife, his motives for doing so, though undoubtedly obscure, were not beyond discernment. Himself a sensitive man, he had found the unintelligent companionship of his wife unendurable. The Wallaces were not sufficiently well-off to afford much diversion, and they were consequently shut up together, evening after evening, with no society but their own.'

Possibly Rhode, who also took the unusual facts of the case as a starting point for *The Telephone Call* (1948), considered Wallace guilty of battering his wife Julia to death with a poker in their Liverpool home. Wallace was convicted of murder in 1931, only to have the sentence overturned on appeal, and the case became a cause célèbre. Dorothy L. Sayers analysed the facts in a long essay included in the Detection Club's book *The Anatomy of Murder* (1936); she was unconvinced of Wallace's guilt, not least because she did not think it made psychological sense for him to have killed Julia. Many years later, researchers identified an alternative culprit, although in 2013, P.D. James published an essay arguing that Wallace was guilty of the crime. On balance, it seems more likely that Wallace was innocent, but the complexity of the puzzle continues to fascinate. As Raymond Chandler said, 'The Wallace case is the nonpareil of all murder mysteries...I call it the impossible murder because Wallace couldn't have done it, and neither could anyone else... The Wallace case is unbeatable; it will always be unbeatable.'

Crime novelists whose work features incidents and characters taken from real life need to take care. This is the lesson of Milward Kennedy's *Death to the Rescue* (page 271), written at the height of the fashion for giving actual cases the thinnest of fictional disguises. Authors in the second half of the century ranging from Patricia Highsmith to Val McDermid, and from Julian Symons to James Ellroy continued to make effective use of material from real-life cases, while avoiding Kennedy's disastrous mistake.

Death to the Rescue
by Milward Kennedy (1931)

No Golden Age detective novel better illustrates the perils of fictionalising real-life cases than *Death to the Rescue*. The storyline is ambitious and experimental, and in dedicating the book to his friend and Detection Club colleague Anthony Berkeley, Milward Kennedy mused about the future of the detective fiction. The bulk of the story is narrated by Gregory Amor, a rich and conceited middle-aged bachelor with an unhealthy interest in young women. When his new neighbours slight him, he embarks on a lengthy investigation into their past, and chances upon a link with an unsolved murder of an old woman more than 20 years earlier. Garry Boon, a conceited actor with an excessive fondness for alcohol, emerges as a prime suspect during the inquest, but no proceedings are taken against him, and Amor comes up with a succession of increasingly elaborate theories about the case.

Eventually, Amor hits upon the truth, but proves to be too clever for his own good. The narrative perspective suddenly switches, and Kennedy shows how the tables are ingeniously turned on the amateur detective. A locked-room murder is discovered, and the cleverness of the method defeats the agents of justice, who satisfy themselves that it is a case of suicide. The irony of the ending is powerful—but there is also an unintended irony in Amor's repeated expressions of anxiety about possible libel claims arising from the record of his investigations.

Six years after the book's publication, Kennedy, his publisher, Victor Gollancz Limited, and the printer, Camelot Press Limited, found themselves in the High Court, facing a libel action brought by an American actor called Philip Yale Drew. In June 1929, Drew had appeared at the County Theatre, Reading for a week that saw the murder of a local tobacconist. Drew was interviewed by the police in connection with the crime, and when he gave evidence at the inquest he was closely questioned about his movements on the day of the murder. The case—and Drew's part in it—attracted extensive publicity, but an open verdict was returned, and he was never charged.

When in 1934 a cheap edition of Kennedy's book was published, Drew was told about it, and concluded that the portrayal of Garry Boon defamed him. The case was settled out of court, with Kennedy acknowledging that he had drawn on the details of the inquest for the purposes of his novel. He maintained that he had 'so disguised the characters and the events so as to prevent anyone thinking that Garry Boon referred to Mr Drew', but he now appreciated that was incorrect. The defendants apologised to Drew, and made a payment of compensation to him. The book was withdrawn from circulation. This was a pity, because it was one of the most notable examples of Kennedy's varied and intelligent crime fiction.

After this unnerving episode, Kennedy's creative powers flagged, and his final detective story in the classic vein, complete with another 'challenge to the reader' was *Who Was Old Willy?* (1940), a story written for children. After the Second World War, he wrote a handful of thrillers, but devoted most of his energies to reviewing the books of others.

A Pin to See the Peepshow
by F. Tennyson Jesse (1934)

A noted historian and criminologist, as well as an author of detective stories, F. Tennyson Jesse was ideally equipped to write a novel based on the story of the woman at the centre of one of the most notorious criminal trials of the Twenties. Edith Thompson, hanged in 1923 (as was her lover, Frederick Bywaters) for the murder of her husband, was the model for Jesse's protagonist, Julia Almond.

Julia is introduced as an imaginative schoolgirl with high hopes for the future: 'She would, of course, get on in the world, she never doubted that. She knew, because of the way she was treated here, at school, that that she was somebody, although she wasn't the prettiest or even the cleverest.' The passing years bring several disappointments, but fail to diminish her spirit. After her boyfriend is killed during the war, she accepts a proposal of marriage from a widower who works for a firm of gentlemen's outfitters. But Herbert Starling does not excite her sexually, and although he treats her kindly during their honeymoon, 'her body still felt battered as well as her soul'. Soon she finds herself attracted to other men, and after she meets Leonard Carr, a young man whom she had known years earlier, a passionate affair develops. One night, while he is drunk, Leo follows Julia and Herbert, and attacks the older man, striking a fatal blow.

But to her 'strange incredulity', Julia, as well as Leo, is arrested and tried for murder.

The events of the story follow those of the Thompson–Bywaters case. Edith Thompson's behaviour was foolish and naive, but Anthony Berkeley was among those who argued that the case resulted in a miscarriage of justice. A scornful phrase used by the trial judge supplied the title of *As for the Woman* (1939), published as by Francis Iles. Berkeley's friend and confidante E.M. Delafield wrote the first novel based on the case, *Messalina of the Suburbs* (1924), while elements of Thompson's personality are to be found in Margaret Harrison, a central character in *The Documents in the Case* (page 186).

A Pin to See the Peepshow was successfully adapted for television in 1973 by Elaine Morgan, with Francesca Annis playing Julia. Writing about the poignant closing scenes, Morgan argued that: 'The last chapters should be compulsory reading for anyone who still believes, for whatever high-minded reasons, that the death penalty ought to be reintroduced.' Sarah Waters, author of *The Paying Guests* (2014), which also draws on the Thompson case, has written of her admiration for Jesse's book, and for 'the intensity of the narrative…its dogged commitment to its flawed, doomed heroine…the fidelity—and the tremendous humanity—with which *A Pin to See the Peepshow* embraces Thompson's tragedy'.

Fryniwyd Tennyson Jesse studied art before becoming a journalist. She married a playwright, H.M. Harwood, and seven of her own plays were produced in the West End. She edited six volumes of the *Notable British Trials* series, and a fascination with criminal psychology prompted her to write *Murder and its Motives* (1924). She also created Solange Fontaine, a French sleuth with the ability—priceless for any detective—to 'smell' evil.

Earth to Ashes
by Alan Brock (1939)

When Maude Ash befriends a stranger while selling poppies, one thing quickly leads to another. George Brooks takes her out for tea to an old mill, and soon finds himself invited to take lodgings with Maude and her invalid husband Dick. Maude is an attractive woman who finds domestic life frustrating, while George is both handsome and persuasive. Although she resists George's overtures for some time, before long Maude succumbs to his charm. To her distress, she discovers that she is not the only woman in his life, and this revelation is swiftly followed by Dick's sudden death.

The focus shifts to the mysteriously unpredictable married life of Ada Strange and her husband Joe. Soon a body is found in a blazing car belonging to Joe Strange. But whose is the corpse? The investigation is led by Inspector Kennedy and his quicker-witted subordinate Constable Vine, and they soon become convinced that Joe Strange has faked his own death. But the man is nowhere to be found.

Alan Brock notes in a foreword that the story was suggested by a 'famous murder trial of a few years ago', but emphasises that his novel departs radically from the facts of that case; he was referring to the 'blazing car murder' committed by Alfred Arthur Rouse. Rouse was a travelling salesman and compulsive philanderer who murdered an unknown victim before setting fire to his Morris Minor, with the body inside, on Guy Fawkes Night in 1930. The case caused a sensation, and Rouse's trial was notable for the forensic evidence of Home Office pathologist Bernard Spilsbury and the deadly cross-examination of Rouse by prosecuting Counsel Norman Birkett.

Rouse may have conjured up his scheme after studying the then recently published spy novel *The 'W' Plan* (1929) by Graham Seton Hutchinson, writing as Graham Seton. The notion of burning a corpse beyond recognition in a blazing car attracted several Golden Age writers, including Dorothy L. Sayers, in her short story 'In the Teeth of the Evidence', J.J. Connington and Milward Kennedy.

Perhaps it was inevitable that Alan St Hill Brock should be intrigued by the blazing-car case, given that his first published book was called *Pyrotechnics*. He came from a family whose fireworks company dated back to the late seventeenth century; the business flourishes to this day. Brock's novels made varied and inventive use of plot material drawn from real life, and he also co-wrote a book about fingerprints with fellow crime novelist Douglas G. Browne.

Dorothy L. Sayers admired Brock's *Further Evidence* (1934), inspired by 'a number of cases...where, though the jury's conclusion was the obvious and probably the true one, an alternative explanation might be made to cover all the known facts'. Brock's aim was 'to construct a case on similar lines and to fill in all the gaps', and although Sayers felt the result 'hovers rather curiously between the detective story and the psychological crime study', she was impressed.

Sayers was less taken with *After the Fact* (1935), based on the unsolved Luard case of 1908, in which Brock 'reproduces the circumstances of the actual murder...but...provides a solution of his own, quite extraneous to the facts of the real case and not intended to elucidate them'. *The Browns of the Yard* (1952) is a post-war novel, featuring three generations of detectives, who grapple successively with a Victorian mystery reminiscent of the Constance Kent case.

The Franchise Affair
by Josephine Tey (1948)

The Franchise is a large, isolated country house, recently inherited by Marion Sharpe and her elderly mother, but this story is a far cry from the country-house murder mysteries so common a few years earlier. Indeed, the book is a rare example of a successful crime novel which lacks a murder. Fifteen-year old Elisabeth Kane accuses the Sharpes of kidnap. She claims they attempted to force her, by whipping and starvation, to work as their maid, and her account seems, thanks to supporting circumstantial evidence, to have the ring of truth, but Marion Sharpe engages a staid but kindly local lawyer, Robert Blair, to defend her and her mother, and he becomes convinced of their innocence.

As well as dispensing with a murder, Tey also relegates her series detective, Inspector Alan Grant of Scotland Yard, to a walk-on part, while Blair occupies centre stage. But the risks she takes pay off. Suspense mounts as Blair battles against the odds on his clients' behalf, but the book owes its outstanding reputation to Tey's flair for compelling depiction of human character. The ending is compassionate but realistic; Tey realised that a book as strong as this deserved something more thoughtful than a facile happy-ever-after resolution.

The book was filmed in 1951, with Michael Denison as Blair, and has been televised twice, most recently in 1988 with Patrick Malahide in the lead. The plot's origins lay in the strange case of

Elizabeth Canning, a maidservant of eighteen who disappeared for almost a month in 1853, and claimed that she had been held against her will in a hay loft. Two of her alleged captors, Mary Squires and Susannah Wells, were put on trial and convicted, but an investigation by Sir Crisp Gascoyne, the Lord Mayor of London, established that Canning's accusations were false. She was found 'guilty of perjury, but not wilful and corrupt', and was transported to Connecticut.

The case provoked a public furore, and Canning's disappearance was never conclusively explained. Three years before Tey's novel appeared, the American author Lillian de la Torre, best known for her short stories featuring Dr Samuel Johnson as a detective, wrote up the case in *Elizabeth is Missing* (1945). An earlier book about the case, *The Canning Wonder* (1925), was written by the Welsh author and mystic Arthur Machen.

Josephine Tey was a much less prolific detective novelist than most of her contemporaries. A Scot who spent much of her life caring for an invalid father, her real name was Elizabeth Mackintosh, As Gordon Daviot, she carved a distinct reputation as a playwright, and in 1932, John Gielgud made his name in the title role of her most successful play, *Richard of Bordeaux*. Tey's first detective novel, *The Man in the Queue* (1929) introduced Alan Grant, and initially appeared under the Daviot name. Grant returned in *A Shilling for Candles* (1936), although he did not feature in Alfred Hitchcock's film version, *Young and Innocent*, which bore minimal resemblance to the novel. In all, Tey published a mere eight crime novels, with the last, *The Singing Sands*, appearing posthumously in 1952. Nevertheless, the quality of her writing has ensured that her work has remained popular. *The Daughter of Time* (1951) sees Grant conducting a cold-case investigation into the alleged misdemeanours of King Richard III, and is one of the most celebrated novels concerned with real-life crime.

Chapter Twenty-one

Singletons

The puzzle of why a novelist, having ventured into detective fiction with success, never repeats the trick is sometimes easily solved, but is occasionally perplexing. Several classic crime novels are 'singletons', written by authors who only contributed a solitary, but memorable, novel to the genre. *Tracks in the Snow* (page 17) is a striking example from the Edwardian era, with A.A. Milne's *The Red House Mystery* (page 47) a famous singleton from the early phase of the Golden Age.

The Clue of the Postage Stamp by Arthur Bray (1913), subtitled 'A tale of love and adventure', is an exceptionally rare novel eagerly sought (but almost always in vain; there is not even a copy in the British Library) by philatelists as well as by collectors of crime fiction. The book was published in London and Dublin in a binding of pictorially printed paper-covered boards; it bore a fake postage stamp on the front, an innovative gimmick. Nothing is known of Bray, or whether the name was a pseudonym.

S.R. Crockett's *The Azure Hand* is an unusual singleton: the novel was published posthumously in 1917, and may have been written as much as a decade earlier. Crockett was, in his Victorian hey-day, a popular Scottish author, and may have ventured into crime fiction in the hope of maintaining a wide readership as tastes in fiction changed; if so, it is unclear why the book did not appear during his lifetime.

Several authors of distinction tried their hand at detective fiction early in their careers, before turning their attention elsewhere. T.H. White and James Hilton are among those who wrote enjoyable singleton detective stories before moving on. The popularity of their later work justifies their abandonment of the genre, and the same could be said of C.P. Snow, whose *Death Under Sail* (page 106) stood alone until, at the end of a long and distinguished career, he returned to crime writing, but with a very different kind of whodunit. The trouble was that *A Coat of Varnish* (1979) lacked the zest of his youthful *jeu d'esprit*.

John Beynon introduced Detective Inspector Jordon of New Scotland Yard in his light thriller *Foul Play Suspected* (1935), but although he wrote two more books featuring the same character, *Murder Means Murder* and *Death Upon Death* were rejected by a host of publishers both before and after the Second World War, and never saw the light of day. Beynon, whose full name was John Wyndham Parkes Lucas Beynon Harris, became disillusioned, and he argued in *John O'London's Weekly* in 1954 that science fiction would replace detective stories: 'There has been too much murder going on for too long ... The present outbreak of rockets may be seen as the assault weapons softening up the detectives.' His crystal ball may have malfunctioned on that occasion, but he had already become a bestseller after reinventing himself as John Wyndham, the name under which he published sci-fi novels such as *The Day of the Triffids* (1951).

House Party Murder (1933) by Colin Ward was published both in Britain—under the estimable imprint of Collins Crime Club—and the US, achieving a good enough reception to justify a follow-up, but the author promptly slipped back into obscurity. The same was true of Gathorne Cookson, an accountant whose sole venture into the genre, *Murder Pays No Dividends* (1938) exploited his professional understanding of financial shenanigans.

Sometimes authors wrote follow-up mysteries that publishers rejected; sometimes, as with the Johns, the husband and wife team responsible for *Death by Request* (page 120), life simply got in the way. Ivy Low published her solitary detective story, *His Master's Voice* under her maiden name in 1930. Fourteen years earlier, she had married a revolutionary exile from Russia, Maxim Litvinov, and after he became the People's Commissar for Foreign Affairs under Stalin in the year of the book's appearance, her brief career as a crime writer came to a full stop.

Well-written and entertaining, *The Mummy Case* (1933) was an Oxford mystery which might have launched a successful crime writing career, but Dermot Morrah opted to concentrate on writing leader articles for *The Times* and books about (and speeches for) senior members of the Royal Family. *Murder at Liberty Hall* (1941), set in a progressive school, was a solitary venture into detection by Alan Clutton-Brock, who is not to be confused with the author of *Earth to Ashes* (page 275). Clutton-Brock also wrote for *The Times*, serving as its art critic for a decade from 1945. He became Slade Professor of Fine Art at Cambridge in 1955; in the same year inherited Chastleton House, a Jacobean mansion in Oxfordshire now in the care of the National Trust, but seems not to have been tempted to return to the genre with a 'murder at the manor' mystery.

Stanley Casson's *Murder by Burial* (1938) offers insights into archaeology benefiting from the author's expertise; they compensate for a flimsy plot based on a real-life accident involving two prominent archaeologists at Colchester in 1931. Stanley Casson was a director of the British Academy Excavations at Constantinople and also a Fellow of New College, Oxford. Rather more renowned than his solitary excursion into crime writing is the occasion when his famously absent-minded colleague the Reverend William Archibald Spooner invited him to tea to welcome 'Stanley Casson, our new archaeology fellow'. When Casson pointed out that he *was* Stanley Casson, Spooner said, 'Never mind. Come all the same.'

Ellen Wilkinson was already a high-profile political campaigner at the time *The Division Bell Mystery* (page 286) appeared. Even better known at the time she produced *Twice Round the Clock* in 1935 was Billie Houston. Houston was such a celebrity that two photographs of her appeared on the *front* of the book's dust-jacket. Born in Renfrewshire as Sarah McMahon Gribbin, she and her sister Katherina Valarita Veronica Murphey Gribbin (who prudently changed her name to Renée Houston) formed a music hall act called the Houston Sisters. Singing, dancing and telling jokes (usually with Billie in drag), the duo enjoyed immense popularity for a decade and a half; they even appeared in a short musical film produced with an accompanying soundtrack a year before the first genuine 'talking picture', *The Jazz Singer*.

Houston's novel is a country-house murder mystery, with a prologue featuring the discovery of the corpse of a repellent scientist, followed by an account of the build-up to the crime, and then by the story of its unravelling; a structure of this kind was also adopted by Henry Wade in his masterly novel of police procedure, *Lonely Magdalen* (1940). Houston planned and wrote her story 'in many dressing-rooms all over the country', and the book was said by her publishers to be product of 'a life-long ambition and an absorbing interest in criminology, and its success may mean to its author more than the thunderous applause from a packed theatre'. The joy of achieving publication proved short-lived. In 1938, after one matrimonial quarrel too many, Houston's actor husband Richard Cowper killed himself by drinking poison. She subsequently married a distinguished Australian journalist, and pursued a new life of quiet domesticity, giving up both the stage and crime writing; her sister Renée became a well-known actor, appearing in such diverse films as *A Town Like Alice* and *Carry On at Your Convenience*.

Rarely, a singleton is the product of a novelist who has already established a reputation. *Gory Knight* (1937) was produced by not one but two successful writers, Margaret Rivers Larminie and Jane Langslow. The authors spoof a quartet of

Great Detectives—Hercule Poirot, Lord Peter Wimsey, Reggie Fortune, Dr Priestley—as well as Inspector French. The four famous sleuths are invited separately by the nephews and nieces of Miss Pyke, who want her to see what a 'real' detective is like. The central mystery concerns the disappearance of a cook, and although the plot is too lightly boiled to justify the length of the book, the agreeable prose reflects the joint authors' way with words. Margaret Rivers Larminie was a champion badminton player and a popular novelist, but not—other than with this book—in the field of detective fiction. Her work includes *The Visiting Moon* (1932), a witty novel about people in unhappy marriages. Jane Langslow was an unfamiliar name even when *Gory Knight* appeared. This is because it is a pseudonym, a family name concealing the identity of Larminie's half-sister, Maud Diver, another successful writer of mainstream fiction. Diver was born in the Himalayas, and spent many years in India; colonial life in the sub-continent supplied the background for much of her fiction. At the time *Gory Knight* appeared, both Maud Diver and Margaret Rivers Larminie were past their peak as novelists. They amused themselves with a gentle send-up, unusual if not unique as a detective story co-written by half-sisters. But they never repeated their experiment in crime.

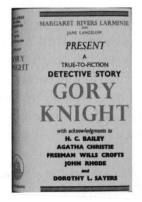

Darkness at Pemberley
by T.H. White (1932)

'Originality in detection seems impossible in 1932,' proclaimed
the front cover of the dust-jacket for the first edition of *Darkness at Pemberley*, 'but doesn't this blend of the "scientific"
detective story and the thriller—by a poet, who can therefore
write English prose—achieve it?' The boldness of this rhetorical
question was characteristic of Victor Gollancz, who published
many of the most remarkable detective novels of the Thirties,
although the claim to originality is dissipated by the additional
promise that 'The climax is a thrilling chase across England in
high-powered cars.'

Flawed yet fascinating, eccentric and extraordinary, the
novel uniquely fuses divergent types of fiction. Not content
with combining a locked-room puzzle and a bizarre manhunt,
White blends an Oxbridge college setting with a country estate
background familiar from *Pride and Prejudice*. The novel's verve,
energy and unevenness mark it as the work of a young, inexperi-
enced author, but the calibre of writing presages a distinguished
literary career.

An unpleasant don called Beedon is found shot in his locked
room in St Bernard's College, Cambridge. The corpse of an
undergraduate is also discovered, and the case appears to involve
murder followed by suicide. The story's initial impression of
conventionality is supported by the inclusion of three plans of

the crime scene. The crime is suitably ingenious, but Inspector Buller solves the case rapidly, and confronts the culprit. He is rewarded with a prompt confession—in private: 'I'm sorry to drag you out. Walls have ears, you know...and we scientific criminals get to be a little pernickety.' The bad news is that although the villain has killed three times in quick succession, Buller is quite unable to prove his guilt.

Disheartened, Buller resigns from the police force, and travels to Derbyshire to meet two old friends. At Pemberley, he tells the lovely Elizabeth Darcy (descended from 'the famous Elizabeth') and her brother Charles the story of his disastrous last case. Charles has personal experience of bitter injustice, and attempts—unsuccessfully—to take the law into his own hands. Like so many crime writers in the Thirties, White was intrigued by the moral conundrums arising when the legal system fails to secure justice. Buller and the Darcys find themselves menaced by a deranged yet infinitely cunning murderer, and the story takes several wildly improbable turns as the characters become increasingly embroiled in what Elizabeth describes as 'this Four-Just-Men business'. Preposterous as the story becomes, it fulfils Gollancz's promise of originality.

Terence Hanbury White, known as 'Tim' to many friends, read English at Queen's College, Cambridge, which is fictionalised as St Bernard's. He worked as a schoolteacher, and experimented with different genres. He co-wrote with Ronald McNair Scott, a light thriller called *Dead Mr Nixon* (1931), while an impossible crime mystery plays a small part in one of the stories told in *Gone to Ground* (1935), an eccentric novel subtitled *A Sporting Decamero*. His breakthrough came when he published *The Sword in the Stone* (1938), a tale of the boyhood of King Arthur. The book eventually formed part of the sequence of Arthurian novels known as *The Once and Future King*, which provided source material for the Lerner and Loewe stage musical and film *Camelot*, and influenced J.K. Rowling's stories about Harry Potter.

The Division Bell Mystery
by Ellen Wilkinson (1936)

A remarkable number of Golden Age detective stories were set in the world of Westminster, presumably because politicians made such popular murder victims. None, however, benefited from as much inside knowledge of the Parliament's corridors of power as *The Division Bell Mystery*, whose author was a former MP and future minister.

The Home Secretary has a dinner meeting with a shady money-man called Oissel, but is required to abandon his guest when summoned by the Commons division bell. During his short absence, Oissel is shot. At first, suicide is suspected, but the police—and Oissel's beautiful daughter Annette—are convinced that he did not kill himself.

Robert West, a young Conservative MP and Parliamentary Private Secretary, is desperate to protect his party's reputation and hold on power. He is entranced by Annette, and decides to play the detective. The story becomes a race against time—the mystery needs to be solved before scandal results in the government's collapse.

West is aided, and sometimes obstructed, by a variety of characters—an old friend, a likeable journalist, a stolid policeman, a suave financier, and a society hostess. The rapid shifts of scene and succession of plot developments help to move the story along at a rapid lick. Fair play is not a conspicuous feature of the slightly anti-climactic solution, and the reader is left bemused by the incompetence of the original investigation of the crime scene, but otherwise the book is thoroughly entertaining. Wilkinson's readable style is characteristic of a gifted communicator, and she presents West sympathetically, even though her outlook on the world was very different from his.

Ellen Cicely Wilkinson was born in Manchester to working class parents. She trained as a teacher and embraced socialism during her teens, becoming national officer for a trade union in 1915, and a founder member of the Communist Party of Great Britain, while remaining a member of the Labour Party. In 1924, having left the CPGB, she was elected to Parliament, and she remained an MP until 1931, when Labour was routed in the general election. She returned to Westminster as Member for Jarrow four years later, and was closely associated with the Jarrow March of 1936.

Wilkinson was known as 'Red Ellen', a reference both to her politics and her distinctive fiery hair. During the Second World War, while serving as Parliamentary Secretary to Herbert Morrison, she also earned the nickname 'the shelter queen' after overseeing the distribution of 'Morrison shelters' to more than half a million households. In the post-war Labour government, she became Minister of Education, but she died of an overdose of barbiturates in 1947. Despite speculation that she might have committed suicide as a result of the failure of her personal relationship with Morrison, the coroner concluded that her death, which followed a period of serious ill-health, was an accident. She wrote two novels, as well as books on political subjects, but *The Division Bell Mystery* was her only excursion into the field of crime fiction.

Death on the Down Beat
by Sebastian Farr (1941)

Music often plays in the background of detective stories, and reaches a dramatic crescendo in a handful of excellent mysteries. In *The Nine Tailors* (1934), Dorothy L. Sayers made bell-ringing central to both plot and theme, and she admired E.C.R. Lorac's similar use of musical knowledge in *The Organ Speaks* (1935). Knowledge of Mozart's Prague Symphony helps in solving the puzzle of Cyril Hare's *When the Wind Blows* (1949), while there is a musical cryptogram in *The Hymn Tune Mystery* (1930) by George A. Birmingham (in real life the Rev. Canon James Owen Hannay). But Sebastian Farr's sole foray into the genre is surely the most extraordinary of musical mysteries.

Farr chose the epistolary form for an unusual story in which the loathsome conductor of the Maningpool Municipal Orchestra is shot dead during a performance of Strauss' tone poem 'A Hero's Life'. Instead of a floor plan of a country house, the reader is provided with a diagram showing the layout of the orchestra, and no fewer than four pages of musical notation—all of which contain information relevant to the plot.

The story is told primarily through indiscreet letters sent by Detective Inspector Alan Hope to his wife, supplemented by information from newspaper cuttings and an extensive selection of letters from members of the orchestra who might be able to cast light on the killing. The late Sir Noel Grampian had many enemies, but there are surprisingly few physical clues to the crime. Eventually, snippets of information gleaned from the documents in the case put Hope on the right track.

The unorthodoxy of the story is appealing, although the indirect narrative method complicates the task of establishing the personalities of the chief suspects. Edmund Crispin (who under his real name Bruce Montgomery achieved distinction as a composer) was among the novel's admirers. Nicholas Blake, in a review for the *Spectator*, acknowledged both the strengths and limitations of Farr's approach: 'Musicians will appreciate both the deductions made from the musical score and the milieu of a provincial orchestra—to say nothing of the amusing feud between Maningpool's two music critics. The detection-fan may find the story's tempo rather jerky and the final clues to the murderer more than sketchy.'

Sebastian Farr's publisher, J.M. Dent, made a mystery of who he was, as Gollancz and Benn did with the identities of Francis Iles and Glen Trevor. 'Who is Sebastian Farr?' was a question emblazoned on the rear cover of the dust-jacket. The blurb proclaims, with some truth, that the novel offers 'something new in detective fiction. "Sebastian Farr" is the pen-name of a well-known musician, who is likely to find new fame as a conductor of criminal investigation. His plot is ingenious. He is, moreover, a writer of uncommon gifts. This is (forgive the pun) a farr, farr better thing than the average detective story.'

Yet the book, like so many novels written during war-time, disappeared almost without trace, and—perhaps disappointed—Sebastian Farr never came back for an encore. In real life, he was Eric Walter Blom, who was born in German-speaking Switzerland. Blom moved to Britain, and spent his working life there, becoming a prominent music journalist and critic for many years prior to his retirement as the chief music critic of the *Observer* in 1954. The following year saw the publication under his editorship of the fifth edition of *Grove's Dictionary of Music and Musicians*, a monumental work in nine volumes. His obituary in *The Times* remarked that 'he had an almost feline wit', but failed to mention his solitary novel. Nevertheless, the book deserves to be remembered for its originality, as well as for providing a pleasing illustration of Blom's sense of humour and love of music.

Chapter Twenty-two

Across the Atlantic

Edgar Allan Poe's first detective stories did not immediately prompt a flurry of imitations. The most successful American detective novel of the nineteenth century was *The Leavenworth Case* (1878) by Anna Katharine Green, dismissed by Julian Symons in his history of the genre, *Bloody Murder*, as 'drearily sentimental'; although it was admired by Stanley Baldwin, Symons suggested that this tended 'to confirm one's gloomy view of politicians' literary taste'.

In the new century, Craig Kennedy, a scientist from Colombia University, created by Arthur B. Reeve was touted as 'the American Sherlock Holmes; if anything, he bore a closer resemblance to Dr Thorndyke, but was neither as handsome nor quite as meticulous. Kennedy investigated mysteries involving such technological innovations as a lie detector, gyroscope and portable seismograph, but like all topical stories, they soon began to date. Jacques Futrelle's Professor S.F.X. Van Dusen, tetchy and cerebral, was known as 'The Thinking Machine', and his cases include several of high quality prior to Futrelle's death in the *Titanic* disaster. Mary Roberts Rinehart produced hugely popular 'woman in jeopardy' novels such as *The Circular Staircase* (1908), written in the literary style derided by Ogden Nash as 'Had-I-But-Known'. Rinehart influenced countless writers of melodramatic suspense, the most gifted being Wales' Ethel Lina White.

Melville Davisson Post created an unscrupulous lawyer, Randolph Mason, who—like the amateur cracksman A.J. Raffles—later sided with the forces of law and order, and became less interesting as a result. Post's major contribution to the genre was a series of historical mysteries set in rural West Virginia during the years before the American Civil War, and eventually collected in *Uncle Abner: Master of Mysteries* (1918). Uncle Abner is guided by his deep religious faith, but he is more of a man of action than Father Brown; in 'A Twilight Adventure', he prevents a mob from lynching an innocent man, and lectures about the dangers of relying on circumstantial evidence. 'The Doomdorf Mystery' offers a celebrated example of an impossible-crime puzzle, but the enduring strength of the stories lies in their evocation of period and place.

Ashes to Ashes (1919) by Isabel Ostrander, impressed Dorothy L. Sayers as 'an almost unique example of the detective story told from the point of view of the hunted rather than the hunter'. Ostrander, like Futrelle, died young, and is now almost forgotten. *The Bellamy Trial* (1927) by Frances Noyes Hart, a highly successful mystery set during a murder trial, was admired by Julian Symons for 'the powerful climax and the semi-hypnotic effect of the courtroom buzz upon the reader'.

Neither Ostrander nor Hart made such an extraordinary impact on the American detective novel as S.S. Van Dine, the pen-name adopted by Willard Huntington Wright. His detective, Philo Vance, was rich, snobbish and self-consciously erudite, but the early novels in which he appeared sold in vast quantities; they made his creator—a failed literary novelist with a damaging cocaine habit—rich and famous. Vance's first two cases were inspired by real-life crimes, and for a while, his popularity soared, aided by successful film adaptations. But Van Dine's blend of artificiality and affectation did not provide a long-term recipe for success, and his reputation declined before his early death.

Ellery Queen's books, in which cleverly conceived puzzles were solved by a detective who shared his name with the author, enjoyed much greater longevity, not least because, as the years passed, they placed more emphasis on characterisation, and slightly less on intricacy of plot. Rex Stout's Nero Wolfe, whose long and distinguished career began with *Fer de Lance* (1934), was the supreme example of the 'armchair detective'. While he savoured beer and admired his orchid collection, his legwork was undertaken by Archie Goodwin, an energetic and engaging 'Watson'.

Erle Stanley Gardner's defence lawyer Perry Mason became a household name, thanks to forty years' worth of novels, which were adapted for radio, film and—most successfully—television. The first Mason novel, *The Case of the Velvet Claws* (1933), was published in a jigsaw edition by Harrap, a distinction shared by J.S. Fletcher's *Murder of the Only Witness* (1933): the books were accompanied by jigsaw pieces which supplied a visual solution to the puzzle.

Game-playing Golden Age mysteries were in stark contrast to the hardboiled crime stories so prevalent in the United States at much the same time. Tough American novels, often featuring private eyes, and written by authors who had served a literary apprenticeship writing for pulp magazines such as *Black Mask*, became so enduringly popular that it is often forgotten that elaborately plotted whodunits continued to flourish in the US prior to the Second World War.

John Dickson Carr and C. Daly King were ingenious exponents of the impossible-crime story whose work was received with particular warmth in Britain, but there was no shortage of American writers writing impressive mysteries in the same vein, such as Clayton Rawson, Joseph Commings, Hake Talbot and Anthony Boucher. Boucher, who also wrote as H.H. Holmes, became an influential editor, critic and translator; the Bouchercon mystery convention, which flourishes to this day, is named after him. Writers such as Rufus King, Milton Propper and

Todd Downing enjoyed their share of success, as did Earl Derr Biggers, creator of Charlie Chan.

The collaborators who, in 1936, joined forces under the name Q. Patrick, Richard Wilson Webb and Hugh Wheeler compiled two 'crime dossiers' in 1938, *File on Fenton and Farr,* and *File on Claudia Cragg,* but soon followed Ellery Queen's lead, and adjusted their approach as reading tastes changed. They adopted a variant pseudonym, Patrick Quentin, and a more hard-bitten style, but still came up with ingenious scenarios, as in *Puzzle for Fiends* (1946), in which series character Peter Duluth wakes up after being attacked to find himself in unfamiliar surroundings, and being taken for someone else by people who claim to be members of his family.

With a few exceptions, notably Dashiell Hammett's *The Dain Curse,* and Joel Townsley Rogers' dazzling *The Red Right Hand,* (pages 297 and 304), hard-boiled novels bore scant resemblance to ingenious whodunits, with not a crossword puzzle clue in sight. The nearest equivalent to the English country house was probably the Sternwood mansion in Raymond Chandler's *The Big Sleep* (1939), in which definitive gumshoe Philip Marlowe ('I was everything the well-dressed private detective ought to be. I was calling on four million dollars.') made his debut. Chandler remains the most renowned of Hammett's contemporaries to have emerged from the pulps, but he was in excellent company. Vivid and often violent books such as *Little Caesar* (1929) and *High Sierra* (1940) by W.R. Burnett, *The Postman Always Rings Twice* (1934) and *Double Indemnity* (1943) by James M. Cain, and *They Shoot Horses, Don't They?* (1935) and *Kiss Tomorrow Goodbye* (1948) by Horace McCoy, all had an immediacy that made them ideal for film-makers. These were not cerebral mysteries, but novels with visceral power.

The same was true of the 'emotional thrillers' of Cornell Woolrich, who also wrote as William Irish and George Hopley. Woolrich had a gift for conjuring up memorable situations. In the William Irish novel *Phantom Lady* (1942), an unhappy husband's alibi for the time when his wife was murdered depends on a woman who seems not to exist. When he is sentenced to death, there is a race against time (a device at which Woolrich excelled) to prove the woman was not a phantom, and identify the real culprit. The movie versions of Woolrich's fiction helped to define the film noir genre.

Laura (1943) by Vera Caspary and *The Big Clock* (1946) by Kenneth Fearing also became superb films. In each book, the contrasting viewpoints of multiple narrators are as effective as in those very different novels, Wilkie Collins' *The Moonstone* and *The Documents in the Case* (page 186). Fearing was also responsible for an extraordinary novel, on the outer margins of the genre, which told a story through the voices of a bewildering number of narrators, *Clark Gifford's Body* (1942), set in a future where an idealist seeks to overthrow a government controlled by Fascists. The only (remotely) comparable crime novel of the period is Bruce Hamilton's *Rex v. Rhodes: The Brighton Murder Trial* (1937).

The vast majority of the celebrated American crime writers of the first half of the twentieth century were men. But as the century's mid-point approached, women authors made their presence felt. Chandler described Elisabeth Sanxay Holding to his publisher as 'the top suspense writer of them all. She doesn't pour it on and make you feel irritated. Her characters are wonderful; and she has a sort of inner calm which I find very attractive.' He started work on a screenplay based on her *The Innocent Mrs Duff* (1946), but abandoned it; she enjoyed better fortune with *This Reckless Moment*, a film version of *The Blank Wall* (1947) which was loosely re-made in 2001 as *The Deep End*.

Holding was far from being the only female crime novelist of distinction to emerge on the other side of the Atlantic during the Thirties and Forties. *Dance of Death* (1938), the dazzling debut of Helen McCloy, introduced the psychiatrist Basil Willing, whose sleuthing career lasted for more than forty years. Elizabeth Daly wrote sixteen mysteries in the classic vein; her series detective, Henry Gamadge, was an antiquarian bookseller, and her admirers included Agatha Christie.

The first novel of Helen Eustis, *The Horizontal Man* (1946) was at the time of its publication hailed as a compelling and original study in morbid psychology, even though today it seems almost as dated as a mystery about murder in a manor house. Eustis did not pursue a career as a crime writer, but the enjoyable detective stories produced by Canada's Margaret Millar during the Forties served as a prelude to a sequence of superb novels during the following decade.

In 1950, the most influential of all American women crime writers appeared on the scene. Patricia Highsmith spent many years living in Europe, and felt she was under-appreciated in her native country, but her books were as transformational as those of Dashiell Hammett and Raymond Chandler. Ironically, in later life she was pleased to become one of the few Americans elected to membership of that most traditional of literary social networks, the Detection Club.

The Dain Curse
by Dashiell Hammett (1929)

The Continental Op, the private eye who recounted the story of his blood-soaked foray into the gangster-cluttered town of Personville in *Red Harvest* (1929) returned to investigate a very different type of mystery in *The Dain Curse*. The earlier book concerned corrupt politicians and crooked police officers, whereas its successor is a dark, elaborate Gothic folly featuring stolen jewels, the sinister Temple of the Holy Grail and a family haunted by tragedy.

The Op is called in to investigate the theft of diamonds from the home of Edgar Leggett, a scientist, and it quickly becomes clear that this case forms part of a much larger drama concerning Leggett's family and spanning a quarter of a century. The first part of the story ends with the unmasking of a killer, who warns Edgar's daughter Gabrielle: 'you're cursed with the same black soul and rotten blood that…all the Dains have had'. As the story twists and turns, and the body count of people close to Gabrielle continues to rise, the challenge for the Op is to defeat the Dain curse and save her.

Both Continental Op novels began life in serial form, in the magazine *Black Mask*, and the episodic origins of *The Dain Curse* are evident from its unusual structure, which stitches together four distinct mystery stories. Hammett's concept was admirably ambitious: he was combining a hard-boiled detective with a plot as extravagant as anything to be found in the outlandish Golden Age novels of his fellow countryman S.S. Van Dine. His execution of the concept is artistically flawed, but although the story is eccentric and melodramatic, it is also oddly compelling.

Hammett was to dismiss the book as 'a silly story…all style', and some critics have agreed with him, including one of his biographers, Julian Symons, who felt Hammett was much more at home 'writing about gunmen, swindlers, crooks…His touch was much less sure with family curses and erotic religious cults.' Another biographer, the crime writer William F. Nolan, was more sympathetic, arguing that this is 'the most romantic of Hammett's Op stories, involving symbolism, allegory and mysticism'.

Dashiell Hammett worked for Pinkerton's National Detective Agency, and drew on his experience when he started writing fiction for magazines. For a time, he reviewed detective fiction, and he regarded Anthony Berkeley's Roger Sheringham as 'of all the facetious amateurs…engaged in solving mysteries that are too much for the police…the most amusing—well, anyhow, the least annoying—to me'. He thought Anthony Berkeley's second novel, *The Wychford Poisoning Case* (1926), brisk and entertaining, but with an 'unsporting' solution. The American critic James Sandoe highlighted the coincidence that *The Dain Curse*, with its multiple solutions, appeared in the same year as Berkeley's *The Poisoned Chocolates Case*. In their contrasting ways, Hammett and Berkeley were both kicking against the stereotypes and conventions of the genre.

The Dain Curse was swiftly followed by two memorable private-eye novels, *The Maltese Falcon* (1930) and *The Glass Key* (1931). *The Thin Man* (1934) was lighter in tone, but also highly successful, spawning a series of popular films. Although Hammett lived for more than thirty years after the book appeared, he was dogged by alcoholism and ill-health, and never produced another novel; however, he had already achieved enough to be guaranteed literary immortality.

The Curious Mr Tarrant
by C. Daly King (1935)

The Curious Mr Tarrant is one of the most renowned collections of stories focusing primarily on impossible crimes. Ellery Queen described the eight 'episodes' narrated by Jerry Phelan, who acts as Watson to Trevis Tarrant's Holmes, as 'in many ways the most imaginative stories of our time'. King's work illustrates the truth that, alongside the more acclaimed 'hard-boiled' crime fiction of the era, some of the most remarkable Golden Age mysteries were written by American authors. Yet this book's publishing history is as unorthodox as the stories it contains; despite being greeted with acclaim in some quarters, it was not even published in the United States until 1977.

Trevis Tarrant is a wealthy young dilettante who believes that cause and effect 'rule the world'. He is described as 'interested in the bizarre', and King supplies him with cases so strange as to verge on the eccentric. Tarrant lives in a modern apartment in New York, and has a Japanese butler, Katoh, who happens to be a doctor in his own country and, as Tarrant casually acknowledges, a spy while in the United States.

The amiable but dense Phelan meets Tarrant for the first time in 'The Episode of the Codex Curse', in which a priceless Aztec manuscript vanishes from a guarded room in a museum. King was skilled at creating an intriguing premise for a story, although he sometimes struggled to resolve the puzzle with equal aplomb.

'The Episode of "Torment IV"' offers an exceptionally outlandish explanation for a *Marie Celeste*-inspired mystery, whereas 'The Episode of the Nail and the Requiem', a classic locked-room puzzle, is deservedly the most anthologised of Tarrant's cases.

The impossible-crime mystery is suited to the short story form, because suspension of disbelief needs to be much less prolonged, and King's habitual wordiness is less in evidence in the Tarrant stories than in some of his novels. *The Curious Mr Tarrant* was published by Collins Crime Club, and the UK first edition is now famously scarce. The cleverness of King's fiction was admired by Dorothy L. Sayers, and C.E. Bechhofer Roberts dubbed him 'the Aldous Huxley of the detective story', yet he failed to achieve popular success in his native country, and never had the same American publisher twice.

Charles Daly King was a Yale-educated intellectual who served as a lieutenant in the field artillery during the First World War. After flirting with a business career, he concentrated on psychology, publishing books such as *The Psychology of Consciousness* (1932). His first detective novel, *Obelists at Sea*, appeared in the same year, and was swiftly followed by *Obelists en Route* (1934). *Obelists Fly High* (1935) is a dazzlingly ingenious Golden Age classic, which like its predecessors featured a variation of the Holmes–Watson duo in New York cop, Michael Lord, and the absurdly named psychologist, Dr Love Rees Pons. In 1937, King appeared in one of the 'candid camera' photographic clues featured in *The Castle Island Case* (1937) by Francis Van Wyck Mason, a historical novelist who occasionally dabbled in detective fiction.

Presumably discouraged by the failure of his novels to make an impression in the US, King did not publish any more detective novels after 1940, and concentrated on academic work, not least 'an electromagnetic study of sleep'. Ellery Queen persuaded him to revive Tarrant in short stories for *Ellery Queen's Mystery Magazine*, while another was published in a fantasy and science fiction magazine, with Jeremiah Phelan named as the author. *The Complete Curious Mr Tarrant*, containing all twelve stories about the character, finally appeared in 2003. King also completed a novel about Tarrant in 1946. Boasting one of King's characteristically odd titles, *The Episode of the Demoiselle d'Ys* remains suitably mysterious, never having been published, either in the US or anywhere else.

Calamity Town
by Ellery Queen (1942)

Ellery Queen arrives in Wrightsville, a small town in New England, calling himself Ellery Smith, and looking for a furnished house to rent. He is hoping to settle down in tranquil surroundings, and make progress with his next novel. The destiny of Great Detectives, however, is to find peace and quiet elusive. Ellery duly tempts fate by moving into the supposedly jinxed 'Calamity House', owned by the wealthy but ill-fated family after whom the town is named. Inevitably, he is soon confronted by a tantalising mystery.

Nora Wright, a member of the Wright family, was inexplicably deserted by Jim Haight three years earlier, shortly before they were due to be married. When Jim returns, just as unexpectedly, he and Nora are reunited. The wedding does take place this time, but before long, the couple's relationship deteriorates. All the signs are that Jim is contemplating the murder of his wife, and a note he has scrawled in red crayon suggests that he is planning her death for New Year's Day. Death does come to Wrightsville on the appointed day, but it is not Nora who is poisoned.

The ingenious plot borrows ingredients from Agatha Christie, Dorothy L. Sayers and Francis Iles, blending them with originality and flair. Wrightsville life, and the passions swirling within its troubled first family, are splendidly evoked, and the literary quality and style of the novel meant that it represented a landmark in the long series of mysteries written by and starring Ellery Queen. The earlier books, starting with *The Roman Hat Mystery* (1929), subtitled 'A Problem in Deduction', were intricate fair-play Golden Age puzzles, which challenged readers to beat Ellery to the solution. The sequence of books from *Halfway House* (1936) onwards saw Queen responding to the lead given by Sayers, Berkeley and others in shifting the focus away from a pure intellectual puzzle, and as Queen's biographer Francis M. Nevins put it, 'making room within its intellectual rigor for more of the virtues of mainstream storytelling'.

Calamity Town, the first of three novels set in Wrightsville, continued the process of evolution, and quickened its pace. Queen signalled that the puzzle was no longer the sole priority by changing the subtitle to 'A Novel', and abandoning the challenge to the reader. Subsequent Ellery Queen novels, such as the serial-killer mystery *Cat of Many Tails* (1949), displayed a similar impressive reluctance to be constrained by the original formula, and a shrewd recognition that times, and readers' tastes, had changed.

Ellery Queen was the pen-name used by two cousins, Frederic Dannay (born Daniel Nathan) and Manfred Bennington Lee (born Emanuel Benjamin Lepofsky; they also wrote four Golden Age mysteries as Barnaby Ross. Broadly speaking, Dannay came up with the plots of their stories, and Lee did the bulk of the writing. Dannay, passionate about the genre, was primarily responsible for a flood of anthologies of crime fiction, including the landmark compilation *101 Years' Entertainment: the Great Detective Stories 1841–1941* (1941). He also masterminded *Ellery Queen's Mystery Magazine*, which continues to be the premier magazine of short mystery stories to this day, more than 70 years after its creation. The Ellery Queen novels are said to have sold over 150 million copies, and although the Queen brand was slightly tarnished by the cousins' decision to allow ghost writers to produce books under the Queen name, the Lee–Dannay duo made an influential and lasting contribution to the crime genre.

The Red Right Hand
by Joel Townsley Rogers (1945)

From its opening lines, *The Red Right Hand* draws the reader into 'the dark mystery of tonight', and a world as surreal as it is grotesque. Where is the killer of Inis St. Erme? What did he do with St. Erme's right hand? And what will he do next? St. Erme was travelling in his car with his fiancée, Elinor Darrie, from New York to Vermont, when they pick up a strange-looking tramp. Shortly afterwards, St. Erme is murdered.

The hallucinatory events of the story are recounted by Dr. Henry N. Riddle Jr., a brain surgeon who can scarcely credit the evidence of his own eyes. A potential witness, Riddle may also be an unreliable narrator and a suspect. Is it true that there was 'something hellish and *impossible* about that rushing car, its red-eye sawed-off little driver and its dead passenger' that caused him to fail to see the tramp, who appears to be a homicidal maniac responsible for St. Erme's death?

The story is set in a rural Connecticut which seems disturbing and dangerous long before a mutilated corpse is discovered in a swamp. Locales such as the Swamp Road and Dead Bridegroom's Pond have names as eerie and evocative as Rogers' feverish descriptions. Character names—Professor MacComerou, McQuelch, Unistaire and Hinterzee among them—are equally sinister and memorable. Even more arresting is the lyrical prose. Riddle is haunted by recollections of 'the distant baying of the hounds', and 'the voices of the locusts…the gray bird fluttering frantically in my face' as he tries to make sense of the inexplicable.

The Red Right Hand was a revised and expanded version of a novella which first appeared in the *New Detective* magazine. It enjoyed a particular vogue in France, where it won the Grand Prix de Littérature Policière, and earned comparison to the work of Edgar Allan Poe and John Dickson Carr. Even Robert Adey, doyen of impossible crime enthusiasts, and author of *Locked Room Murders*, admitted defeat in his attempt to summarise the solution to the mystery: 'The explanation, given little by little, is impossible to describe fully here, and is dazzlingly brilliant.' Suspension of disbelief, especially given the number of startling coincidences, is vital, but entirely justified by the quality of the story and the writing.

Joel Townsley Rogers, like so many crime writers, began his literary career as a poet; later, he concentrated on writing for pulp magazines. His first novel, *Once in a Red Moon*, appeared in 1923, but Rogers did not return to full-length fiction for more than twenty years. Two other novels also expanded shorter pieces of work, but although he produced a vast quantity of stories, his reputation rests on *The Red Right Hand*.

Strangers on a Train
by Patricia Highsmith (1950)

'The germ of the plot for *Strangers on a Train*', Patricia Highsmith said, was: 'Two people agree to murder each other's enemy, thus permitting a perfect alibi to be established'. A similar idea had occurred to Baroness Orczy, and featured in one of her Old Man in the Corner stories, but it seems unlikely that Highsmith had read or heard of it. She had only limited interest in traditional detective fiction, and admitted that *A Game for the Living* (1958), her only novel in the form of a whodunit, was a failure. Her first novel, however, proved far more influential in the development of the crime genre than anything written by Orczy.

Guy Haines, an architect, takes a journey to see his faithless wife Miriam. He wants to be rid of her so that he can marry again, and a casual encounter with Charles Anthony Bruno results in Bruno offering to kill Miriam in return for Guy disposing of Bruno's father. Although Guy does not take the plan seriously, Bruno murders Miriam, and manages to avoid suspicion. Will Guy be able to bring himself to undertake his side of the bargain?

Highsmith's later novels often explore disturbing relationships between two men who find themselves drawn to each other, although few books match the brilliance of her debut. The novel is much closer in its central concerns to *Crime and Punishment* than to the artificial world of Agatha Christie or Ellery Queen.

Nevertheless, Highsmith later became a frequent contributor to *Ellery Queen's Mystery Magazine*—her short stories include some of her most compelling and extraordinary work—and she was even elected to the Detection Club in 1975. The uncertain post-war world was ready for crime fiction that explored the ambiguities of guilt and innocence, and Highsmith's subtle and ambitious writing paved the way for gifted successors such as Ruth Rendell, who wanted to take detective stories in a fresh direction.

Shortly after *Strangers on a Train* was published, Alfred Hitchcock bought the film rights for a modest sum, and his 1951 movie version of the story, with a screenplay co-authored by Raymond Chandler, is itself a classic of suspense. The memorable climax at a fairground was not, however, based on a passage from Highsmith's novel. The source was the Botley Fair scene at the end of *The Moving Toyshop* (page 157) by Edmund Crispin, who was not given a credit.

The troubles that plagued Patricia Highsmith (born Mary Patricia Plangman) began early; her parents divorced ten days prior to her birth. She had a difficult relationship with her mother and step-father, and a series of failed sexual relationships, mostly with women. But her first-hand experience of emotional instability infused her novels and short stories with a rare depth and power.

Her fourth novel, *The Talented Mr Ripley*, arguably her masterpiece, was the first of a quintet featuring a charming but amoral murderer. It remains the outstanding example of a crime novel with an anti-hero, but was published in 1955, four years after *The West Pier* (1951), first in a trilogy about Ernest Ralph Gorse, a British forerunner of Ripley whose misadventures were televised as *The Charmer* in 1987. Gorse's creator was the undervalued Patrick Hamilton, brother of the even more underservedly neglected Bruce.

Chapter Twenty-three

Cosmopolitan Crimes

In *Murder for Pleasure* (1941)—which until the appearance of Julian Symons' *Bloody Murder* in 1972 was the principal history of the genre—Howard Haycraft talked about 'the marked inferiority of the Continental detective story—even that of France, with a few exceptions—when measured against the English and American product'. Haycraft reckoned that the explanation for this lay in 'origin and tradition. In America the detective story was founded by one of its greatest men of letters of all time. In England it was fostered and advanced by such literary giants and near-giants as Dickens, Collins, and Conan Doyle. But in France the form began with a hack writer...As for the remainder of the Continent, it simply lacked the essential political and legalistic backgrounds of the established democracies and was consequently able to produce at best feeble imitations of the real thing.'

Today, crime in translation is in vogue. Yet even during the period covered by this book, crime writers whose first language was not English were more active, and their work was more noteworthy, than Haycraft's remarks suggest. In the past, British and American readers were more parochial in their tastes, and publishers had little incentive to pay for translations; even now, there is no English translation of many fascinating crime novels and short stories by gifted writers. It is admittedly true that the cosmopolitan rivals of Sherlock Holmes were not, by and large, as striking as Arthur Conan Doyle's Great Detective, and their cases did not have an impact comparable to that of Agatha Christie, Dorothy L. Sayers, Ellery Queen and the other leading English-language exponents of classic crime fiction. To a modern reader, however, the early examples of cosmopolitan crime offer much the same fascination as the forgotten gems of Britain's Golden Age of Murder.

Haycraft made no mention of the Russian literary giant, Anton Chekhov, and was perhaps unaware of Chekhov's forays into the crime genre. The early short stories about crime collected in *A Night in the Cemetery* (2008) are interesting, although minor in comparison to his finest work. *The Shooting Party* (1884) boasts a plot twist anticipating a similar device in a story by Agatha Christie, and so do early crime novels from Norway and Sweden, Stein Riverton's *The Iron Chariot* (1909), and Samuel August Duse's *Dr. Smirnos Dagbok* (1917). Duse's detective, the lawyer Leo Carring, is modelled on Sherlock Holmes, and appeared in no fewer than thirteen novels.

Even in their home countries, Riverton and Duse were not regarded as rivals to Doyle. Introducing the story collection *A Darker Shade* (2013), John-Henri Holmberg pointed out that 'the first internationally successful Swedish crime writer, the pseudonymous Frank Heller…enjoyed considerable popularity not only throughout Europe but also in the United States during the 1920s', but added that, apart from Heller, 'the relatively few Swedish authors writing before the 1940s were highly derivative and were considered unworthy of critical notice'.

A similar pattern was evident elsewhere on the Continent. The Hungarian-born Balduin Groller, for instance, was one of numerous European writers inspired by the popularity of Sherlock Holmes; eighteen of his stories about a Viennese Great Detective were collected in six volumes of *Detective Dagobert's Deeds and Adventures* in and around 1909. Germany's Paul Rosenhayn created another sub-Holmesian sleuth, the American

Joe Jenkins, who enjoyed enough success to merit translation into English at a time when the Anglo-American reading public's taste was much narrower than it is today. Friedrich Glauser, born in Vienna, wrote a series of interesting detective novels in Swiss-dialect German about Sergeant Studer; they were unknown to British crime fans during the Golden Age, but were finally translated and published with considerable success in the late twentieth century.

In France, the picture was rather different. *The Mystery of the Yellow Room* (1907) by Gaston Leroux was a popular locked-room mystery which introduced the journalist and amateur sleuth Joseph Rouletabille. Haycraft approved of the originality (at the time the book was written) of the crucial plot twist, and the fact that Leroux 'unlike most of his contemporaries, played religiously fair with his readers', but was properly sceptical about the story's reliance on 'the long arm of coincidence'. Leroux's contemporary, Maurice Leblanc, created Arsène Lupin, another of those literary rogues who became progressively more law-abiding and less exciting as the years passed. Haycraft complained that Leblanc, even more than Leroux, over-used disguises and aliases to the point of tedium, but felt that he was 'a rewarding author for those who will meet him half-way'.

Haycraft admired the work of the Belgian Georges Simenon, but made no mention of Stanislas-Andre Steeman, or Noel Vindry, or of Pierre Boileau. Vindry remains little known in the English-speaking world, but during the Thirties he wrote a dozen novels which matched John Dickson Carr's for inventive-ness; like Carr's Henri Bencolin, Vindry's Monsieur Allou was an examining magistrate with a knack for unravelling impos-sible crimes. Boileau's career as a crime novelist began in the Thirties, although it was not until he started collaborating with Pierre Ayraud, who wrote under the name Thomas Narcejac, that he earned widespread attention in the English-speaking world. Several of Boileau-Narcejac's atmospheric post-war novels were adapted into highly successful films, such as Clouzot's *Les*

Diaboliques, and Alfred Hitchcock's *Vertigo*, but some of their early work has yet to be translated into English.

The story in South America was much the same as in Europe. In *Latin Blood* (1972), Donald A. Yates pointed out that the success of Edgar Allan Poe and Doyle prompted Alberto Edwards to create Roman Calvo, dubbed 'the Chilean Sherlock Holmes', and quoted Abel Mateo, an Argentinian writer whose work was influenced by Ellery Queen, as saying: 'For me, one of the requirements of the detective story is an Anglo-Saxon background...just as the picaresque novel has to be told in Spain.' But Mateo's fellow countrymen, Jorge Luis Borges and Adolfo Bioy Casares led the way in writing stories with a distinctive Latin American flavour.

Taro Hirai played a leading role in developing Japanese detective fiction, writing under the name Edogawa Rampo, which was itself a tribute to English-language detective fiction, being a corruption of 'Edgar Allan Poe'. His first mystery story, 'The Two-Sen Copper Coin', appeared in 1923; as John Apostolou noted in *Murder in Japan* (1987), this is 'generally accepted as the first detective story written in the Japanese language. However, many Japanese crime stories...were written before 1923. In fact, Japanese crime fiction can be traced back to the seventeenth century.' Hirai's work influenced successors, and although the Second World War saw the writing of mysteries banned by the Japanese government, in 1947 he formed the Detective Authors' Club, which later became the Mystery Writers of Japan.

From uncertain, and often derivative, beginnings, foreign crime writers grew rapidly in confidence, and their work became increasingly important. Julian Symons devoted a whole chapter of *Bloody Murder* to Simenon (whose work influenced such English-speaking authors as Alan Hunter, Gil North, W.J. Burley and John Banville, who writes crime fiction as Benjamin Black). The leading Swiss dramatist Friedrich Durrenmatt digressed occasionally into crime fiction, and *The Judge and His Hangman* (1950) and *The Pledge* (1958) were both successfully filmed. The series of ten books about Martin Beck published by

Maj Sjowall and Per Wahloo from 1965 onwards was a highly significant forerunner to the globally popular 'Scandi-noir' fiction of Henning Mankell, Stieg Larsson, Jo Nesbø and others. Seicho Matsumoto and Shizuko Natsuki led the way in adding depth of characterisation to the ingenious plotting that has become a trademark of Japanese mysteries. There is nothing inferior about the work of these authors, but the debt that they owe to the pioneers of cosmopolitan crime is perhaps yet to be fully appreciated.

Six Dead Men
by Stanislas-André Steeman (1931),
translated by Rosemary Benet

Tontines feature in crime fiction written by authors ranging from Robert Louis Stevenson to Agatha Christie, and make ideal starting points for the 'who will be next?' type of mystery such as *Six Dead Men*. Half a dozen young men have agreed to spend five years seeking their fortunes all over the world, before returning to Paris to share their gains equally. One by one, they are murdered, presenting a baffling puzzle for Inspector Wenceslas Vorobeitchik to solve. When the detective, nicknamed Wens, reveals all in the final chapter, he begins his explanation in classically enigmatic fashion: 'what first roused my suspicions was the disappearance of the bedspread'.

The story's pace and multiple plot twists were key to its success. The trick at the heart of the novel anticipates a similar device in Agatha Christie's masterpiece *And Then There Were None* (1939) the storyline of which was also foreshadowed—in a different way—by a rather less distinguished mystery written before Steeman's novel. *The Invisible Host* (1930), filmed in 1934 as *The Ninth Guest*. This was a collaboration between an American husband-and-wife team, journalist Gwen Bristow and screenwriter Bruce Manning; the story is said to have begun life as a facetious scheme to dispose of a neighbour who played his radio too loudly.

Six Dead Men won the Grand prix du roman d'aventures, and Steeman was dubbed 'the Continental Edgar Wallace'. Mention of Steeman in *The New Yorker* caught the interest of the Pulitzer Prize-winning writer Stephen Vincent Benet, once a well-regarded poet, but today best remembered for his story 'The Devil and Daniel Webster', which became an Oscar-winning film. Benet recommended the novel to an American publisher, and his wife Rosemary undertook the translation.

Stanislas-André Steeman was, like Georges Simenon, a French-speaking Belgian born in Liège, who left school young and displayed a precocious talent for writing, working as a journalist before becoming renowned as a crime writer. However, the similarities end there. Steeman's novels place less emphasis on character and setting, and are more notable for their ingenuity. The puzzles are clever, and Steeman's work displays a commitment to fair play, plotting in the Golden Age manner, and a willingness to experiment mirroring that of his contemporaries in the Detection Club.

Wens reappeared from time to time over more than a quarter of a century, but is absent from *The Murderer Lives at Number Twenty-One* (1939), which became the first film made by the distinguished director Henri-Georges Clouzot. *Legitimate Défense* (1942), a psychological crime story, became Clouzot's third film, *Quai des Orfèvres*. Only two of Steeman's novels were translated into English during his lifetime, which accounts for the neglect his fiction has suffered among Anglo-Saxon commentators on the genre, despite its considerable reputation in continental Europe. The surrealist and poet Adolfo Casais Monteiro, for instance, translated *The Murderer Lives at Number Twenty-One* into Portuguese, so enthused was he by the surreal quality of Steeman's writing.

Steeman's first crime novel was conceived, rather like *Trent's Last Case* (page 36), with humorous intent. He and fellow journalist Herman Sartini, who used the pen-name Sintair, co-authored *The Mystery at Antwerp Zoo* (1928) as a parody of the genre's conventions. They sent it to a French publisher who took the story seriously; after he published it, the pair collaborated on three more mysteries before Steeman struck out on his own.

Pietr the Latvian
by Georges Simenon (1930),
translated by David Bellos

This short, snappy novel, originally published as a serial in the magazine *Ric et Rac*, introduced one of the most celebrated of fiction's police officers. Detective Chief Inspector Jules Maigret is hunting a mysterious fraudster known as Pietr the Latvian. He learns that Pietr ('extremely clever and dangerous' according to the official file) is travelling by train to Paris, and heads for the Gare du Nord. When the train arrives, Maigret learns that a body has been found on board.

Pietr has, it seems, been shot dead, but Maigret is not satisfied. On a hunch, he pursues a passenger from the train to the luxurious Hotel Majestic. Calling himself 'Mr Oppenheim', the traveller appears to be hand in glove with a rich couple called the Mortimer-Levingstons. Puzzlingly, he bears a strong resemblance to the description of Pietr—but if he is Pietr, who was the murdered man?

Maigret's pursuit of the truth becomes relentless after one of his colleagues is killed. A plot twist about identity was well worn even in 1930, but the strength of the Maigret stories lies in the spare writing rather than the puzzles. Above all, the appeal of the books lies in the portrayal of a detective who is extraordinary in his relentless ordinariness: 'his frame was proletarian. He was a big, bony man. Iron muscles shaped his jacket sleeves and quickly wore through new trousers. He had a way of imposing himself just by standing there...It was something more than self-confidence but less than pride...His pipe was nailed to his jawbone. He wasn't going to remove it just because he was in the lobby of the Majestic.'

The setting is painted with crisp, economical brush strokes, and the wind and rain chasing Maigret as he closes in on his quarry match the bleakness of the storyline. Maigret disguises himself, but 'Maigret in make-up was still Maigret in some aspect of his being—in a glance or a tic.' It is while wondering about Pietr's ability to inhabit more than one persona that he cracks the case. His genius as a detective is unglamorous but effective: 'what he waited and watched out for was the *crack in the wall*. In other words, the instant when the human being came out from behind the opponent.'

Maigret was eventually to appear in no fewer than 75 novels and 28 short stories. Julian Symons contrasted 'the realism of the character and background and the sensationalism of the plots...One is disconcerted by things in Simenon that can be taken for granted in John Dickson Carr...The art of Simenon lies in making the implausible acceptable.' Maigret is French, but Georges Joseph Christian Simenon was born in Belgium, and worked as a journalist, writing fiction under a pen-name, prior to establishing himself as an astonishingly productive crime novelist. His non-series work included highly successful '*romans durs*', such as *The Man Who Watched the Trains Go By* (1938), *The Strangers in the House* (1940), and *Dirty Snow* (1948).

Six Problems for Don Isidro Parodi
by H. Bustos Domecq, translated by
Norman Thomas di Giovanni (1942)

Often cited as Argentina's first home-grown book of detective stories, this collection of tales was an early collaboration between Jorge Luis Borges and Adolfo Bioy Casares. The playfulness of the half-dozen mysteries, in keeping with the finest traditions of Golden Age fiction, is underlined by their choice of surname for their detective. A foreword contributed by Gervasio Montenegro ('Member, Argentine Academy of Letters'), who pays tribute to 'the blood-curdling cruelties of the *roman policier*', and talks about Sherlock Holmes, Lecoq and Max Carrados, as well as Edgar Allan Poe, M.P. Shiel and Baroness Orczy. Even John Dickson Carr and Lynn Brock earn a mention. Montenegro has no hesitation in putting the book 'on the same level as those recommended to keen London enthusiasts by the incorruptible Crime Club'.

Before coming to the end of the essay, readers will have deduced that Montenegro is a figment of the authors' imagination, and he becomes a character in their stories. In similar vein, a biographical note about H. Bustos Domecq supplied by a schoolteacher, Miss Adelina Badoglio, ends with the ironic claim that the stories 'are not the filigree of a Byzantine locked in an ivory tower but are the voice of a true contemporary, who is sensitive to the human pulsebeat and from whose generous heart flows the torrent of his truths'. In-jokes abound; some are lost on a modern British reader, while Montenegro's anti-Semitism represents the authors' scorn for racism; Nazi-supporting extremists had previously suggested that Borges was secretly Jewish, and not a 'true' Argentinian.

Parodi is introduced in 'The Twelve Figures of the World' as a victim of a miscarriage of justice which, for the authors, typifies corruption in Argentina. Fourteen years earlier, a butcher taking part in a carnival parade was killed by a blow on the head inflicted by the member of a gang, but the police found a convenient scapegoat in Parodi, whom 'some claimed was an anarchist, by which they meant an oddball'. He was neither, just the owner of a barbershop who was owed a year's rent by a police clerk. The gang members' false evidence led to his conviction, and Parodi was sentenced to twenty-one years in prison: 'He was now in his forties, sententious and fat, and had a shaved head and unusually wise eyes.'

Parodi never leaves his cell, but proves to be a master of armchair detection, solving the weird problems brought to him, including one puzzle, 'Tai An's Long Search', which is dedicated to the memory of Ernest Bramah, and amounts to a variation on Poe's 'The Purloined Letter'. Another story, 'Tadeo Limardo's Victim', is dedicated to Franz Kafka, while characters are named after Father Brown, and Wilkie Collins' most memorable villain, Count Fosco.

Jorge Francisco Isidoro Luis Borges became one of Argentina's most distinguished men of letters. His love of detective fiction is reflected in his reviews, as well as intriguing and much-admired stories such as 'Death and the Compass' and 'The Garden of Forking Paths'. Adolfo Bioy Casares, also a writer and translator of distinction, became a close friend of Borges. The pair collaborated regularly, often under the Domecq pseudonym, and in 1943, they produced an anthology of crime fiction featuring the work of fellow countrymen alongside that of Arthur Conan Doyle, Agatha Christie and Ellery Queen.

Chapter Twenty-four
The Way Ahead

Crime fiction evolved during the first half of the twentieth century, and has kept evolving ever since, because the genre responds to changes in the world at large. Just as the pioneering work of Edgar Allan Poe, Wilkie Collins and Arthur Conan Doyle paved the way for the classic crime fiction discussed in this book, so the stories written by early Detection Club members and their contemporaries have exerted an influence on their successors. This is so despite the fact that some attitudes evinced in classic crime stories seem at best dated, and at worst intolerable.

At first glance, Agatha Christie's work may seem parochial, even though her settings are, in geographical terms, extraordinarily varied. Yet the universal nature of the behaviours at play in her mysteries contributes to their long-lasting global appeal. Readers can recognise the humanity in Christie's retired colonels and flighty housemaids, even if they have never encountered a retired colonel or housemaid in their lives. *Death Comes as the End* (1944), set in ancient Egypt, illustrates her strengths as well as her limitations. The characters are not portrayed in depth, but the emotions that drive their actions seem equally powerful in modern times. The novel is also an example of Christie's knack of anticipating trends; when the book was first published, historical mysteries were uncommon. Now they crowd bookshop shelves.

Psychology is frequently mentioned in Golden Age mysteries, although often its treatment is superficial. Anthony Berkeley was right to identify the 'puzzle of character' as the central theme for exploration in crime fiction, although to this day other forms of puzzle retain a pull on readers. Golden Age writers' love of playing games led them to experiment with tricky structures for their story-telling. Christie, Berkeley and Nicholas Blake deployed unreliable narrators with great skill, even in novels featuring their Great Detectives of the traditional kind. Although most of Richard Hull's structural experiments commanded less attention, his witty and inventive stories demonstrated the almost endless range of possible ways for telling a story about crime. Clever writers used multiple viewpoints, so effective long before in *The Moonstone*, to achieve different effects—to pull the wool over the reader's eyes in Robert Player's *The Ingenious Mr Stone*, to help amplify a theme in *The Documents in the Case* (page 186) or to supply insight into character in *Birthday Party* (page 122).

As the high spirits of the Twenties gave way to a darker mood, crime writers responded to changes taking place in the world around them. By the early to mid Forties, the Golden Age was to all intents and purposes at an end. Dorothy L. Sayers, Berkeley, Ronald Knox, R.C. Woodthorpe and Rupert Penny, among others, had all stopped writing detective novels. Their place was taken by a new generation of writers, some of whom produced highly ingenious mysteries. In the vanguard were Christianna Brand, Michael Gilbert, Edmund Crispin, and even, for a short time in the Fifties, Anthony and Peter Shaffer, identical twin brothers who later became famous as playwrights. They in turn were followed by the likes of P.D. James, Robert Barnard, and Colin Dexter accomplished storytellers who understood the value of strong plotting and a commitment to entertaining the reader.

The newcomers also included Shelley Smith and Margot Bennett, whose perspectives on politics and social issues were very different from those of Christie and Sayers. Smith and Bennett found their feet as novelists in the Forties, and Bennett's characteristically witty and clever debut, *Time to Change Hats* (1945), struck a distinctive note from the start, with a dedication 'To my creditors' and a first paragraph beginning 'It is difficult to become a private detective; the only recognised way is to be a friend of the corpse. My friends were disobliging'. They proceeded to produce some of the finest British crime novels of the Fifties, including Smith's dazzling *An Afternoon to Kill* (1953) and Bennett's very different but equally original *The Man Who Didn't Fly* (1955).

Julian Symons' praise for both women in *Bloody Murder* helped to maintain their reputations; his career followed a roughly similar pattern to theirs, but lasted much longer. He first tried his hand at crime fiction after working out a plot for a satiric mystery with his friend Ruthven Todd. Todd, a poet and artist, did none of the writing, although he later produced a handful of mysteries at great speed under the name R.T. Campbell as a money-making exercise; his series detective, Professor John Stubbs, bore a strong resemblance to John Dickson Carr's principal sleuths, Gideon Fell and Sir Henry Merrivale. Years later, after leaving the army, Symons sent the novel to a publisher, and *The Immaterial Murder Case* finally appeared in 1945. Partly because of its inferior quality, and partly because Todd objected to the caricature of him, Symons never allowed the book to be reprinted, but many of his later novels achieved distinction. His advocacy on behalf of the modern psychological crime novel was even more influential than his fiction.

Symons' work included whodunits in the classic mould, novels inspired by real-life crimes, historical mysteries and Sherlockian pastiche. His contemporary Michael Gilbert's first novel was also begun before the Second World War and not published until after its end. Gilbert demonstrated similar versatility as well as a high level of professionalism, and an unyielding commitment to writing entertaining storiest. Neither man became a household name, perhaps because of their failure to create a truly memorable series character, but together they led the way in exploring the possibilities of the well-made British crime novel.

Before he died, Symons had the satisfaction of knowing that his crusade had 'been won in the sense that...Highsmith, Le Carré, and Sjowall and Wahloo, along with some other writers are now treated as serious novelists'. He was also wise enough to recognise that the success was not, and will not, be total. But he probably underestimated the range, quality, and durability of classic crime fiction, and like many others, he would no doubt be astonished by its recent resurgence in popularity.

The Beast Must Die
by Nicholas Blake (1938)

Fusing a psychological crime story with an investigation in the traditional style conducted by an erudite Great Detective is a challenge to test the skill of even the most accomplished author. Nicholas Blake, a young writer of distinction, pulled off the trick with such aplomb that this novel earned high critical praise, and has twice been made into a film.

The book's opening paragraph is as memorable as anything in the Francis Iles canon: 'I am going to kill a man. I don't know his name, I don't know where he lives, I have no idea what he looks like. But I am going to find him and kill him.' These are the words of Felix Lane, a successful detective novelist and widower whose young son has been knocked down by a car and killed. It was a hit-and-run calamity, and the police have proved unable to trace the guilty motorist. The grieving father determines to take the law into his own hands, and exact his own form of justice, or retribution.

The first part of the novel takes the form of an extract from Felix Lane's diary, and records the steps he takes to fulfil his goal; the second part, taking the story a stage further as Lane closes in on his quarry, is told in the third person. Nigel Strangeways, Blake's series detective, is only introduced in the third of the four sections, after murder has occurred. The question he has to answer is whether Felix is guilty of the crime. In an epilogue, Strangeways describes the investigation as 'my most unhappy case'.

In a very different way, Blake was trying to do what Freeman Wills Crofts—in the same year—attempted with *Antidote to Venom*, namely to combine an 'inverted' story with a more conventional inquiry into a mysterious crime. Unlike Crofts, he was not seeking to tell a story with a hammered-home moral, or have his criminal indulge in a highly elaborate means of committing murder; these factors, coupled with his superior gift for characterisation, explain why Blake's book seems the more realistic.

Nicholas Blake was the nom de plume of Cecil Day-Lewis, whose primary reputation as a poet conceals the fact that he was a crime novelist of distinction. His debut novel, *A Question of Proof* (1935) was set in a private school, and introduced Strangeways, a wealthy private investigator. *Thou Shell of Death* (1936), a superb impossible-crime novel, swiftly followed. By early 1939, the Marxist detective-fiction fan John Strachey was citing Blake as one of the outstanding writers of detective fiction, in an article which seems the first to have proclaimed that the Thirties were a 'Golden Age' for the genre.

After the Second World War, Blake continued to write crime novels of quality, and Strangeways adapted to changing times in books such as *End of Chapter* (1957), set in a publishing house. In 1968, the year when he was appointed Poet Laureate, he produced his final crime novel. Strangeways does not appear in *The Private Wound*, set in the author's native Ireland and containing thinly disguised autobiographical elements, but some judges regard it as the best of the Nicholas Blake books.

Background for Murder
by Shelley Smith (1942)

The title of *Background for Murder* implies a crime story with greater depth than the conventional whodunit, and Shelley Smith delivers on that promise. Her first book displays the energy of youth, as well as one or two of the hallmarks of inexperience. Smith uses the apparatus of the traditional detective story—a floor plan of the crime scene is supplied, and the sleuth writes out a list of suspects, with notes on motive, opportunity and likelihood of guilt. In the self-referential tradition of Golden Age mysteries, she makes frequent references to the genre: Holmes and Watson, Poirot's 'little grey cells', Dorothy L. Sayers' *Unnatural Death* (1927) and G.K. Chesterton are all name-checked.

The story is, however, narrated by a private investigator, Jacob Chaos, in a wisecracking style influenced by the more 'realistic' American school of writers such as Raymond Chandler—and mental illness, abortion and sexual promiscuity are discussed more freely than in typical Golden Age mysteries. The result is a book reflecting a genre in transition, yet entertaining in its own right.

Chaos has been called in by Scotland Yard to investigate a murder which has baffled the local police. Dr Maurice Royd, in charge of a hospital for the mentally ill, has been battered to death in his office with a poker. Improbably, the Yard have passed the case to Chaos because they want to hush up any possibility of scandal, and he soon establishes that Royd was an odious character whom many people, including his attractive and pregnant wife, had cause to wish dead. Chaos' list of potential culprits runs to fifteen names, most of whom are either doctors or patients. He whittles down the options, but two more deaths occur before he reveals the truth in a scene which, although set in a doctor's consulting room, is entirely in keeping with Poirot's method of disclosing whodunit in a library crowded with suspects.

In one passage, Smith breaks the fourth wall, as Chaos addresses the reader directly: '(The hell, you say, what's this man Chaos up to? Do we need this subtle exposition of his reaction to atmosphere? Let us…return to our dead bodies—or else, hand me my copy of Mrs Christie's latest. All right.)' For Smith, atmosphere is important. The uncertain boundaries between sanity and insanity supply a central theme of the novel, reinforced by the setting. Three-quarters of a century after the book's publication, the presentation of mental illness seems outdated, despite Smith's progressive views, but like so many classic crime novels, the book supplies a fascinating insight into the attitudes of its time.

Smith was a confident and accomplished writer, but little has been written about her personal life. Her real name was Nancy Hermione Courlander, and her sister Barbara also dabbled in crime fiction under the name Elizabeth Anthony. Smith was educated in France, and in her twenties she married and then divorced Stephen Bodington, a Marxist economist who later turned to writing about computers and socialism. Her second book, *Death Stalks a Lady* (1945), was a 'woman in jeopardy' mystery worthy of Ethel Lina White, and although Chaos—having made a transition to Scotland Yard—returned to solve a seemingly impossible crime in *He Died of Murder!* (1947), she promptly abandoned him.

Smith and her contemporary Margot Bennett were leading exponents of the post-war British crime novel. *An Afternoon to Kill* (1953) boasts a stunning climax, while *The Lord Have Mercy* (1956) is a powerful update of the village mystery. After publishing *The Ballad of the Running Man* (1961), which was filmed, Smith produced only two more crime novels, but her work bridges that of the 'Crime Queens' of the Golden Age and high-calibre novels of the leading women writers of the next generation, notably P.D. James and Ruth Rendell.

The Killer and the Slain
by Hugh Walpole (1942)

'A strange story' is the apt subtitle of Hugh Walpole's macabre, posthumously published novel. It was the fifth of his books to be flavoured by the fantastic, and in introducing a collection of the first four, he wrote: 'It is not just now the fashion to believe in Good and Evil; at any rate no one pays them the compliment of decorating them with capital letters…It is a matter of reconciling two opposite worlds, a feat possibly too difficult for me, but one well worth attempting.' His final attempt was the most gripping of all.

The narrator, James Ozias Talbot, describes how his early years were haunted by a fellow pupil at school who shared his initials but whose personality was corrupt and malign, the polar opposite to his own. James Oliphant Tunstall is selfish and immoral, and although he sets himself up as Talbot's protector, in reality he is a controlling bully who has spotted Talbot's vulnerability, and is determined to have sport with him. Talbot comes to loathe him, and reprieve only comes when Tunstall moves away.

In adulthood, Talbot marries the beautiful but chilly Eve, who runs their antique shop so that Talbot can pursue his career as a novelist in the seaside town where they live. Tunstall, now a successful painter, re-enters his life, and soon proceeds to re-establish his dominance, not least by seducing Eve. Talbot is driven to murderous revenge, but in a nightmarish twist on the

Jekyll-and-Hyde scenario, he finds himself taking on Tunstall's characteristics.

The Killer and the Slain is a compelling novel, very distantly reminiscent of James Hogg's *The Private Memoirs and Confessions of a Justified Sinner* (1824), yet distinctive in its treatment of cruelty and murderous obsession. Walpole conceived the storyline years before the start of the Second World War, but by the time he came to start writing, Britain was under attack from the air. The nightmarish atmosphere created by the threat from a ruthless oppressor translates into a book of genuine power.

Hugh Walpole was a highly regarded novelist whose reputation began to fade during his lifetime, and has never fully recovered. The four books in *The Herries Chronicles*, his series of historical romances set in the Lake District, were especially popular. For a time he worked in Hollywood, where he wrote the screenplay for David O. Selznick's film of *David Copperfield*, and he was knighted in 1937. On the strength of his occasional 'shockers', he was invited to become a founder member of the Detection Club, and he was a contributor to their first round-robin mystery, *Behind the Screen* (1930). Julian Symons chose *Above the Dark Circus* (1931) as one of his 'hundred best crime stories', saying it was Walpole's 'feeling for fear and cruelty that gives a curious distinction' to the book. Even darker emotions swirl through *The Killer and the Slain*, a book whose admirers included Jorge Luis Borges, yet which remains unaccountably neglected.

The 31st of February
by Julian Symons (1950)

Julian Symons worked as a copywriter after leaving the army, an experience which provided him with the background for his second novel, *A Man Called Jones* (1947). His fourth novel, which appeared three years later, was set in Vincent's Advertising Agency, but the similarities ended there. Symons came to have little or no regard for his first three whodunits, but *The 31st of February* marked a new beginning for him, and signposted the way ahead for post-war crime writers.

In a personal memoir included in a posthumous bibliography of his vast body of work, Symons said: 'I must at that time have had some nascent idea about doing all the things in a crime story that one can do in a "straight" novel, in the way of character development and saying something about the form and shape of society...There is a puzzle to be solved—did copywriter Anderson kill his wife or did she just fall down the cellar stairs?—but this goes along with a vision of the nightmare world Anderson inhabits and the mechanical nature of his reactions to the events that eventually overwhelm him.'

For the light-heartedness of *Bland Beginning* (1949), his third novel, Symons substituted a study of a man whose self-belief disintegrates under pressure. Much of that pressure is applied by Inspector Cresse, whose portrayal reflects Symons' interest in the story of the Grand Inquisitor in *The Brothers Karamazov*

(1880). Towards the end of the novel, when he is accused of 'playing God' with Anderson, Cresse mounts a robust defence of his methods: 'A policeman is God—or he is God's earthly substitute. Justice should be intelligent, not blind. If we are obstructing by the forms of legality in reaching the ends of justice, the forms of legality must be ignored.' In one way or another, many of the Great Detectives held similar views. But the final lines of this thought-provoking story suggest that such an assumption of power can corrupt.

The novel was much praised (despite earning the disfavour of traditionalist critics such as Jacques Barzun and Wendell Hertig Taylor), and although some of Symons' writing at this stage of his career was heavy-handed, his fiction demonstrated growing confidence and skill.

Julian Gustave Symons wrote poetry, history, biography and literary studies of distinction, but is remembered chiefly for his contribution to crime fiction. In 1976 he succeeded Agatha Christie as President of the Detection Club, and more than four decades after its first edition appeared in 1972, his history of the genre *Bloody Murder* remains admired and influential, even if the development of the detective story into the crime novel has proved less clear and straightforward than Symons suggests.

One regrettable consequence of *Bloody Murder*'s success is that it has overshadowed Symons' achievements as a novelist. He combined the study of criminal psychology and the examination of social mores with dazzling plots in books such as *The Man Who Killed Himself* (1967), *The Man Whose Dreams Came True* (1968) and *The Plot against Roger Rider* (1973), while *The Name of Annabel Lee* (1983) reflects his enthusiasm for Edgar Allan Poe, whose biography he wrote. A particularly innovative and successful late novel, *Death's Darkest Face* (1990), has been mysteriously overlooked by commentators. Patricia Highsmith reciprocated Symons' admiration for her work, and said that he was 'a first class writer...his suspense novels illustrate the scope possible to this genre'. For a crime novelist, this is an epitaph to die for.

Select Bibliography

The primary sources for *The Story of Classic Crime in 100 Books* are the novels of the writers discussed, but a vast literature deals with the topics covered. For those seeking to research further, this highly selective list of books, many of which I have referred to in researching the story of classic crime, should provide a good starting point.

Adey, Robert, *Locked Room Murders* (London, Ferret Fantasy: 1979, rev. ed. 1991)

Bargainnier, Earl. F. ed., *Twelve Englishmen of Mystery* (Bowling Green, Ohio: Popular Press, 1984)

Barnes, Melvyn, *Murder in Print: A Guide to Two Centuries of Crime Fiction* (London, Barn Owl Books, 1986)

Barnes, Melvyn, *Francis Durbridge: A Centenary Appreciation* (Stowmarket: Netherall Books, 2015)

Barzun, Jacques and Taylor, Wendell Hertig, *A Catalogue of Crime* (New York: Harper & Row, 1971, rev. ed. 1989)

Barzun, Jacques and Taylor, Wendell Hertig, *A Book of Prefaces to Fifty Classics of Crime Fiction 1900–1950* (New York: Garland, 1978)

Binyon, T.J., *Murder Will Out: The Detective in Fiction* (Oxford, O.U.P., 1989)

Clark, Neil, *Stranger than Fiction: The Life of Edgar Wallace, the Man who Created King Kong* (Stroud: The History Press, 2014)

Cooper, John and Pike, B.A., *Detective Fiction: The Collector's Guide* (Aldershot: Scolar Press, 1988, rev.ed.1994)

Craig, Patricia and Cadogan, Mary, *The Lady Investigates: Women Detectives and Spies in Fiction* (London: Gollancz, 1981)

Curran, John, *Agatha Christie's Secret Notebooks: Fifty Years of Mystery in the Making* (London: HarperCollins, 2009)

Curran, John, *Agatha Christie's Murder in the Making: Stories and Secrets from Her Archive* (London: HarperCollins, 2011)

Dean, Christopher, ed., *Encounters with Lord Peter* (Hurstpierpoint: Dorothy L. Sayers Society, 1991)

Donaldson, Norman, *In Search of Dr Thorndyke* (Bowling Green, Ohio: Popular Press, 1971, rev. ed. 1998)

Drayton, Joanne, *Ngaio Marsh: Her Life in Crime* (Auckland: Collins, 2008)

Edwards, Martin, *The Golden Age of Murder* (London: HarperCollins, 2015)

Edwards, Martin, ed., *Taking Detective Stories Seriously: The Detective Fiction Reviews of Dorothy L. Sayers* (Witham: Dorothy L. Sayers Society, 2017)

Evans, Curtis, *Masters of the 'Humdrum' Mystery: Cecil John Charles Street, Freeman Wills Crofts, Alfred Walter Stewart and the British Detective Novel, 1921–1961* (Jefferson, North Carolina: McFarland, 2012)

Evans, Curtis, ed., *Mysteries Unlocked: Essays in Honor of Douglas G. Greene* (Jefferson, North Carolina: McFarland, 2014)

Gilbert, Michael, ed. *Crime in Good Company: essays on criminals and crime writing* (London, Constable, 1959)

Girvan, Waveney, ed., *Eden Phillpotts, an Assessment and Tribute* (London: Hutchinson, 1953)

Greene, Douglas G., *John Dickson Carr: The Man Who Explained Miracles* (New York: Otto Penzler, 1995)

Haste, Steve, *Criminal Sentences: True Crime in Fiction and Drama* (London: Cygnus Arts, 1997)

Haycraft, Howard, *Murder for Pleasure: The Life and Times of the Detective Story* (New York: D. Appleton-Century Company, 1941)

Haycraft, Howard, ed., *The Art of the Mystery Story: A Collection of Critical Essays* (New York: Simon & Schuster, 1946)

Herbert, Rosemary, ed., *The Oxford Companion to Crime and Mystery Writing* (New York: Oxford University Press, 1999)

Hubin, Allen J., *Crime Fiction 1749–1980: A Comprehensive Bibliography* (New York: Garland, 1984)

James, P.D., *Talking About Detective Fiction* (Oxford: Bodleian Library, 2009)

Jones, Julia, *The Adventures of Margery Allingham* (Pleshey: Golden Duck, 2009)

Keating, H.R.F., *Murder Must Appetize* (London: Lemon Tree, 1975)

Keating, H.R.F., *Crime & Mystery: The 100 Best Books* (London: Xanadu, 1987)

Kestner, Joseph A., *The Edwardian Detective, 1901–1915* (Aldershot: Ashgate, 2000)

Lewis, Margaret, *Ngaio Marsh: A Life* (London: Chatto & Windus, 1991)

Light, Alison, *Forever England: Femininity, Literature and Conservatism Between the Wars* (London: Routledge, 1991)

Lobdell, Jared, *The Detective Fiction Reviews of Charles Williams, 1930–1935* (Jefferson, North Carolina: McFarland, 2003)

Mann, Jessica, *Deadlier than the Male* (Newton Abbot: David and Charles, 1981)

Meredith, Anne, *Three-a-Penny* (London: Faber, 1940)

Murch, A.E., *The Development of the Detective Novel* (London, Peter Owen, 1958)

Osborne, Charles, *The Life and Crimes of Agatha Christie* (London, Collins, 1982)

Panek, Leroy, *Watteau's Shepherds: the Detective Novel in Britain, 1914–1940* (Bowling Green, Ohio: Popular Press, 1979)

Pedersen, Jay P., ed., *The St James Guide to Crime and Mystery Writers* (Chicago: St James Press, 1991)

Quayle, Eric, *The Collector's Book of Detective Fiction* (London: Studio Vista, 1972)

Queen, Ellery, *Queen's Quorum: A History of the Detective-Crime Short Story* (US, Biblo & Tannen, rev.ed. 1969)

Reynolds, Barbara, *Dorothy L. Sayers: Her Life and Soul* (London: Hodder, 1993)

Routley, Erik, *The Puritan Pleasures of the Detective Story* (London: Gollancz, 1972)

Scott, Sutherland, *Blood in their Ink: The March of the Modern Mystery Novel* (London, Stanley Paul, 1953)

Stewart, A. W., *Alias J. J. Connington* (London: Hollis & Carter, 1947)

Symons, Julian, *Bloody Murder: From the Detective Story to the Crime Novel* (London: Faber, 1972, rev. eds. 1985, 1992)

Symons, Julian, *The 100 Best Crime Stories* (London: Sunday Times, 1956)

Thomson, H. Douglas, *Masters of Mystery: A Study of the Detective Story* (London: Collins, 1931)

Turnbull, Malcolm J., *Elusion Aforethought: The Life and Writing of Anthony Berkeley Cox* (Bowling Green, Ohio: Popular Press, 1996)

Van Hoeven, Marianne, ed., *Margery Allingham: 100 Years of a Great Mystery Writer* (London: Lucas, 2003)

Various authors, *Meet the Detective* (London: George Allen & Unwin, 1935)

Walsdorf, John J., *Julian Symons: A Bibliography* (Winchester and New Castle, Delaware: St. Paul's Bibliographies and Oak Knoll Press, 1996)

Watson, Colin, *Snobbery with Violence: English Crime Stories and their Audience* (rev. ed. London: Eyre Methuen, 1971, rev. ed. 1979)

Whittle, David, *Bruce Montgomery/Edmund Crispin: A Life in Music and Books* (Aldershot: Ashgate, 2007)

CADS, an irregular magazine edited by Geoff Bradley, has been crammed with interesting information about classic crime fiction for more than thirty years. I have also learned a great deal from members of the Golden Age Detection Facebook group, and from the excellent blogs specialising in classic crime fiction listed at www.doyouwriteunderyourownname.blogspot.com/.

Acknowledgements

Writing is usually a solitary activity, but all authors depend on the support of others, and I am very grateful for the help that I have received from a wide range of people. I must thank my editor, Rob Davies, and his colleagues at the British Library for their enthusiasm and support throughout the writing of this book, and their work on the indexes, as well as my agent, James Wills. Barry Pike and Nigel Moss, two friends who have forgotten more about classic crime fiction than most of us will ever know, were kind enough to comment on a draft of this book, and Nigel also read through the final draft; their input unquestionably improved it. Family members and other heirs of several of the authors whose books are published in the British Library's Crime Classics series have proved to be invaluable sources of information. I have benefited from the help of so many friends and fellow enthusiasts for classic crime that it is almost invidious to highlight a few individuals, but I must express my particular appreciation of the expertise and support of Jamie Sturgeon, John Cooper, Lyndsey Greenslade, Mark Sutcliffe, James M. Pickard, Arthur Robinson, Geoff Bradley, John Norris and Douglas G. Greene, who have provided books, illustrations and other information with their customary generosity.

Index of Titles

Index of Authors

To see more Poisoned Pen Press titles:

Visit our website: poisonedpenpress.com/
Request a digital catalog: info@poisonedpenpress.com